Workforce Transitions from the Profit to the Nonprofit Sector

NONPROFIT AND CIVIL SOCIETY STUDIES
An International Multidisciplinary Series

Series Editor: Helmut K. Anheier
> *London School of Economics and Political Science*
> *London, United Kingdom*

CIVIL SOCIETY AND THE PROFESSIONS IN EASTERN EUROPE
Social Change and Organizational Innovation in Poland
S. Wojciech Sokolowski

MEASURING THE IMPACT OF THE NONPROFIT SECTOR
Edited by Patrice Flynn and Virginia A. Hodgkinson

NEIGHBORHOOD SELF-MANAGEMENT
Experiments in Civil Society
Hillel Schmid

PRIVATE FUNDS, PUBLIC PURPOSE
Philanthropic Foundations in International Perspective
Edited by Helmut K. Anheier and Stefan Toepler

WORKFORCE TRANSITIONS FROM THE PROFIT TO THE NONPROFIT SECTOR
Tobie S. Stein

A Continuation Order Plan is available for this series. A continuation order will bring delivery of each new volume immediately upon publication. Volumes are billed only upon actual shipment. For further information please contact the publisher.

Workforce Transitions from the Profit to the Nonprofit Sector

TOBIE S. STEIN

Brooklyn College
Brooklyn, New York

KLUWER ACADEMIC / PLENUM PUBLISHERS
NEW YORK, BOSTON, DORDRECHT, LONDON, MOSCOW

Library of Congress Cataloging-in-Publication Data

ISBN 0-306-46720-8

©2002 Kluwer Academic/Plenum Publishers, New York
233 Spring Street, New York, New York 10013

http://www.kluweronline.com

10 9 8 7 6 5 4 3 2 1

A C.I.P. record for this book is available from the Library of Congress.

Printed in the United States of America

This book is dedicated to my mentors Professors Paul Attewell, Cynthia Fuchs Epstein, Gerald Handel, and Benito Ortolani, for helping me make the transition to professor. It is also dedicated to the memory of Charles E. Inniss, my dearest mentor and friend, whose own career inspired the career transitions of so many of those portrayed in this book.

Preface

Over the last twenty years, the numbers of professionals and managers displaced from U.S. corporate jobs has increased dramatically. This has coincided with a rapid expansion of employment in the U.S. nonprofit sector, a sector that has a high proportion of managerial and professional workers among its employees. This raises the possibility of shifting unemployed private sector managers into new jobs in the nonprofit sector. However, occupational stereotypes on both sides hinder such movement: suspicions by corporate managers that nonprofit management is unskilled or inefficient confront suspicions by nonprofit recruiters that corporate managers lack value commitments and correct orientations for nonprofit work. It is clear that movement from corporate to nonprofit employment requires resocialization of the individuals making the transition, as well as surmounting negative stereotypes via the creation of new professional networks, new skills, and new ways to present oneself.

My research addresses these issues by examining the existence of occupational stereotyping as it relates to dislocated white-collar managers moving as employees from the profit to the nonprofit sector and the methods used to alter workplace stereotypes based on occupation: occupational networks and anticipatory socialization. The research utilizes open-ended interview techniques with 19 dislocated corporate managers who were preparing to transition to the nonprofit sector and 35 corporate managers who were successful in changing careers. The majority of the data were collected from participant observation of training classes specifically designed by the researcher to help resocialize 117 dislocated managers for new careers in the nonprofit sector. Through the development of a training class that utilized 120 nonprofit managers as peer socializers, the dislocated corporate managers were able to learn and practice their nonprofit occupational identities in preparation for entering new organizational cultures.

I would like to acknowledge Helmut Anheier and Eliot Werner for giving me the opportunity to write this book and for steering its development. I want to thank Paul Attewell, Reynold Levy, and Mark H. Moore for granting me permission to use their copyrighted materials in this book. I am also indebted to Paul Attewell, Cynthia Fuchs Epstein, and Gerald Handel for supporting me in my research on this very topic. I am grateful for the ongoing support of my chair Benito Ortolani, my husband Richard Grossberg, and my parents Elaine and Bernard Stein.

Contents

Workforce Transitions from the Profit to the Nonprofit Sector

Chapter 1

Introduction

Since the early 1980s (Bureau of Labor Statistics, 2000a; Gardner, 1995; Hipple, 1999), the downsizing of corporate America has shattered the workforce identities of thousands of long-term white-collar managerial workers. Among the casualties profiled in this study are Sam, a 35-year employee of the financial services industry; Jim, also a 30-year veteran of the financial services industry; and an investment banker named Pat who was downsized after working in the private sector for almost 15 years.[1]

Regardless of their ambiguous and tarnished statuses as unemployed managers (Newman, 1988), these three managers all remember an organizational corporate culture which treated their employees as family, rewarded them for their loyalty, and gave them job satisfaction. Of course, while they reflect that many of the rewards gained in their organizational cultures came at the cost of playing the undeniable rules of the corporate game (Jackall, 1988), they were basically satisfied, that is, before the culture changed.

For these three white-collar managers and the 114 others represented in this study, losing their jobs in the corporate sector was followed by a time of disenchantment and disengagement and a time of downward mobility which Katherine Newman (1988) calls a "falling from grace" (p. 11). Managers like Sam, Jim, and Pat created their occupational identities around the statuses and rewards they achieved as members of the corporate sector. Now that they joined the ranks of the unemployed, what would their colleagues and family members think of them? What did they think of themselves? If employment opportunities were limited due to the shrinking of their industries, what kinds of occupational opportunities awaited them?

As U.S. corporations continue to downsize, ridding themselves of middle and senior managers, another sector of the U.S. economy—the nonprofit sector—is expanding (Bureau of Labor Statistics, 2000b; *The Chronicle of Philanthropy*, 2000; Hodgkinson et al., 1996; Ruhm and Borkoski, 2000; U.S. Census Bureau, 2000). The good news for Sam, Jim, and Pat is that during their corporate careers, they became involved, as volunteers, in voluntary organizations within the nonprofit sector. Sam served on several boards and actually worked with nonprofit organizations as part of his management portfolio. Jim spent more than 15 years raising money for his university and various arts organizations, and Pat was the treasurer of a religious organization. One might think that since Sam, Jim, and Pat had volunteer experience in the nonprofit sector, as well as management experience in the corporate sector, they would be likely managerial candidates for the nonprofit sector. Unfortunately, this was not the case. They were having difficulty convincing nonprofit employers that they were suitable candidates for employment. Why?

The subject of this book *Workforce Transitions from the Profit to the Nonprofit Sector*, focuses on the career sequences of dislocated white-collar managers like Sam, Pat, and Jim, who want to move from the corporate to the nonprofit sectors. It highlights their motivations, the structural barriers that prevent them from making the transition, and the methods of penetrating the barriers. It uncovers the reasons why some corporate managers are able to make the transition and why others do not. Finally, it exposes the methods of adaptation as well as the frustrations incurred, with culture shock, as they struggle to adapt within their new environment.

My investigation utilizes participant observation of the Nonprofit Management and Communications Program (Program). This Program consisted of training classes I designed to help 117 dislocated white-collar managers become reemployed in the nonprofit sector. From 1991 to 1996, I taped 130 two-hour classes involving interactive sessions between and among the trainer, 120 nonprofit managers, and the 117 dislocated corporate managers.[2] I also conducted in-depth interviews with 19 corporate managers, from the Program, to gain an understanding of their corporate culture before it changed and 35 corporate managers, from the Program, who successfully made the transition from the profit to the nonprofit sector. Through analyzing these empirical data, I discovered that stereotypes on both sides hinder the successful transition of corporate managers to the nonprofit sector. Specifically, suspicions by corporate managers that nonprofit management is unskilled or inefficient confront suspicions by nonprofit recruiters that corporate managers lack value commitments and correct orientations for nonprofit work. Shinar (1975) in Lipton et al. (1991) identified this type of stereotyping as occupational stereotyping. Occupational stereotyping is "a preconceived attitude about a particular occupation, about people who are employed in that occupation, or about one's own suitability for that occupation" (p. 129). Since there is little written on occupational stereotyping, I have linked my empirical research to the literature on gender and racial-based stereotyping found in white-collar hiring and promotion practices. I also used this particular literature to explain how the use of mentors, occupational networks, and anticipatory socialization can alter workplace stereotypes.

It is clear that movement from corporate to nonprofit employment requires a training process which emphasizes anticipatory socialization or a resocialization of the individuals making the transition, as well as surmounting negative stereotypes via the creation of new professional networks, new skills, and new ways to present oneself.

For Sam, Jim, and Pat, as well as for the others written about in this book, finding a new job becomes a process of reinvention—of restructuring an individual's occupational identity to meet the expectations of nonprofit managers.

RESEARCH PROBLEMS AND METHODOLOGY

This study of workforce transitions from the profit to the nonprofit sector analyzes how the process of career transition and organizational assimilation occurs. It analyzes how dislocated corporate managers encounter the behaviors and attitudes of a new reference group—nonprofit managers.

The study focuses on 117 displaced managers who participated in the Nonprofit Management and Communications Program during 1991–1996. (For a more detailed description of the Program, see Chapter 5; for information on recruitment of participants, see Appendix C.) These 117 managers provide the central source of data focusing on the managers' responses to the socialization efforts of the Program's trainer and the 120 nonprofit peer socializers within the classroom.

One aspect of the research was to characterize the culture of profit as compared to nonprofit. Nineteen managers from the Program were taped during interview sessions to gain a picture of the old corporate culture as they experienced it prior to being displaced (see Appendix A). Thirty-five managers from the Program who had successfully made a transition to a nonprofit organization were taped during interview sessions to get their insights into contrasts between the sectors and the transition process that they had gone through (see Appendix B). I observed all 117 dislocated managers within the Program and collected data on them through taped classroom sessions (130 two-hour sessions); all were also interviewed at intake (one to two hours each). The 76 dislocated managers, who were enrolled in the Program from 1991 to 1995, were contacted again during 1995 or 1996 to inquire about their work status.

Finally, I also wanted to obtain the viewpoint of established managers in the nonprofit sector. These were **not** people displaced from the corporate world. They were lifetime successful nonprofit career managers as well as career changers who had transitioned to the nonprofit sector from the corporate world. Their perspective was important in determining cultural expectations in the nonprofit sector. I collected data on nonprofit managers and the interaction between the displaced managers and nonprofit managers in over 260 hours of taped classroom sessions.

The following section provides a summary of the topics and research questions to be covered in each chapter.

Chapter 2, "Culture Change and Career Transition," provides a theoretical framework for this study in the areas of organizational culture, social stratification, and adult socialization. Its main components include: the downsizing of corporate America and its implications for career transition to the nonprofit sector; growth of the nonprofit sector and the need for corporate management models; obstacles faced in changing careers; differences between the profit and nonprofit sectors; and reshaping organizational identity.

Chapter 3, "Differences and Barriers between the Two Worlds," provides two sections of analysis: (1) "The Nonprofit View on Cultural Differences and the Need for Culture Change" and (2) "Hiring Processes and Biases in the Nonprofit Sector." Data collected for this portion of the study came from the taped classroom sessions and interviews with career changers.

"The Nonprofit View on Cultural Differences and the Need for Culture Change" focuses on three views held by nonprofit managers concerning the differences between the sectors, the problems which face the nonprofit sector, and the need for corporate managers to overcome these challenges.

The following questions are analyzed:

- To what extent do nonprofit managers perceive differences between profit and nonprofit cultures? What form do these differences take?
- What problems and challenges does the nonprofit sector face?
- Why do some nonprofit managers perceive a need for culture change and the hiring of corporate managers to initiate this change?
- What types of culture change have benefited the nonprofit sector, what types have not?

The second section "Hiring Processes and Biases in the Nonprofit Sector" examines the consequences that arise from an investment in cultural differences by nonprofit organizational members. The internalization of these cultural differences by nonprofit organizational members leads to hiring bias and stereotyping. Structural barriers that perpetuate these stereotypes such as the absence of peer networks and volunteer experience are also discussed.

I address the following questions:

- How do nonprofit managers describe their hiring processes and biases?
- Under what circumstances will a nonprofit manager hire a corporate manager?

- What part do peer networks and volunteer experience/board membership play in the hiring process?
- Under what circumstances are nonprofit managers more or less likely to change their impression or previous bias about a corporate manager?

Chapter 4, "The Nonprofit Management and Communications Program," introduces one particular anticipatory socialization process in which 117 dislocated corporate managers were selected to participate during 1991–1996. It focuses on the selection process for determining their eligibility for inclusion in the Program, as well as their occupational backgrounds, and motivations for changing careers.

Utilizing in-depth interviews with 19 dislocated managers as well as data collected from intake interviews of 117 dislocated managers, I describe the attitudes of displaced corporate managers toward their corporate work roles and job satisfaction in the corporate sector before the culture changed. Displaced managers were asked to describe the processes that led to corporate culture change, and their motivations for career change to the nonprofit sector. The field work observations are used to illustrate the processes which determined the selection of students for participation in the Program (e.g., processes for determining motivations and commitment to career change) and the structure employed in "setting the stage" for the presocialization process within the classroom.

Chapter 5, "The Program Components," focuses on five processes that helped presocialize the dislocated managers, assisting them in relinquishing the ingrained habits learned in their prior corporate culture. Field work and interview materials are used to answer the following questions:

- When corporate managers first entered the Program, how do they communicate their occupational identity nonverbally (dress); verbally (language); and in writing (résumé, cover letter)?
- What types of verbal and nonverbal communication do they use to express their motivations for changing careers?
- With the intervention of the classroom trainer, how does the corporate manager reconstruct his occupational identity to avoid being labeled an outsider? What types of intervention are used to help the manager achieve this change in occupational identity, motivation, and self-description?
- What is the role of the trainer in helping to transform occupational identities within the classroom?
- Why does the facilitated interaction between members of the profit and nonprofit sector transform the occupational identities of the corporate managers? What processes are used to facilitate this interaction?

Chapter 6, "Transition from the Profit to the Nonprofit World," provides three sections of analysis. The section "Learning Cultural Expectations" outlines the ways in which dislocated managers learn and assimilate the expectations and orientations of nonprofit sector managers. Utilizing the taped interactive sessions between nonprofit and corporate managers, as well as the interviews of career changers, the following questions are explored:

- What does the successful career changer's career path look like? What methods do the corporate managers use to secure a job in the nonprofit sector? How important are anticipatory socialization and the use of networking with reference group members in getting a job?
- What are the roles of the executive director, the financial manager, the communications manager, the grantmaker, the volunteer, and board member?
- How is volunteerism used as a socializing method?

The section "An Odyssey of the Self" utilizes intake and in-depth interviews with dislocated managers, and taped classroom sessions to expose the odyssey of the self or the struggles that dislocated workers encounter as they attempt to transform their occupational identities.

It addresses these questions:

- What are the consequences of the disengagement of self from the corporate sector?
- As dislocated managers struggle to reconstruct their identities, what types of self-imposed barriers create frustration and self-doubt?
- How is cohort solidarity used to both resist and support the transformation of identity?
- How do the dislocated managers find reference group acceptance?
- To what extent is some type of deviance or resistance functional for career change?

The section "Nonprofit Career Transition and Adaptation in the Workplace" examines, through interviews with career changers, the extent to which socialization techniques are successful and raises the following issues:

- What are the numerical outcomes of those who participated in the Nonprofit Management and Communications Program?
- What expectations do for-profit managers bring when first entering the nonprofit arena? What are their fears and apprehensions, and what do they see as the attractive aspects of the nonprofit sector?

- What unexpected aspects of the nonprofit work world emerge during the job? How do career changers respond to these?
- What types of socialization techniques (training) are used by non-profit organizations to prepare these managers for their roles?
- What job demands are described by those who have successfully made the transition into the nonprofit sector? What skills and capacities do they feel they have transported from their for-profit background? What have they not used? What new skills or orientations do they have to develop?
- Under what conditions are career changers forced to leave their non-profit employers?

Chapter 7, "Conclusion—Implications for Management Approaches," summarizes my findings and explores their future implications for the recruitment, training, and retention of nonprofit managers—career changers and career managers, as well as a growing segment of the population, the older worker. Given the tight labor market and a competition for qualified managers in all sectors of the economy, I recommend that the nonprofit sector create organization development models that emphasize nonprofit traditional values, anticipatory and peer socialization processes within graduate education programs and on-the-job training designed to support all entering nonprofit employees, and the implementation of corporate reward systems.

Notes

1. These names are pseudonyms. All names of individuals and organizations have been changed in this paper.
2. This ethnography is written from the point of view of a researcher who was also an active participant who played the role of "trainer" within the classroom. It was within this context that I not only observed identity change throughout the Nonprofit Management and Communications Program, but was actively engaged in influencing that change by serving as a transmitter of nonprofit organizational culture between corporate and nonprofit managers. In an effort to create some distance between the two distinct roles of participant and observer, I have distinguished "the trainer" from "the observer" throughout the ethnography, and have used the third person in describing various events.

Chapter 2

Culture Change and Career Transition

THE GROWING TREND OF WHITE-COLLAR DISPLACED MANAGERS 1980–2000

Starting with the recession of the early 1980s, white-collar workers in America began to experience layoffs or displacement at an increasing rate. In a February 2000 survey conducted by the U.S. Employment and Training Administration, they found that "managerial and professional specialty occupations[1] account for 30 percent of all displacements. This proportion has doubled since the early 1980s" (Bureau of Labor Statistics, 2000a, p. 3). During the period 1979–1995, 18.7 million white-collar jobs were eliminated ("More Than 43 Million Jobs Lost," p. 27). U.S. firms continue to downsize, having eliminated 179,144 jobs in the first four months of 2000 (Joyner, 2000, p. 1R). Despite the booming U.S. economy of the late 1990s, older workers aged 55 to 64 have a reemployment rate of 56 percent, and persons aged 65 years and older have a reemployment rate of 26 percent (Bureau of Labor Statistics, 2000a, p. 2). Two percent of the current U.S. workforce or 4.4 million people are considered "discouraged workers," those who want to work but have essentially given up (Joyner, 2000, p. 1R).

THE GROWTH OF THE NONPROFIT SECTOR 1977–2000

A Definition of the Nonprofit Sector

Because so many white-collar corporate jobs have been eliminated, some corporate managers have begun to look outside their original industries for reemployment. One sector that has been growing across the United States is the nonprofit sector. According to the U.S. Internal Revenue Service, there are 1.3 million tax-exempt organizations in the United States. The Internal Revenue Service lists 26 different categories of tax-exempt organizations (nonprofit) which are exempted from federal income tax[2] (*The Chronicle of Philanthrophy*, 2000, p. 1). These organizations vary widely in their scope of activity and purpose. The Independent Sector, which conducts extensive research on the nonprofit sector in the United States, studies the "independent sector" or those nonprofit organizations that fall under the tax-exempt categories of 501(c)(3) and 501(c)(4). Salamon (Salamon and Anheier, 1997, p. 296) categorizes 501(c)(3) and 501(c)(4) organizations as "public serving organizations." In his book (coauthored by Helmut K. Anheier) *Defining the Nonprofit Sector: A Cross-National Analysis,*" he maintains that the distinctions made between the tax-exempt categories are based on the purpose of the organization. 501(c)(3) organizations, which numbered 733,790 in 1998, are classified as religious and charitable organizations, and include educational, social service, arts and culture, and healthcare institutions.[3] 501(c)(4) organizations,[4] which numbered 139,533 during the same period, are social welfare organizations which lobby on behalf of social concerns such as gun control, environmental conservation, and healthcare ("Tax-Exempt Organizations," 2000, pp. 1–2).

The documented growth of the nonprofit sector in terms of numbers of organizations and employment rates, as well as other workforce characteristics including the age, race, and gender of its employees is often described comparatively with the other two sectors: corporate and government. For purposes of this study, the following section compares the workforce characteristics of the corporate and nonprofit sectors.

WORKFORCE CHARACTERISTICS

Organizational Growth

The Independent Sector reports that from 1977 to 1992 there was a 70 percent increase in the number of 501(c)(3) and 501(c)(4) organizations (Hodgkinson et al., 1996, pp. 25–26). Since 1992, there has been a 90 percent increase in the number of nonprofit organizations in the United States. Nonprofit organizations now account for 8 percent of the U.S. gross domestic product (Cohen, 1999, p. 11).

Revenue Growth

Smith and Lipsky (1993) suggest that the U.S. federal government as well as local and state governments were largely responsible for the proliferation of nonprofit social service organizations between 1960 and 1980. Between 1960 and 1980, total federal spending, on nonprofit social service organizations, went from $1.14 billion to $13.5 billion (p. 54). This dramatic increase in federal spending was influenced by public pressure to expand social services such as day care, legal services, family planning, employment, and training. State spending for social services almost doubled from 1975 to 1980 ($2.6 billion to $4.8 billion, p. 57). When the Reagan administration reallocated federal funding to the states, state and local spending on social services rose from $4.8 billion in 1980 to $7.3 billion in 1988 (p. 63). The total expenditures of government for nonprofit social services (including the federal government) went from $13.6 billion in 1980 to $15.24 billion in 1988 (p. 63).

When we look at total funding, rather than government funding alone, we find that from 1977 to 1992 there was an increase in total annual funds to the independent sector of 112 percent (Hodgkinson et al., 1996, p. 156). In 1992, the three largest sources of revenue to the entire sector were private payments in the form of dues, fees, and charges (39 percent); government payments in the form of contracts and/or grants (31 percent); and private contributions from individuals, corporations, and foundations (18 percent). As a percentage of total revenue, private contributions declined from 26 percent in 1977 to 18 percent in 1992. This was due to several factors including the high rate of inflation from 1977 to 1982; the passing of the 1986 Tax Act which eliminated the charitable deduction for nonitemizers of deductions, and altered the rules for taking the full deduction for appreciated property for gifts and other charitable deductions; and the recession of the early 1990s. Payments and grants from government increased from 27 percent to 31 percent of total revenues over the same period. Increases in payments to Medicaid resulting from the increase in uninsured individuals, children, and the elderly and increases to Medicare pushed a lot of money into the medical segment of the nonprofit world thus accounting for this percentage growth. Private payments increased from 37 percent to 39 percent during this period due to the cost of private insurance, the costs of health services, and an aging population (Hodgkinson et al., 1996, pp. 159–162).

Hodgkinson et al. (1996, p. 158) report that in 1992, the health services subsector received the largest share of total annual nonprofit sector funds (51 percent) followed by education and research (19 percent). The religious sector received 12 percent of the total annual funds and social services received 11 percent.

Health services increased its share of revenues from 46 percent in 1977 to 51 percent in 1992. Education's share of funds declined from 25 percent in 1977 to 19 percent in 1992. Social services increased its share from 9 percent to 11 percent during the same period. Religion was stable at 12 percent during this period and arts and culture showed a modest increase from 2 percent to 3 percent. The latest statistics compiled by the U.S. Census Bureau on tax-exempt service organizations[5] show that between 1992 and 1997, there was an 89.8 percent increase in social services revenue; a 76.8 percent increase in home healthcare services revenue; and a 35.4 percent increase in noncommercial research revenue (2000, pp. 1–2).

Employment Growth

According to the Independent Sector's analysis of the 1990 U.S. Census, total paid employment grew faster in the independent sector (75 percent) than in the business sector (36 percent) from 1977 to 1994 (Hodgkinson et al., 1996, p. 29).

Lynn Burbridge's (1994) working paper *Government, For-profit, and Third Sector Employment: Differences by Race and Sex, 1950–1990* found that executive and managerial positions in the nonprofit sector grew 185 percent from 1970 to 1990 compared to 66 percent in the corporate sector during the same period (p. 36). The Independent Sector's 1993 study *National Summary: Not-For-Profit Employment from the 1990 Census of Population and Housing* reports that more than half of all nonprofit jobs are managerial or professional (51 percent) as opposed to only 19 percent in the corporate sector. Since this category of workers for both sectors is projected to increase by 16 percent from 1998 to 2008, one can make an assumption that there will be increasing opportunities for managers in the nonprofit sector (Bureau of Labor Statistics, 2000c, p. 1; Hodgkinson et al., 1993, p. 4).

Nonprofit Industries and Type of Manager Employed

According to the Independent Sector's 1993 study on the nonprofit sector, five major industries account for six out of ten nonprofit jobs: hospitals, elementary and secondary schools, religious organizations, colleges, universities, and social services (p. 7). Furthermore, the Independent Sector's *Nonprofit Almanac 1996–1997* states that 60 percent of all managers in service organizations, one-third of healthcare managers, and over one-quarter of educational administrators are employed by the independent sector (Hodgkinson et al., 1996, p. 133). According to the U.S. Department of Labor's Bureau of Labor Statistics, employment growth is expected for each of these occupational groups through 2008 (Bureau of Labor Statistics, 2000c, p. 1; *Occupational Outlook Handbook* Web site).

Managerial Diversity

Women

Burbridge's study (1994, p. 84) establishes that over a 20-year period from 1970 to 1990, the percentage of white, Latina, and black female managers and professionals was lower in the corporate sector than in the nonprofit sector. Accordingly in 1990, the Independent Sector's 1993 study found that there is a higher percentage of women in professional specialties and managerial jobs as a proportion of their total employment in the nonprofit sector (37 and 15 percent, respectively) than in the corporate sector (8 and 14 percent, pp. 5–6). However, professional and managerial women earn less in the nonprofit sector (mean salaries: $25,575 and $25,833, respectively) than in the corporate sector (mean salaries: $27,668 and $26,151) (p. 22).

African-Americans

There is a higher percentage of African-American professionals and managers as a proportion of their total employment in the nonprofit sector (25 and 13 percent, respectively) than in the corporate sector (5 and 7 percent, pp. 5–6). African-American professional occupational groups earn a lower mean salary in the nonprofit sector than in the corporate sector ($25,702 and $29,004, respectively). The mean salaries for nonprofit and corporate African-American managers are about the same ($27,595 and $27,466) (Hodgkinson et al., 1993, p. 25).

Latinos

Hodgkinson et al. (1993) found that Latinos also accounted for a higher percentage of managerial and professional jobs as a percentage of their total employment in the nonprofit sector (12 and 22 percent, respectively) than in the corporate sector (8 and 4 percent, pp. 5–6). However, the mean professional and managerial salaries are higher for Latinos in the corporate sector ($31,469 and $28,835) than in the nonprofit sector ($26,005 and $26,965, p. 26).

Older Workers

Finally, there is documented growth in the transition of workers from the profit to the nonprofit sector as these workers age. Burbridge (1994, p. 98) found that as "cohorts age, most workers shift out of the for-profit sector, into the two other sectors. The biggest within-cohort shift over this period was into the third sector." In 1980, 69 percent of those aged 45–54 worked in the for-profit sector and 8.6 percent of the same cohort worked in the nonprofit sector. Ten years later in 1990, 66 percent of those aged 55–64 were working in the corporate sector and 13 percent were working in the nonprofit sector (Burbridge, 1994, p. 109). One reason for this workforce shift may be that nonprofits are more likely to hire older workers than is the corporate sector. In 1990, 19.7 percent of the nonprofit workforce was aged 45–54 and 11 percent was aged 55–64. During the same period, 16.4 percent of the corporate workforce was aged 45–54 and 9 percent was aged 55-64 (Hodgkinson et al., 1993, p. 16).

Neither the Burbridge nor the Independent Sector studies document the transition of specific occupational groups from the profit to the nonprofit sector such as the transition of managers and professionals from one sector to another. However, based on the growing social problems of society (Salamon and Anheier, 1996), the government's response to the public outcry for fiscal accountability of nonprofits (Smith and Lipsky, 1993), and the fundraising needs of nonprofits to combat these increasing social needs, there is evidence that there is a demand for cross-sector managerial expertise.

THE DOCUMENTED NEED FOR MANAGERS IN THE NONPROFIT SECTOR

The enormous growth in the nonprofit sector necessitates the need for qualified managers to lead nonprofit institutions. A global study of the nonprofit sector, conducted by Lester M. Salamon and Helmut K. Anheier (1996), found that as government cuts back direct aid to citizens, nonprofit organizations are having greater difficulty in meeting demands for their services. As this demand for social, healthcare, and educational services increases, there is a growing problem in finding competent managers to lead nonprofit organizations. According to Salamon, "untrained managers will be less and less appropriate as nonprofits play central roles in dealing with social problems" (Greene, 1994, p. 28). The abundance of untrained nonprofit managers is increasingly evident in the United States. Gayle A. Brandel, an executive recruiter, asserts that "managers now need to have business backgrounds or skills." Executive recruiter James Abruzzo believes that even with the increase in nonprofit salaries over the last 5 years, "there aren't enough good people to fill top nonprofit jobs" (Souccar, 2000, pp. 23, 28). According to a survey conducted by The Chronicle of Philanthropy, one-third of those surveyed changed chief executives since 1997. Charity leaders are having a difficult time recruiting qualified managers with expertise in fundraising, computer technology, accounting, and communications (Billitteri, 2000, p. 1).

Within the human or social services sector, the need for fiscal accountability and professional management has been fueled by the sector's reliance on the government for support (Smith and Lipsky, 1993). Since the human services sector is dependent on the government for 50 percent (Hodgkinson et al., 1996, p. 181) of its total annual revenues, it is inclined to adhere to the government's demand for greater fiscal and managerial accountability. Wolpert (1993) believes that "nonprofits have become locked into a process of providing services and amenities to their own local donors" (p. 37).

The government's insistence that nonprofits be accountable for the allocation of shared and central costs, knowledge of social security tax reporting, insurance issues, personnel policies, and affirmative action procedures all demand the recruitment of skilled managers (Smith and Lipsky, 1993). In fact, as the level of government support increases, so does the pressure of public officials to justify these expenditures to organizations. The consequence of this pressure is the "gradual displacement" of the founding executives, originally trained as social workers and clinicians, and their replacement by professional managers (Smith and Lipsky, 1993, p. 83).

The professional manager not only provides accountability, but brings with him a "network of colleagues, peers, and expectations that are outside of the founding community of the organization" (Smith and Lipsky, 1993, p. 85). While the "new" professional helps the organization become more competitive in securing government contracts, Smith and Lipsky (1993) are concerned that this professional orientation conflicts with the "commitment to the client and a particular mission which provides the raison d'être for many community organizations" (p. 86). In addition, if nonprofits become more like government agencies or corporations and they lose their "quasi voluntary" character, will the skilled professional be agreeable to working for a lower wage than could be obtained in another sector of the economy? Nonprofit organizations such as the American Red Cross in Washington, D.C. and the American Lung Association in New York City admit that they have lost their technology managers to higher-paying jobs in the corporate sector (Sommerfeld, 2000). While movement of managers from the nonprofit to the corporate sector is uncommon, it is important to consider if Smith and Lipsky's assertions are accounting for this mobility between sectors. Are nonprofit managers moving to the corporate sector because of higher compensation, or because the sectors are more and more perceived as resembling each other, making high compensation a prominent value in both sectors? Smith and Lipsky raise extremely interesting questions that require new research on the degree to which funders are creating nonprofit organizations in their own image and if so, whether the funding relationship with a nonprofit organization impacts the retention and recruitment of nonprofit managerial talent.

A SHORTAGE OF NONPROFIT MANAGERS

With an obvious shortage of skilled nonprofit managers, from where will the next generations of skilled managers come? One likely and obvious choice is the corporate sector. From the nonprofit organization's point of view, corporate sector managers would appear to be a likely source of applicants. However, this is not the case. Dislocated corporate managers are more likely to be reemployed in their same occupation and industry.

Low Proportion Change Careers

Statistics show that while corporations continue to displace their managers and nonprofit organizations appear desperate for managerial talent, a very small proportion of displaced workers in general change industries or occupations. Of those dislocated managers who lost their jobs during 1995–1996 and were reemployed by 1998, 60 percent were reemployed in the same occupation (Hipple, 1999, p. 23). Ruhm and Borkoski found that **only 3 percent** of individuals dislocated from corporate jobs switched to the nonprofit sector (2000, p. 18). Henry Farber (1998) explains:

> The labor market … in the United States and other developed countries is not primarily a spot market characterized by short-term employment relationships between workers and firms. There is not a high frequency of movement by workers from firm to firm …. It may be that long-term employment relationships enable firms and workers to invest in firm specific capital. (pp. 1, 48)

Large proportions of the U.S. workforce make long-term investments in their companies. In February 1996, 35.4 percent of workers between the ages of 35 and 64 had been with their employers for at least 10 years; 20.9 percent of those aged 45–64 had been with their employer for 20 years (Farber, 1998, p. 1).

The Lack of Mobility between Sectors

What accounts for the lack of mobility between sectors? On the surface, it appears as though employees and their employers profit from the experience of long-term employment. Employers benefit from having "presocialized" workers who have, over time, internalized the requisite values and behaviors that the industry seeks (Schein, 1990, p. 115). Long-term benefits for employees include healthy salaries, social and workplace networks, authority, autonomy, and status within the workplace and community (Trice and Beyer, 1993). Another reason for the lack of mobility during the last 10–20 years is that the economic recessions of the 1980s and 1990s created fewer opportunities within many industries. When this occurs, it is likely for employees to have greater dependence on the organization in which they are affiliated (Rosow, 1965). Since most occupational networks of managers with rates of low mobility consist of within-industry contacts, there are fewer opportunities to receive informal leads to jobs outside of one's chosen industry (Blau, 1964; Granovetter, 1995; Trice and Beyer, 1993).

Given the fact that the economy and the perpetuation of hiring practices which serve both the employee and the employer significantly affect the mobility of workers, it is no wonder that only 3 percent of corporate employees move to the nonprofit sector! For those corporate managers who are motivated to make the change, there are additional obstacles.

Corporate Managers Face Obstacles

Loss of Identity

Goffman (1963) explains that the identity of an individual is generated by interactions with others and that an actor's identity is the "photographic image of the individual in the others' mind" (p. 56). Similarly, George Mead (1934) observed that the "self is a reflection of the complete social process" (p. 144). Furthermore, Gregory Stone (1962) analyzed the "role of appearance in interactions and its effect through the reflected image of others back on the self" (p. 86).

Professional and managerial workers derive much of their sense of self from their work role and the expectations which significant others (employers, peers, family, and friends) have of this role in our society. When corporate managers lose their jobs and are unable to quickly find another, they become emotionally devastated in part not only because of financial problems that beset them, but also because their identity or claims to a certain self are now open to question. In her work, *Falling from Grace* (1988), Newman explains that being "unemployed is clearly a stigmatized condition in this society. It broadcasts to employers that there is something not quite right about this person. It prevents the job seeker from constructing an appealing image of himself" (p. 57). This inability to construct an appealing self-image is rooted in the loss of the social group or culture that imparts the individual's self-image. One study of 1000 retired midlevel managers who returned to work found that one-third "wanted contact with people rather than the social emptiness of retirement" (Gray and Morse, 1980, in Trice and Beyer, 1993, p. 167). "Retirement from work means more of a social loss for the professional class, whose friends are more likely to be work associates, than for the working-class whose friends are more likely to be drawn from the neighborhood" (Hochschild, 1973, p. 20).

When corporate managers are forced to retire early or are terminated, they often experience a loss of their workforce identity. Rather than admit defeat by taking a lower-paying job (in the nonprofit sector), the worker may remain retired or unemployed, emphasizing the success, values, and rewards of his former status (Hutchens, 1988; Wilensky and Edwards, 1959, in Rosow, 1974). Hence, loss of identity acts as a barrier to change. It implies that people find it difficult to give up their old occupational identity and embrace a new occupational identity. Unfortunately, the longer the corporate manager invests in his prior occupational and industrial statuses, the more difficult it is to change careers.

The Cost of Commitment

According to Blau (1964), employees do indeed invest time to gain the rewards within their organization. Corporate managers invest time at the expense of seeking other opportunities that may be found through networking outside of the corporation. Their corporate loyalty impedes their mobility into other industries. Granovetter (1995) maintains that people who have stayed in a job for a long time, those who have few personal acquaintances, and those not well placed in the labor market such as the unemployed, discouraged older worker will not have a large network of professional ties to facilitate the development of the next job.

Absence of Networks and Mentors

The absence of networks or people who can support the manager's transition from one industry to another is a significant barrier to "getting in." Wethington and Kessler (1986) discovered that the perception of having a network that is ready to support the individual with advice, coping methods, listening, cheering, and referrals can be important, if not more important, than an actual supportive network. A manager's introduction to new occupational networks can be facilitated more easily if the manager has access to a mentor who will "sponsor and back" the manager's transition. The "reflected power" of a mentor eases the transition of the newcomer (Kanter, 1977, p. 182). Without the support of occupational networks and mentors, the dislocated corporate manager faces the nonprofit hiring process as an outsider—perceived as not being capable of understanding the value system or culture of the nonprofit sector.

Those who are "sponsored" by industry insiders are more likely to achieve desirable jobs. In Zuckerman's (1977) study of Nobel laureates, those apprentices who had mentors were more likely to learn the appropriate behaviors and attitudes, ask the right kinds of questions, and propose the right kinds of solutions. She also found that those apprentices with mentors were more likely to have the confidence needed to achieve success in their profession. In her study of "glass ceilings" within law firms, Epstein et al. (1995)

found that a mentor gives female attorneys high visibility and insights into the corporate culture.

Those without mentors may have to depend on formal procedures both in getting into the organization (Granovetter, 1995) and once in, working their way up through a multilayered chain of command (Kanter, 1977). Thus, building the appropriate occupational network with one or more mentors, and creating a bridge between the nonprofit insider and the corporate outsider, appear to be significant career strategies for those in the process of changing careers.

Occupational Stereotyping

Perhaps more than any other factor, I argue that occupational stereotyping contributes in large part to the low incidence of workforce transition from the profit to the nonprofit sector. Different organizational cultures in the profit and the nonprofit worlds are marked by unflattering stereotypes of the other and tend, therefore, to prefer hiring from within their own sector. What accounts for the creation of occupational stereotypes or "preconceived attitude[s] about a particular occupation, about people employed in that occupation, or about one's own suitability for that occupation?" (Shinar, 1975, in Lipton et al., 1991, p. 129). Within the social stratification literature, it is recognized that social boundaries create insiders with greater access to wealth, power, knowledge, and the elite occupations, and outsiders who are prevented from attaining these rewards based on the perception that "one must be one to understand one" (Merton, 1972, p. 15). Especially stigmatized are outsiders who are in a transitional state (such as being unemployed or retired early). Since this means that one is not a member of any in-group, they are believed by others to be marginal human beings or "placeless" individuals (Douglas, 1966, p. 95). Those without a definite status in our society are thought to be "dirty" because their actions and values are thought to be uncertain (Douglas, 1966, p. 95).

What accounts for or explains the maintenance of such boundaries? Those who create boundaries are interested in maintaining their identities and the economic power associated with their identities. Intruders threaten those with power. Additionally, there is a need to reduce the anxiety and dilemma that are produced when status boundaries are not maintained (Hughes, 1945). Furthermore, contact with people who are different "may produce embarrassing and unpleasant experiences ... people prefer to interact with others whose behavior can be predicted" (Blalock, 1982, p. 97). Stereotyping which involves labeling in the magnification of one or two attributes out of proportion to others (Schur, 1984) is used by insiders as a mechanism of control to preserve the in-group's majority status and their privileged allocation of resources, rewards, and power.

Though very little has been written about the stereotyping of nonprofit managers by corporate managers, a few examples do exist. One corporate executive addressed a group of displaced managers in New York City and said that "motivation is not their strong suit, they are there because they love it" (Smith, 1996, p. 4). In her article supporting the transition of nonprofit managers into the corporate sector, Rosemarin (1995) warns that corporate managers believe that nonprofit managers "lack the *hard* skills necessary for the change" (p. 28).

Stereotyping is more evident on the nonprofit side. Eisenberg (1997) believes that the "cult of the CEO ... is dangerous to the long-term health of the nonprofit sector because it diminishes collegiality and teamwork and detracts from organizational mission" (p. 334). In David Mason's (1992) article "Invasion of the Soul Snatchers: Aliens in Our Midst: Are the invaders from the business world stealing our sector's soul?" he cautions that business values such as the profit motive and personal gain are displacing nonprofit values such as "altruism, caring, fidelity, stewardship, and safeguarding the public trust" (p. 27). Furthermore, Mason believes that, in the corporate world, money is the measure of success and that corporate managers therefore "think we're (nonprofit managers) still playing around with our lives, and that someday we'll grow up and get serious jobs .... Business managers assume that people's success can be roughly measured by their salaries—that's the way it's done in their culture" (p. 29). Another example of occupational stereotyping is found in Merchant's (1991) "Letter to the Editor" in *Nonprofit World*. She believes that corporate superiority is a myth and concludes that corporate leaders use resources and money to cover up mistakes passing them along to "unsuspecting customers." In addition, she argues that "generally, corporate leaders don't have an understanding as to why the third sector exists in the first place and they have very little insight into social missions and are unable to meet the nonprofit sector's high expectations of them for knowledge, skills, and resources" (p. 3).

Another nonprofit manager, who makes her living writing grants, advises against using business venture models to create new revenue streams for nonprofit organizations at the expense of building strong fundraising programs. "Nonprofits are mission-driven; as opposed to making money," she states. And, she views the nonprofit's use of the business venture as an "invasion of their [corporations'] turf" (McMahon, 1996, p. 38).

Additional evidence of occupational stereotyping appears in Jennifer Moore's 1992 article, "Charity Workers' Job Market Jitters." Moore interviews nonprofit managers who confirm worries about hiring corporate executives because "they don't have previous experience in charity work" (p. 28). In addition, nonprofit managers question the commitment of corporate managers who have recently been laid off, perceiving the corporate manager as wanting a quick fix and fearing they will leave if offered a better high-paying job. Finally, nonprofit managers "don't want to take a chance on people who are trying to do something different from what they have done in the past" (p. 28).

Tschirhart (1998, p. 78) found that "nonprofit managers place most hiring emphasis on the applicant's work experience in a similar organization." This is of course underscored in job advertisements which state "a familiarity with and understanding of educational fundraising," "a minimum of 10 years' experience in education/community development fundraising," or "this position requires 2–3 years of development experience, preferably at a highly selective liberal arts institution" ("Professional Opportunities," 2000, p. 73). The job advertisements make it apparent that an individual who does not share the same occupational status as an employee who already works for a university or educational institution will be disadvantaged when seeking employment within these types of organizations. These job advertisements, in essence, are a means of attracting those of like mind, those with a shared perspective. They are used to create a "homo-social reproduction" of the workplace (Kanter, 1977, p. 63).

Although corporate managers may want to make a transition to the nonprofit sector, they may not be eligible if the nonprofit organization wants to maintain a closed social structure where distinctive social relations—social relations which share a similarity of status—are to be maintained (Merton, 1968). Shared statuses are a feature of many professional communities (Goode, 1957). A profession is defined as a community that shares values and language in common and established role definitions for members and non-members. Control over access to training and recruitment sustains the professional community (Abbott, 1988; Goode, 1957). By maintaining control over recruitment, occupations and industries are "in an excellent position to pre-select new members who fit within or to reinforce preferred elements of their occupational culture … to preserve the status quo" (Trice and Beyer, 1993, p. 220). Furthermore, "the more stake observers have in the status quo, and hence the more to lose, the more likely they are to stereotype out-groups" (Reskin, 2000, p. 5).

Dominant members of a group control opportunities by recruiting members like themselves from homogeneous networks. The networks are comprised of people who have been trained, educated, or socialized together and are thought to have the same values about work as well as shared class, race, and gender (Epstein et al., 1995; Lorber, 1984). Occupations are able to maintain their homogeneous networks of employees through socializing those who wish to enter, or finding those who are "presocialized" and already have acquired the requisite values and behaviors that the occupation seeks. If the entering recruit is presocialized, the organization needs to do less formal socialization (Schein, 1990, p. 115). These homogeneous networks control access to educational institutions, entry to types of organizations, and the referral networks needed to advance (Epstein et al., 1995; Lorber, 1984).

The next section provides a description of the general socialization techniques occupations use to sustain the homogeneity of their occupations and industries.

ADULT SOCIALIZATION: A TYPOLOGY

Scholarship on adult socialization identifies the ways in which adults become socialized, or learn the requisite values and behaviors, in various occupations such as medicine (Becker et al., 1961), accounting (Montagna, 1975), teaching (Lortie, 1975), and nursing (Davis et al., 1966).

I will discuss the processes of adult socialization and the consequences of socialization within each of these studies by using Van Maanen's (1976, 1983) socialization typology. The typology, delineated below, compares and contrasts formal and informal socialization; sequential and nonsequential socialization; fixed and variable socialization; tournament and contest socialization; serial and disjunctive socialization; and investiture with divestiture socialization within the context of occupational studies described above. If the assumption is made that all types of organizations use one or more of these socialization techniques to indoctrinate their members with the organization's requisite values and behaviors, one can understand how profit and nonprofit organizations are able to distinguish their organizational cultures through the socialization of their members as well.

Professions such as medicine (Becker et al., 1961) and accounting (Montagna, 1975) use greater degrees of **formal socialization** to train recruits than do nurses (Davis et al., 1966) and teachers (Lortie, 1975). In the formal socialization process the recruit is separated from the workplace and trained or educated off-site. Within the formal educational process (e.g., medical school) the newcomer's role is made explicit, and there is a strong attempt to influence the newcomer's values and behaviors to reduce dependence on prior skills learned in previous organization settings. Problems arise when participants are forced to learn everything presented to them, as in the case of Becker's medical students. In their study, Becker and his colleagues found that the students form their own perspectives apart from the professors that allow the students to cope with the situation. Problems also arise when there is a gap between the values and behaviors learned in school and those expected by the profession (Davis et al., 1966; Lortie, 1975). For example, while Davis's collegiate nurses are socialized to be humanistic in school, the hospital workplace setting requires a bureaucratic approach to healthcare. When there is a gap between what is anticipated or learned and what is expected by the profession, the individual experiences culture or reality shock (Hughes, 1981). A study of Dade schoolteachers (Lortie, 1975) shows an enormous degree of culture shock when the new teachers enter their schools, because their formal education focuses on the process of learning as opposed to processes of teaching and problem solving which are expected of them in the workplace.

Informal socialization or learning by trial and error occurs when there is no differentiation between the workplace and the learning setting. The recruit is dependent on learning the requisite behaviors and attitudes from his peers. Success depends on the newcomer convincing others to teach him the ropes. Peer groups often set the rules within an organization. Becker et al. illustrate that the peer group's (students) shared ordeal of mastering uncertainty, forces it to form a collective perspective to share workloads and make a united good impression before the professors. In the absence of a unified peer subculture, the individual is forced to learn on his own as Lortie described in his study on Dade county schoolteachers.

Van Maanen's next two socialization strategies are called sequential and nonsequential socialization. **Sequential socialization** is found in professions such as medicine and accounting which have identifiable stages through which an individual must pass in order to achieve a defined status. A medical student's career sequence has 4 years of medical school, 1 year as an intern, and 3 to 5 years as a resident (Becker et al., 1961). The accounting career sequence consists of four to five stages during a 14-year period. Problems arise for recruits who cannot adhere to a predetermined schedule. Accountants who could not reach the "senior" stage by age 34 could not become a partner in the firm (Montagna, 1975, p. 46).

An occupation that utilizes **nonsequential socialization** does not have defined career steps. For example, one does not have to be an assistant manager to be a manager in many occupations.

Sequential socialization and fixed socialization are related processes. **Fixed socialization** refers to the precise amount of time it takes to complete a step within an occupation. For instance, medical students know it will take a minimum of 5 years of formal education before they will be able to practice medicine (Becker et al., 1961). The accounting profession is age graded: 4 years as a junior; the CPA exam passed by age 29; manager by age 32; partner by age 36. If recruits undergo fixed socialization, it is likely that strong peer relationships will develop and continue.

Variable socialization refers to a minimum number of years the recruit must have received training, before entering an occupation, and it does not specify when the recruit will be able to perform the role within the occupation. Evidence of variable socialization is found in both Lortie's and Davis's studies. Although the schoolteachers acquire a minimum amount of education, they are not skilled enough to perform their roles adequately within the schools. Even though college-trained nurses undergo training within the university, there is no guarantee that they will obtain jobs in the hospital if the hospital continues hiring nurses without college degrees. Since the training is minimal for teachers and not standardized for nurses, it is unlikely that trainees will bond as peers in either profession. Furthermore, since the period between training and practice in the professional role is ambiguous, this type of socialization divides and drives the recruits apart, creating less loyalty between the recruits and the profession.

Tournament socialization fosters separate clusters of selected recruits into different socialization programs and tracks the recruit based on presumed ability, ambition, and background. Men, historically, have been tracked into accounting and medical professions and women into nursing and teaching professions. If tournament socialization is used, the accomplishments of employees are more likely to be explained by the tracking process than by the achievements of the individual. **Contest socialization** avoids this type of tracking system and allows equal access to professional education and training.

When **serial socialization** is used, it provides the best guarantee that the organization will not change over time. Experienced members of the organization execute serial socialization. A mentor governs the individual serial socialization process. Mentors are important in transmitting organizational culture. Van Maanen (1983) maintains that this process is only used when the incumbent is perceived as the only one who can shape his successor. The newcomer is only accorded full membership in the organization when he conforms to the older member's expectations that are embedded in the values and norms of the organization. This type of socialization is important to women in blue- and white-collar occupations that face sex role socialization that is potentially contradictory to organizational socialization. Sex role socialization presumes that women are trained for specific jobs based on their gender and not on their qualifications for the job. This type of socialization is perpetuated by cultural beliefs that since men and women have different personality traits, they are capable of only holding jobs which coincide with these traits. Recruitment processes perpetuate the concentration of the sexes in different occupations (Epstein, 1970; Reskin and Hartmann, 1986). Using this social process as a model, one could argue that each industry's recruitment practices are based on the perceived similarities of personality traits between the recruit and the members of the industry.

Women are able to diffuse sex role socialization when they have mentors (Epstein, 1988). Mentors of white-collar women teach them to speak the language of the organization (Collins, 1983); apprenticeship helps blue-collar women develop competencies in skilled jobs and demonstrate these competencies on the job (Deaux and Ullman, 1983; Walshok, 1981). Zey (1991) found that problems arise within this type of socialization process when the role expectations of the mentor and protégé are not defined in advance.

Collective serial socialization implies that recruits share a similar fate and it is the peer group itself that develops the method of problem solving to deal with situations. Of course, the peer group's solution may run contrary to the governing authority's solution as is stressed in Becker's study. In addition, medical school does not socialize students in taking on a professional role in that it does not prepare them with the attitudes and behaviors for professional practice. Becker and his colleagues found instead that it is the situations of medical school which influence student actions and values, and that students form perspectives in order to cope with these situations.

Disjunctive socialization gives the recruit the opportunity to be inventive and original because there is no individual or group present to socialize the individual. The individual or the group is expected to be his own socializing agent (Brim and Wheeler, 1966). In the case of the individual teacher in Lortie's study (1975), there is no peer group to help new teachers solve problems. The teacher is forced to "learn by doing" (p. 60). In the case of Becker's medical students, they are forced to find collective solutions to "work overload" in the absence of predecessors. Conflict arises when the peer group has greater influence over the new recruit than does the superior with formal authority. Wheeler (1966) contends that when this occurs, the recruit will follow the direction of those he has spent the most time with—his peers. Becker et al. (1961) observe that medical students favor the student perspective of "learn what the faculty wants you to know" rather than the faculty perspective of "learning it all" (p. 111).

The **investiture socialization** process establishes the usefulness of the characteristics the individual already possesses (e.g. skills, behaviors and attitudes, relationships with previous organizational members) and the **divestiture** process aims to strip away the entering characteristics of the recruit (e.g., prior attitudes and behaviors learned from a prior organizational culture). In the divestiture process, individuals are expected to suffer, participate in "dirty work," and work for low pay. This treatment detaches the individual from former roles. Schein (1964, in Van Maanen, 1976) calls this the "unfreezing process" (p. 99). Through the shared experience of suffering, recruits in the medical and accounting profession identify with peers. Those who survive these ordeals are viewed as committed members.

Using Van Maanen's (1983) typology, individuals are more likely to conform when formal, serial, sequential, fixed, divestiture, and tournament socialization techniques are used. If an organizational culture allows for individual creativity, it will be more likely to use informal, disjunctive, investiture, variable, and contest socialization techniques.

Factors which Influence Socialization Methods

Environmental factors, the status of the organization within the social structure, and organizational factors influence the success of socialization methods (Van Maanen, 1976).

Environmental Factors

The cultural environment may undermine professional socialization or contribute to it (Van Maanen, 1976). In Davis and co-workers' (1966) study of collegiate nurses, the values of marriage and motherhood are more salient in socializing the collegiate nurses than the university's attempt to train them for positions as leaders in the nursing profession. Other examples of strong cultural values influencing socialization techniques are found in Trice and Beyer (1993) and Rosow (1974). Trice and Beyer found that values of capitalism undermine employees' dedication to humanitarian issues within a corporation. In conforming to society's capitalistic values, the downwardly mobile corporate employee may feel reluctant to take a job for less pay. If he does take a job for less pay, he may still feel the need to aspire to the rewards that accompanied his old status. If this is the case, the socializing efforts of his new organization may fail to be effective (Wilensky and Edwards, 1959, in Rosow, 1974).

Status of Organization

The higher the status of the organization within the social structure, the greater the aspiring member will be motivated to accept socialization. Since the college-educated nurses do not hold the statuses of the hospital and the university in high esteem, they sought to be socialized by other healthcare professions or the broader cultural values of the time, which favored domestic roles for women (Davis et al., 1966). The high rank of the accounting and medical professions within society motivates recruits to become socialized to their professional roles (Becker et al., 1961; Montagna, 1975).

Organizational Factors

An organization's ability to influence new members depends on its control over rewards valued by new members. These include suitable levels of comfort, health, safety, and limits on effort exerted (Goffman, 1961). Katz's (in Van Maanen, 1977) study on work satisfaction found that the same rewards such as autonomy, salary, and feedback are not salient for all workers. He establishes that the degree to which autonomy is valued depends on the length of time a worker has been with the organization. Autonomy is less important for newcomers than for veterans, because they are more likely to value feedback on the effectiveness of their work. The degree to which rewards are salient also depends on the values of employees. Mirvis and Hackett (1983) discovered that intrinsic rewards such as worker satisfaction are more salient for nonprofit employees, while monetary rewards are more salient for corporate employees.

Factors which Influence the Control of Rewards

Three factors influence a profession's ability to control rewards: size, degree to which the profession is homogeneous, and the extent to which the profession is insulated from the larger society (Van Maanen, 1976). The smaller the profession, the more powerful it is in controlling rewards. The more homogeneous and the more insulated the profession is from the broader society, the more influential the profession is in controlling rewards. Accounting and medicine control size through a rigorous selection and socialization process. The prestigious accounting firms recruit the top 10 percent of business school graduates. One-half of those selected are weeded out after the first year (Montagna, 1975). In addition, not all recruits continue to make a good impression in medicine (Becker et al., 1961).

Thus, through control of recruitment and training, a common body of knowledge, and language enable professions to be distinctive. Formal socialization, such as graduate education, provides the nonprofit sector with a "presocialized" group of applicants who understand the differences and similarities between the profit and nonprofit sectors. While a formal education is not mandatory for nonprofit managers, there are some 70 nonprofit educational programs operating in the United States (O'Neill and Fletcher, 1998, p. 1). According to O'Neill, "the development of nonprofit management education is based on the theory that there are significant differences in the (1) organizational reality of nonprofits, as distinguished from the for-profit and government entities, and therefore in the (2) knowledge, skills, attitudes, and values needed to manage nonprofit organizations" (O'Neill and Fletcher, 1998, p. 2). This type of formalized training shapes the attitudes and behaviors of the nonprofit recruit, acting as a barrier to those who do not have this training.

EDUCATIONAL AND PROFESSIONAL TRAINING

The trained manager of a nonprofit organization is a manager who understands the mission or goal of the organization and the special requirements which are unique to nonprofits, namely, fundraising, advocacy, dealing with volunteers, and nonprofit boards of directors. It is the recommendation of Salamon and Anheier (1996) that a greater emphasis be placed on institutionalizing the training function within the sector.

In order to appreciate the need for replacing "untrained managers" with nonprofit managers who have managerial expertise, it is important to understand that historically, "many new organizations were established by lay persons, social activists, or human services workers with no formal training in organizational management" (Smith and Lipsky, 1993, p. 83).

The need to create professional nonprofit educational programs has been a topic of concern within the nonprofit community since the 1970s. It was not until the 1980s, when the federal government reduced its role and the nonprofit sector was forced to "do more with less," that nonprofit leaders recognized the need for formalized managerial training. In 1977, Yale University became the first university to offer a curriculum dedicated to nonprofit management; the University of San Francisco was the first to offer a graduate degree in nonprofit management in 1985 (O'Neill and Fletcher, 1998).

Within the nonprofit academic community, educators and practitioners argue the pros and cons about creating a generic curriculum which is aimed at educating the nonprofit manager, regardless of his chosen discipline (e.g., arts, education, human services) versus orienting management programs around the nonprofit manager's discipline of choice. In 1986, the Alfred P. Sloan Foundation sponsored a conference on "Educating Managers of Nonprofit Organizations" which focused on this debate (O'Neill and Young, 1988). DiMaggio (1988) and Levy (1988) have discussed this debate in great detail. According to Levy (1988), there are those who believe that "discipline is destiny" and that "graduate education must be rooted in traditional professional experience and credentialing, not in a generic nonprofit course of study" (p. 24). Levy proposes that since the nonprofit sector is facing reductions in government funding, and increased demands for its services and greater regulation, it is crucial that nonprofit managers be well versed in generic management or functions such as fundraising, finance, planning, and marketing. Furthermore, as educators decide on generic versus discipline-based curricula, he urges educators to take a look at the recruitment trends of nonprofit organizations such as the Metropolitan Museum of New York, the Kennedy Center for the Performing Arts, and the Metropolitan Opera who have selected their managers from government, business, and education. In making their hiring decisions, these nonprofit employers obviously placed more importance on generic management skills rather than on the prior occupational discipline of the manager.

DiMaggio (1988) writes that while nonprofit discipline-oriented professionals (e.g., service delivery professionals) who want to upgrade their managerial skills may seek generic training, nonprofit crossover managers (e.g., those wanting to move from the arts sector to the education sector) as well as neophytes need "field-specific knowledge and networks" (p. 68). Finally, he suggests that the best solution "would be to create nonprofit general management programs at large universities wherein students could supplement their generalized management training with sector-specific courses in professional schools" (p. 68). It is this model that the Hauser Center on Nonprofit Organizations at Harvard University's John F. Kennedy School of Government has selected (Miller, 1997).

While DiMaggio, Levy, and others have discussed the need for specialized versus generic nonprofit management programs, Mark H. Moore's (1996) *Notes Toward A Curriculum in Nonprofit Policy and Management* argues for creating a program which specializes in nonprofit management, maintaining that the nonprofit sector differs from other sectors on specific issues including leadership through values, governance, fundraising, mission, recruitment, and management of volunteers. Attention to the development of nonprofit management curricula which is inclusive of the perspectives of the corporate and government sectors was addressed by the W. K. Kellogg Foundation. In 1997, the Foundation introduced a 5-year initiative to "help develop more comprehensive educational programs that respond to the wide range of management and leadership needs of Third Sector leaders" ("Philanthropy and Volunteerism in Higher Education Initiative," 1997).

The Cross-Sector Student and Management Pool

The literature on nonprofit formal education raises questions with regard to the types of students being recruited and the attention the programs have given to the nonprofit sector recruitment of employees outside the field. Nonprofit educators and practitioners discuss four groups of students: nonprofit midcareer leaders trained in a specific discipline such as social work, education, or the arts who seek to return to school for managerial training; crossover midcareer nonprofit managers who are seeking to change disciplines within the nonprofit sector; students who are entering the nonprofit management field and want to be trained in nonprofit management for a specific discipline; and those board members who seek to be educated so that they are better able to perform their role. While all four groups of students represent a pool of talent for the nonprofit sector as well as income-generating markets for the university, is there room for a fifth student group—the mid-career corporate manager who wants to move into the nonprofit sector? In addition to studying the history, culture, and networks of nonprofit disciplines within the sector, this type of student needs to understand what functional imperatives distinguish the sectors. And if, as Levy (1988) states, the nonprofit sector has determined that the crossover or cross-sector candidate is gaining attention as a likely candidate within the recruitment pool, might not it be important to include the rationale for cross-sector employment within the curriculum of a nonprofit program?

With rare exception, there has been little written about cross-sector employment—its origins and rationale. At an Independent Sector Professional Forum in 1985, Reynold Levy, president of the AT&T Foundation, gave a speech entitled "Talent Matters: Attracting and Retaining Gifted Managers in the Third Sector." Levy challenged the sector to consider the concept of recruiting cross-sector employees:

> How extensive is the search for the CEO and other high-level manage-ment posts? Is it and must it be confined to the profession with which the institution is historically associated—physicians for the hospital, academ-ics for the university, social workers for community centers, psychiatrists for mental health institutions, and former musicians for orchestra man-agers? Wittingly or otherwise, do searches screen away able candidates by sex, marital status, race, ethnic, or religious background? (p. 7)

His speech further elaborated on the need to look beyond traditional recruitment practices and to expand the applicant pool to include people from government and business:

> What patterns of mobility, if any, can one discern within nonprofit insti-tutions and between them and government, on the one hand, and for-profit firms, on the other? Is it desirable to encourage circulation of personnel between and within sectors through executive release time, sabbatical leaves, and executive loan? Indeed, if scale of enterprise is a critical variable in executive functioning and if loneliness and isolation are frequent plaints of upper management in the Third Sector, what can be done to stimulate professional exchanges outside of noninstitutional boundaries? (p. 9)
>
> That being so, a hard look ought to be taken on the neglected pools of management and trustee talent being insufficiently tapped for non-profit service—by age, by gender, by racial and ethnic background, and by professional training. (p. 10)
>
> I've counseled hundreds of men and women—professionals in need of career change and others fresh out of school—people of energy, ideal-ism, vitality, and resourcefulness who have not even thought of nonprofit service as an option for themselves. When they do, more often than not the pathways to employment are bewilderingly primitive and complex, the barriers to the Third Sector entry formidable. (p. 11)

Such barriers to entry in the nonprofit sector are sustained by a nonprofit belief system that the structural and cultural differences between the profit and nonprofit sectors necessitate the recruitment of those who have been socialized in the nonprofit sector. It is in understanding the differences and similarities that one begins to understand the criteria used to categorize and label the members of each sector. The next section explores the structural and cultural differences and similarities between the profit and nonprofit sectors.

DIFFERENCES AND SIMILARITIES BETWEEN THE PROFIT AND NONPROFIT SECTORS

Cross-Sector Similarities and Interdependence

In his plan to create a curriculum for Harvard University's John F. Kennedy School of Government's nonprofit center—Hauser Center on Nonprofit Organizations—the Center's director Mark H. Moore begins with a statement that draws attention to the similarities between sectors:

> Managers in all three sectors must figure out to whom and for what they are accountable, and how relationships to their overseers must be managed. They must all be engaged in defining the mission and purpose of their organizations, and the shaping of organizational identity. They must all be able to account for and control their use of financial resources. They must all be able to motivate and develop the people on whom they are relying. They must all be able to analyze and understand their production processes and be able to re-engineer and innovate to enhance efficiency, effectiveness, or quality. They must all be able to do strategic planning that fits their current organization into anticipated future environments. (p. 13)

Furthermore, in addition to these similarities, corporations and nonprofit organizations depend on each other. O'Neill (1989) reminds us of the important linkages including the purchasing of services between sectors, corporate philanthropy of nonprofits, corporate donations of volunteer time and board service, and nonprofit contributions of research and employees to the corporate sector.

While linkages and similarities do exist between the nonprofit and corporate sectors, the majority of the comparative literature focuses on the differences in structures, cultures, and work styles of people working within the corporate and nonprofit sectors.

Organizational Structures

Structural theorists argue that organizations are rational or culturally oriented institutions with a primary purpose of accomplishing set goals. Within organizational structures, goals are achieved through defined rules, formal authority, and a chain of command. Dimensions of organizations can be measured and quantified. Organizational members are rewarded for achieving set goals.

Mirvis and Hackett (1983) found that profit and nonprofit organizations differ in their goal orientations. Corporations exist to make a profit while nonprofits attempt to make a difference in society. Moore (2000) argues that corporations strive to "enhance shareholder wealth" and nonprofit organizations seek to "achieve social mission" (p. 189). Similarly, Etzioni (1975) writes that normative or nonprofit organizations have culturally oriented goals such as education, healthcare, and research while corporations have economic rational goals. Consequently, results in each sector are measured differently. Mirvis and Hackett found that corporations view profit as the measure of success. Within the nonprofit sector, accomplishment of mission is not necessarily connected to an increase in revenue. Moore (2000) contends that nonprofit organizations have two bottom lines: "mission effectiveness and financial sustainability" (p. 194). It is this difference in goal orientation that necessitates nonprofit organizations finding a way to measure their success in something other than financial terms.

Additionally, profit and nonprofit organizations receive their revenues from different sources. O'Neill and Young (1988) report that corporations depend on market sources of funds such as fees for services. While nonprofits rely to some extent on fees for service, they are largely dependent on non-market sources of funds such as grants from individuals, foundations, and corporations. These marked differences in revenue sources are linked to profit and nonprofit goal orientations. Moore (2000) writes that "the performance of [a nonprofit organization] in producing this [social] value is not reliably connected to its ability to attract revenues to pay for its continuing costs, because the [nonprofit organization] secures revenues not by selling products and services to customers but by persuading ... voluntary contributors ... that the social mission they are pursuing is a valuable one" (p. 195).

In his examination of for-profit and nonprofit differences in goal orientation, measures of performance, and revenue sources, Moore (2000) concludes that for-profit and nonprofit organizations must have different strategies for implementing their goals. The corporation's strategy must be centered on the achievement of financial performance and the nonprofit organization's strategy should be oriented around the achievement of social purpose through the creation of public value. The creation of public value extends beyond "the willingness of clients to pay for services" (p. 199). Public value is also generated "by interacting with individual donors in transactions that lend significance to their gifts and on building a network of people who share the cause" (p. 202).

The two sectors differ in their employee composition and the degree to which employees profit from revenues. Corporations have paid staff. Nonprofits also have paid staff, but often they depend heavily on nonpaid staff (volunteers). Nonprofits are extremely reliant on professionals who have credentialed expertise in executing service delivery (social workers, educators, artists) (O'Neill and Young, 1988). Nonprofit organizations legally are required to impose a nondistribution constraint where no member benefits excessively from a surplus. Corporations have no such requirement (O'Neill and Young, 1988).

On average, there is a 20 percent difference between wages of managers and professionals in the profit and nonprofit sector (Preston, 1989, in Emanuele, 1997, p. 57). Different types of rewards are used to secure employee commitment in the profit and nonprofit sectors. Etzioni (1975) reveals that normative organizations, of which nonprofits are one type, use symbolic rewards such as praise and esteem to secure employee commitment to cultural goals. Mirvis and Hackett's study found that nonprofit organizations emphasize intrinsic rewards that include variety, challenge, and satisfaction from the work itself. Wages are less salient, according to Mirvis and Hackett, because nonprofit organizations are themselves nonmonetary in orientation. Nonprofit employees are willing to work for lower wages because they are "donating some of their time" (Preston, 1989, in Emanuele, 1997, p. 57). Emanuele (1997) also discusses that nonprofit employees working in education and healthcare may be willing to work for less because their benefit packages are attractive and can be offered without incurring great costs (e.g., free tuition or health services). In contrast, Mirvis and Hackett and Etzioni view salaries as the most salient rewards for corporate employees.

Cultural Differences

In examining the differences between profit and nonprofit organizations, it is important to explore the cultural differences between the two. The "organizational culture" perspective goes beyond structure and looks at organizational language, rituals, belief systems, and assumptions that are not formalized. Deal and Kennedy (1982) maintain that values or the basic beliefs of an organization form the heart of the organizational culture. Organizational culture guides the behaviors of its members and affects everything from who gets promoted, what decisions are made, and even how employees dress. In strong cultures, Deal and Kennedy assert, there is little uncertainty because strong cultures have clear-cut structures and value systems. It is the culture which determines if the workers are fast or slow; tough or friendly; team players or individualistic in their approach. It is the culture which governs what kind of information is taken seriously for decision-making purposes, what kinds of people are most respected, and what types of strategies are important for achieving the goal of the organization.

Ott (1989) found through ethnography that every organization's culture is different and what works for one may not work for another. For example, when the president of a small human services organization tried to make the organization more business-like by creating a computerized office and increasing income through the attraction of media coverage, the employees resisted, and the president eventually left the board of directors. Bush (1992), echoing the conclusions of organizational cultural theorists, contends that conflict will arise in nonprofit organizations when corporate values such as "competition" are imposed on nonprofits which value "collaboration" (p. 394). Trice and Beyer (1993) write that the reverse sequence of imposing humanitarian values within a corporation will generate conflict as well.

Both structural and organizational cultural theorists argue that value conflict is apparent in both profit and nonprofit organizations. The literature stresses, however, that the source of conflict for each sector is likely to differ. The source of value conflict in nonprofit organizations is oriented around the mission and the best way to achieve it. Etzioni (1975) establishes that when dual leadership, in a nonprofit organization, consists of an expressive (mission-oriented leader) and an instrumental leader (profit-oriented leader) and these roles are not clearly defined and separated, conflict will occur. Liedtka's (1991) model of value contention reveals that since goals are not often specified in nonprofit organizations, conflict will arise when two highly regarded goals compete for primacy such as goals of maintaining employee versus constituency satisfaction.

Since the goals in the corporate sector revolve around profit, it is unlikely that the employee's satisfaction will take precedence over the customer's satisfaction. In fact, Jackall's *Moral Mazes* (1988) discusses the employee's imperative for avoiding conflict. At all costs, one adheres to the "moral rules of the corporation" (p. 4). Individuals show loyalty to their boss and never contradict him. Employees sacrifice their families for the corporation, mask emotions, and separate consciousness from action. Additionally, employees avoid all blame and never leave a track that traces responsibility. In the event that contradiction does occur, the consequence is the severing or termination of corporate upward mobility. Conflict in corporations, therefore, originates around issues of internal and external competition and the best way to make a profit.

Work Styles

Differences in structure and culture also influence the governance and communication styles of corporate and nonprofit organizations. Hodgkin (1993) found that corporate and nonprofit boards of directors differ in their governance styles and in their style of communicating and setting policy. He asserts that corporate boards are dominated by insiders or senior managers who are responsible for executing policy. Furthermore, the board members are usually paid and the chief executive is likely to have a vote (O'Neill and Young, 1988). Since the board is made up of insiders, there is less need to consult other board members when an important decision is to be made (Hodgkin, 1993). In contrast, the only insider who sits on a nonprofit board is the executive director who is not likely to have a vote (and nonprofit board members usually do not receive compensation) (Hodgkin, 1993; O'Neill and Young, 1988). Since many nonprofit boards consist of community members, there is a greater need in a nonprofit than in a corporation for the insider or the executive director to communicate the organization's goals to the other board members. There is also a greater need in a nonprofit than there is in a corporation for the board members to understand the pressing "mission-oriented" needs of the nonprofit.

With regard to setting policy, corporate boards concern themselves with the straightforward policy of making money and leave the day-to-day management of earning a profit to the chief executive officer. For example, based on the board's policy about a strategic approach to pricing (e.g., maximizing profit), corporate management sets and implements a pricing system of products. Pricing changes, as long as they maximize profits, will not require board approval. Hodgkin contends that nonprofit managerial decisions regarding pricing changes will require board approval because many of their value-oriented decisions involve "significant policy issues" which affect people's lives (1993, p. 419). While the raising of prices in a nonprofit organization may increase its income, it may also make it impossible for the constituency it serves to afford its services. The board of the nonprofit will have to decide which course it wants to take based on the underlying values that support the organization's mission. Since so many of the management decisions in a nonprofit organization are policy decisions which affect the public interest, there is a greater need to include the board in the discussion before making the decision.

Finally, Hodgkin maintains that profit and nonprofit boards differ in their level of managerial expertise and this affects their governance and decision-making processes. Corporate board members tend to have considerable training and expertise for the industry they represent. Their primary responsibility is to their shareholders and they have no fiduciary responsibility to other constituencies. Every decision made is based on whether it will make money for the corporation. In nonprofit organizations, board members, as stated above, are outsiders and are more likely to have a poor understanding of their role and responsibilities. They are probably selected for their commitment to the organization rather than for their ability to address organizational problems. Since they are not experts in resolving the issues of organizational values and the conflicting constituencies of their organizations, they probably need a slower approach to problem solving.

Hodgkin (1993) concludes that value-based decision-making in the nonprofit sector differs drastically from the profit-based decision-making of the corporate sector. While decisions in the corporate sector are often made for short-term gain, decisions in the nonprofit sector are often made to support the long-term interests of the community. This severe difference is articulated by career changer Nancy Moses in the *Wall Street Journal* (1997): "I was used to making decisions whose consequences would be felt for 60 days or 60 months—not 60 years" (p. 5). O'Neill and Young (1988) maintain that it is important to stress this difference within the context of nonprofit educational curricula.

Etzioni (1975) and Mirvis and Hackett (1983) insist that nonprofit and corporate executives have different styles of leadership, language, and giving feedback on performance. Etzioni (1975) argues that corporate or utilitarian organizations have instrumental leadership because goals are rational. He asserts that it is functional for expressive leaders such as teachers, ministers, professors, and doctors to dominate the leadership roles in nonprofit or normative organizations because it is expressive leaders who build up commitments of organizational members and initiate goals.

Etzioni also contends that corporate organizations use instrumental or technical language and that communication within these types of organizations is more likely to be vertical. While expressive language or expressions of praise and acceptance do exist in corporations, Etzioni maintains that the degree to which it exists depends on the existence of peer relationships and the extent to which these actors are members of the same external organizations (e.g., churches, unions, and volunteer organizations). Language in nonprofit organizations is more likely to be expressive, and horizontal communication predominates in many voluntary organizations. However, Etzioni points out that organizations such as universities which sustain a dual leadership structure [(e.g., president (instrumental leader) and provost (expressive leader)] will have vertical communication structures.

Mirvis and Hackett (1983) found that nonprofit employees are less likely to receive feedback on their performance than are their corporate counterparts because results are difficult to measure in the nonprofit sector. Corporate employees, on the other hand, are more likely to receive feedback on their performance because results are easier to quantify.

The preceding section illustrates that there are indeed structural and cultural differences between the nonprofit and profit sectors. In making a transition from the profit to the nonprofit sector, the displaced corporate manager must be motivated to identify with a new organizational culture and a new set of organizational values. In reshaping his organizational identity, he must be willing to be socialized by a new reference group—the nonprofit sector.

THE RESHAPING OF OCCUPATIONAL IDENTITY

A New Reference Group

"A successful transition ... requires a shift in the actor's reference groups as a source of norms about a new role for him" (Rosow, 1974, p. 119).

Reference groups (Merton, 1968, p. 292) serve as "frames of reference" for self-evaluation and attitude formation. It is through the acquisition of new reference groups that one is able to "abandon the earlier status." It is through this abandonment of the previous status that the individual is able to identify with the norms of a new reference group (Rosow, 1974, p. 126). In identifying with the new reference group, the individual must be willing to be resocialized or to adapt the new values and behaviors of a new organizational culture. This is accomplished through learning the language (both spoken and nonverbal) and developing skills required to succeed in a new organizational culture, developing the required relationships with "significant others" such as peers and superiors, internalizing organizational norms, and surviving barriers created by the organization, as well as discrepancies between expectations and reality (Brim and Wheeler, 1966; Elkin and Handel, 1984; Rosow, 1974; Van Maanen, 1976, 1977, 1983).

The theory behind the process of reshaping one's occupational identity is explained in the writings of symbolic interactionists Mead and Goffman. They discuss that the type of self revealed is based on understanding the role requirements and prescriptions of others (Goffman, 1959). In other words, the response of the individual is based on the attitudes of others (Mead, 1934). Both Mead and Goffman write that there are many different selves that make up the identity of an individual. Mead (1934) asserts that "different situations call for different selves" and that there are "all sorts of selves answering to all sorts of different social reactions" (p. 142). Thus, in changing one's occupational identity, one must learn the role and value orientations of employees within a specific organizational culture. One must adopt the requisite expectations of significant others including the appropriate values, knowledge, attitudes, behaviors, and motivations that correspond to a specific organizational culture. One must go through a process of adult socialization (Brim and Wheeler, 1966; Elkin and Handel, 1984; Rosow, 1974; Van Maanen, 1983). In order for successful socialization to occur, three conditions must be met by the socializing organization (Brim and Wheeler, 1966). First, the individual must understand what is expected of him in the social role and this may be acquired through formal training programs or through informal means (e.g., peers). Second, the recruit must meet the requirements. Finally, the trainee must be motivated to learn. The process of socialization within an organization may be preceded by anticipatory socialization processes.

Anticipatory Socialization

It is through anticipatory socialization processes (Brim and Wheeler, 1966; Elkin and Handel, 1984; Rosow, 1974; Van Maanen, 1983) that one learns "the recipes of being" (Goffman, 1963, p. 112). Anticipatory socialization or role rehearsal and preparation (Elkin and Handel, 1984) allow the employee to learn and practice the feelings, actions, and values before he actually enters the organization. It helps reduce anxiety by allowing the employee to learn who the significant others in an organization are and how they relate to him (Van Maanen, 1977). Anticipatory socialization helps reduce culture shock in which a huge gap exists between the entering employee's expectations about the job and the actual demands of the job (Hughes, 1981). Deal and Kennedy (1982) assert that "culture shock may be one of the major reasons why people fail when they leave one organization for another. Where they fail, however, is not necessarily in doing the job, but in not reading the culture correctly" (p. 17). Brim and Wheeler (1966) recommend using peer socialization to facilitate the anticipatory socialization process. Peers provide the "means of adaptation" within an organization (Rosow, 1974, p. 94). Reskin believes that work groups which are made up of in-group and out-group members "expose people to individualizing information about out-group members, challenge out-group stereotypes, and hence should reduce bias" (Reskin, 2000, p. 6).

In the same study that found that nonprofit managers were more likely to hire employees with previous nonprofit experience, Tschirhart (1998) also found that nonprofit employers are more likely to hire managers with volunteer experience in an organization similar to their own. Volunteerism for corporate managers who want to be hired as nonprofit employees is a necessary part of the anticipatory socialization process. Clary et al. (1996) found that a group of individuals who utilize volunteer work in nonprofit organizations develop and practice skills that might otherwise go unpracticed; others use the volunteer experience to gain experiences that will benefit their careers. People also volunteer to combat feelings of inferiority and to enhance self-esteem (Clary et al., 1996). Volunteering may help the individual expand his "role repertoire." "The broadening of a role repertoire promotes human development by facilitating interaction with persons occupying a variety of roles" (Bronfenbrenner, 1979, in Moen et al., 1992, p. 1634). "Roles have a magic-like power to alter how a person is treated, how she acts, what she does and what she thinks and feels" (Bronfenbrenner, 1979, in Moen et al., 1992, p. 1634). The individual's engagement in multiple roles leads to increased networks, resources, and emotional gratification.

In addition to volunteer experience, preemployment training programs that emphasize role rehearsal or exposing the trainee to interaction with his role set (peers) help the trainee learn the appropriate skills as well as gain insight into a particular role. The trainee's interaction with his prospective role set is the only meaningful way to learn one's role. It is through this interaction that a trainee becomes invested or committed to the role and "changes his self-image in a manner appropriate to the role" (Rosow, 1974, p. 135). Training programs that divorce the classroom from practical application on the job do not allow for this interaction with the peer group. Furthermore, trainers who cannot demonstrate the actual practice of a role are weak role models as are younger employment counselors who hold statuses that the older worker achieves earlier in life—statuses which have been lost (Rosow, 1974).

OBSTACLES TO ASSIMILATION

Inefficacious Socialization

The unsocialized member of an organization is a product of inefficacious (Van Maanen, 1976) or ineffective socialization methods. For example, if the individual learns outdated workplace skills in a formal educational setting, he will not be able to survive or perform his role adequately within the organization (Hughes, 1981). Another example of inefficacious socialization is the use of divestiture socialization (the stripping away of entering characteristics) when an organization initially desires a fresh perspective from the new recruit. If, for example, an organization is hiring a manager because he brings a fresh or an objective perspective, "any divestiture tactics could work at counter purposes" (Trice and Beyer, 1993, p. 411). On the other hand, if a manager is expected to divest his previous occupational identity which is comprised of ties and loyalties to members of a prior occupational group and the status earned within that group, resistance would be a likely response on the part of the manager. Of course an actor's motivations to be socialized or to conform are influenced by the environmental values, organizational status, and control of reward factors which Van Maanen (1976) writes about. Depending on the strength of these factors, a newcomer entering an organization will not be motivated to divest all ties with his previous occupation because he has a fear of the unknown; is invested in performing in a certain way; is insecure about adopting new patterns of behaviors and/or is tied to self-interests which may be linked to his previous occupational status (e.g., reputation and rewards) (Trice and Beyer, 1993). In this case, if divestiture socialization is inefficacious, the individual will be competent in performing his job, but will not be able to internalize the values and norms of the organization. This would lead the individual to become a chameleon[6] or refuse to be socialized at all (Rosow, 1965).

One final example of inefficacious socialization occurs when there is no peer acceptance of the newcomer. It is the peer group that is essential in helping the new recruit learn the ropes within a new organizational culture (Becker et al., 1961; Brim and Wheeler, 1966; Rosow, 1974; Van Maanen, 1976, 1983). As Epstein has observed, if the individual does not develop the support systems within an organization and is not taught the "trade secrets" of the organization, as occurs with women who want to break into non-traditional occupations, she will not be motivated to accept the socialization process of the organization (Epstein, 1970, 1981, 1988, 1992, 1995).

Lack of Individual Motivation

The degree to which socialization is successful depends on the extent to which the individual is motivated to be socialized (Brim and Wheeler, 1966). "If a person's motivation to belong is not sufficiently strong to induce the personal changes that allow the individual to adjust to the situation, he will leave" (Schein in Van Maanen, 1976, p. 94). An individual may not be motivated if his values are different from the values of the organization. Merton (1968) argues that the individual's attitude toward becoming a member in a reference group is associated with the relevance of the group's values to his own. The individual's values are influenced by the broader cultural values of society—if these broader cultural values are viewed as relevant by the individual (Davis et al., 1966; Trice and Beyer, 1993; Van Maanen, 1976; Wilensky and Edwards, 1959, in Rosow, 1974). If the individual embraces or internalizes the broader cultural values (Van Maanen, 1976) which emphasize self-interest, he may not be motivated to adhere to the values of a humanitarian organization (Ott, 1989; Trice and Beyer, 1993). If the worker's self-image and self-esteem are so aligned with their previous statuses (Trice and Beyer, 1993) and he does not have the confidence to learn the values and belief systems of a new culture, he may not be motivated to accept a new organizational culture.

Creative individualism and autonomy respectively are important to the success of socialization (Gecas, 1989; Schein, 1968, in Van Maanen, 1976). The individual's ability to have some control over his actions leads to increased motivation to accept socialization processes.

When socialization methods are inefficacious and/or when the worker is not motivated to accept the prevailing organizational method of socialization, workers experience varying degrees of alienation and the outcome leads to deviance (Van Maanen, 1976), absence of continuous commitment (Moore, 1969), or resistance to career transition (Brim, 1968). Within the life cycle literature, career transition is viewed as an integral part of the life cycle.

CAREER TRANSITION AND THE LIFE CYCLE

The degree to which workers resist an unrewarding work environment depends on the extent to which they have access to wealth, social status, and political influence. The greater number of interpersonal networks the worker has outside the organization, the greater autonomy he has in seeking out people with the same interests and restructuring his relationships to fit his interests (Brim, 1968). This attempt to find new role relationships within work is part of the life cycle.

The Life Cycle

The individual is able to "repot" himself (Brim, 1968, p. 204) or go through a "change of soul" (Van Maanen, 1976, p. 101) because the socialization process is a continuous one. Throughout the life course or life cycle, there are a succession of roles and multiple role changes. One makes the transition from childhood to adulthood; marriage and parenthood; employment to retirement (George, 1993; Neugarten and Datan, 1973). Moen et al. (1992) maintain that women who occupy multiple roles over a period of 30 years are likely to lead healthier lives. Furthermore, they found that nonprofit volunteer roles such as "churchgoer" and "member" of a socially related club are positively related to health and longevity (p. 1613). They argue that multiple role occupancy might be especially important in later life, when role reduction increases within American culture. In addition, the researchers believe that more needs to be known about the health consequences of volunteer work. They hypothesize that volunteer work may provide "gratifying social involvement and recognition, reduction in anxiety, and self-preoccupation, and many forms of socioemotional support" (p. 1617).

In summary, life cycle theorists agree that individuals experience changing roles throughout their lifetimes (e.g., volunteer, employee, member of organization). In this book, I examine one example of changing adult roles: changing one's occupational status (from the corporate to the nonprofit work world) through preparation, rehearsal, and internalization of new nonprofit organizational values and behaviors. In doing so I will draw on the literature discussed above and will also extend it into a previously unstudied area.

Notes

1. The U.S. Department of Labor's *Occupational Outlook Handbook* (2001) defines "managerial" occupations as including but not limited to: accountants, budget analysts, financial managers, personnel, training, labor relations managers, marketing, public relations managers, general managers, and top executives. "Professional specialties" include but are not limited to: engineers, architects, computer scientists and systems analysts, lawyers, economists, writers, and editors.
2. The nonprofit sector is a diverse sector. However, scholars cited throughout this study argue that there are enough similarities among nonprofit organizations that it is meaningful to look at the sector as a whole and contrast it with the profit sector.
3. Though religious organizations are classified as 501(c)(3) organizations, they need not apply for tax-exempt status from the Internal Revenue Service and thus are not included

in the Internal Revenue Service reporting of charitable organizations or in the number of organizations cited in this book.
4. The remaining nonprofit organizations are classified under various Internal Revenue tax codes including veterans' associations, employee-funded pension plans, and credit unions and are not considered for purposes of this book.
5. The U.S. Census Bureau's statistics are based on tax-exempt service organizations with a payroll.
6. According to Rosow (1965), a chameleon is an organizational member who is competent in his performance, but will not embrace the values of the organization.

Chapter 3

Differences and Barriers between the Two Worlds

THE NONPROFIT VIEW ON CULTURAL DIFFERENCES AND THE NEED FOR CULTURE CHANGE

Every displaced corporate manager trying to enter the nonprofit world wonders how different this sector is compared to the corporate sector with which he is already familiar. Every manager also wonders to what extent his prior stock of knowledge, skills, and experiences will carry over, or to what extent he will have to develop new competencies and attitudes. The larger the differences between the two sectors, the higher the hurdle for the career changer to get over, the greater the body of new information to absorb.

However, the issue of sameness and differences goes beyond any particular person trying to get over the hurdle. Powerful people inside the nonprofit world, the gatekeepers who hire new staff, often have strong views on this issue. If a gatekeeper believes that the nonprofit culture is very unlike the culture in the corporate world, then that gatekeeper will not look favorably on a displaced manager who keeps stressing in an interview, how useful his corporate skills and experiences are. The situation is made even more difficult by the fact that opinions on this issue vary dramatically within the nonprofit world. Other gatekeepers within nonprofit organizations believe that nonprofits share many features with the corporate world; and yet others believe that nonprofits need to become more like the corporate world, in terms of managerial technologies, systems of accountability, speed of decision-making, and so on. These kinds of gatekeepers will welcome displaced managers whose corporate skills seem useful.

These splits in opinion among gatekeepers inside the nonprofit world are documented in other studies: some researchers view nonprofits as quite different, in fact contrasting or opposite kinds of organizations from corporations, while others perceive large numbers of similarities between the two sectors.

In this chapter, I will examine differences between the sectors, drawing on the work of researchers, on the works of gatekeepers inside the nonprofit world, and the experiences and comments of career changers. By identifying what the differences and similarities are between the two sectors (whether perceived or real), we see the extent to which the hurdle between employment from the corporate to the nonprofit sector is a matter of stereotyping, and to what extent it reflects real differences which can be overcome through training.

The Cultures Are Different

Managers in the nonprofit sector, researchers of both sectors, and career changers, from the profit to the nonprofit sector, argue that the corporate and nonprofit sectors differ in their structure, goal setting, and the ways in which results are measured.

Structure

This corporate manager turned "professional board member" describes distinct differences in structure between the corporate and nonprofit sectors:

> *Board Member of Three Nonprofit Organizations*: There is a distinct jargon used in both sectors that is influenced by the cultural values of each sector. The organizational model used by the corporation is the military hierarchy. It employs an authoritarian management style. The watchwords are command, communication, and control. Accountability focuses on the bottom line. The chief executive officer and the board of directors are accountable to the shareholders. The measure of success is linked to increasing the bottom line.
>
> In nonprofit organizations, the measure of strength is the mission of the organization. The watchwords in the nonprofit sector are oriented around cooperation, community, and collegiality. Many constituencies are appealed to in order to secure a balance including students, alumni, clients, faculty, board, volunteers, federal, state, and local regulatory agencies.

While some career changers argue that the corporate sector is more hierarchical than the nonprofit sector, some insist that the corporate sector is "getting flatter" while the nonprofit sector is more hierarchical:

> *Career Changer, Healthcare Organization*: In the for-profit sector, there are many more layers. The further from the top you are, the further you are from the decision-makers. In the nonprofit sector, there are many less layers and there is interaction among all levels. Senior management is accessible and open to ideas and input.

Not all nonprofit employees agree, however:

Career Changer, Educational Organization: In my small educational organization, where we have 25–30 employees, I thought that the structure was pretty hierarchical. The corporate sector, on the other hand, is getting flatter and there are fewer layers between senior management and the other managers.

Career Changer, Human Services Organization: Within my human services organization I had to talk to many people above. My immediate superiors and I had to sell the idea to them, and they had to sell it to their bosses, and they to theirs.

Goal Orientations

In addition to differences in structure, corporations and nonprofit organizations have very different goal orientations (Drucker, 1990; Hodgkin, 1993; Mirvis and Hackett, 1983; Moore, 2000). Corporations exist to make money for their shareholders (Mirvis and Hackett, 1983; Moore, 2000) and nonprofits exist to make a difference in society (Drucker, 1990), reflect the values of society (Hodgkin, 1993), and achieve a social mission or purpose (Moore, 2000). This view is widespread among nonprofit employers, and is often used as an explanation for why nonprofit salaries are markedly lower than corporate ones and why nonprofit employees are more cooperative, or less competitive.

A career changer in the healthcare field believes that "corporations focus on the individual's achievement of making money for the company. In the nonprofit sector, the goal orientation focuses on the collective achievement of mission. There are more people involved in the achievement of the mission— the board, staff, and volunteers."

A career changer in a housing organization found this to be true as well:

Career Changer, Housing Organization: In the corporate sector, people are acting to achieve money on their own so cutting the throat of an associate is not uncommon. Goals, in the corporate sector, are achieved by being able to spend the least and achieve the most.... Nonprofit managers are not motivated by how much money they make, but by helping others.

Another career changer also discusses the different goal focus:

Career Changer, Human Services Organization: The driver in nonprofit organizations is altruism, not money. Don't go into the nonprofit sector expecting to make a lot of money. Because the primary driver is altruism, they [nonprofit employees] are not as professionally oriented as in the corporate sector.

Career changers also observe that there is a difference in the way goals are set and achieved. Corporations have an individual focus in the setting and achievement of goals; nonprofits have a collective focus:

> *Career Changer, Human Services Organization*: In the corporate sector, people in charge set most goals, be it the head of the division or the company. These decisions are made without the participation of the supervised. The attainment of the goals is not necessarily only because of the effort of the senior managers. However, it is always viewed and rewarded as their achievement.
>
> In the nonprofit sector, goals are actually set by funders, as well as accepted by funders. The [nonprofit] agency must deliver the goals, even when it doesn't get the funding. It matters that the senior staff is aware of the goals and that they all have a part in achieving them.

A career changer now working for a school discusses how goals are set and achieved in both sectors:

> In my financial services corporation, the goals were linked to the bottom line and dictated by the higher levels. At the school, we make our goals in a collegial fashion. They are always realizable goals and are more easily achieved on a team basis. If I have questions about a business decision, I call up the other administrators in the organization and discuss it. We aren't in competition [with each other]. In the corporate sector, there was a fair amount of team play, but you really had to watch what you were communicating to others because you were in a competitive situation.

Some managers report that goals are more clearly defined in the profit sector than in the nonprofit sector. Goals are also thought to be more short-term than long-term in the nonprofit sector. Hodgkin (1993) and Liedtka (1991) maintain that goals are clear in the corporate sector because they are driven by the bottom line. Since nonprofit organizations are responsible to many constituencies and they each have their own set of values, it is more difficult to establish and achieve goals as reported by these three career changers:

> *Career Changer, Service Organization*: I don't see any hard-and-fast goals in my service organization. I have to raise one million dollars for a project and that's the goal. Here, the goals are met, but they aren't quite as organized as they are in the corporate world. I'm not sure that they have a strategic plan and the ways to achieve what you set out to do.
>
> *Career Changer, Human Services Organization*: Goal-setting is much more casual here [than in my previous job]. We have some kind of objective settings in our department, but we are one of the few. In the corporate sector, you have objectives and you have to meet them. In this organization, goal setting is much freer flowing. Here we are meeting the day-to-day goals of the organization. The longest objective is one year. In my previous job, we had five-year strategic plans.

Career Changer, Housing Organization: Goals are vague and they change as time goes on. For instance, you build houses for the homeless, and then you realize that you weren't successful in getting them to live in these houses, or helping them get back into society. Then you have to change your goals.

Measuring Results

According to Moore (2000), since nonprofit organizations produce value in terms of meeting social objectives, their performance in producing this value cannot be solely linked to their ability to earn revenues from selling services. Nonprofit organizations also earn revenues from "persuading... voluntary contributors... that the social mission they are pursuing is a valuable one" (p. 195).

Mirvis and Hackett (1983) discovered that there are so many links between nonprofits and their various constituencies (e.g., donors, board, staff, members, clients) that it is difficult to measure results. Corporations, they found, measure results "based on computing the rate of return on resources expended" (p. 4). A career changer now working for an educational organization asserts that since there is pressure to achieve goals in the corporate sector, they are reviewed frequently and success is measured in terms of the amount of money generated. A healthcare career changer concurs that the amount of money generated is compared with the budgeted expectations in the corporate sector. An educational career changer found vast differences comparing how results are measured:

The corporate sector does a wonderful job on reporting its bottom line to the shareholders. In my educational organization, there was no visible means of measuring results. In fact, this was one of the things that we struggled with the most: "How do you define when you are successful?" I don't think that nonprofits invest the time in monitoring whether results are successful.

However, another career changer believes that "there is a lot more accountability in the nonprofit sector if the agency is funded. In the corporate sector, there is more room for manipulation of the results."

Rewards

The reward system of the two spheres differs. Normative or nonprofit organizations use symbolic rewards such as praise and esteem to secure the commitment of people to cultural goals (e.g., arts, education, human, and healthcare services) (Etzioni, 1975). Several career changers reported receiving more feedback of this kind in the nonprofit sector. A healthcare career changer explains:

> I receive more feedback in the nonprofit sector. I get more feedback because I work on more projects and events [than I did in the corporate sector]. Since there are a lot of people involved in putting these projects together, there is more feedback. People are encouraged to get and receive feedback. Since there is a better rapport with managers in the nonprofit sector, you're able to seek out feedback.

A healthcare career changer also found the same to be true:

> In the corporate world, the feedback is not good. Most of the time, supervisors spend more time getting done what they need to get done. They are less interested in developing their subordinate. Most people in the corporation don't like or know how to give good feedback.
>
> In the agency where I work, from the executive director on down to the head of each unit, we have mandatory weekly or biweekly meetings to discuss agency and departmental issues.

As a fundraising consultant, the following career changer found nonprofit organizations are more likely than corporations to give feedback to their employees:

> In the corporate sector, you see that an employee is failing and you don't want to take the time and effort to do anything about it. I have twenty-five nonprofit clients and I haven't seen anyone who doesn't give immediate feedback after the project was done to the person who was responsible for the project. People in the nonprofit sector seem to get a lot of feedback on how well they did, or what else they can do next time to improve.

Another human services career changer receives more behavioral feedback at his agency:

> I receive feedback on things that helps me perform in a better way. For example, they told me not to make a funding presentation with my hands in my pockets. In the corporate sector, they expect you to do the job, period. You are expected to do that and if you bring in a lot of business, then you might get a pat on the fanny.

Because results are difficult to quantify, there is less likely to be feedback on performance in the nonprofit sector (Mirvis and Hackett, 1983). Career changers also observe problems in receiving feedback on their performances:

> *Career Changer, University*: Big corporations have a system for feedback that they have to follow; they must give you feedback. Feedback, in the nonprofit sector, depends on the relationship you have with your supervisor. It isn't necessarily implemented.

Career Changer, Arts Organization: There is no feedback here. I've been here for a year. My one-year [anniversary] came and ended, and no one has said anything about a review. The policy is, if you want to call something unwritten a policy, there are supposed to be annual reviews.

Last year, I had been here just a few months, and my boss sent around a memo to his directors, asking them to rate him- or herself. I have no expectation here that I will get an increase in salary and that has nothing to do with performance. In the corporate sector, feedback, in the form of salary increases, are a given.

Career Changer, Human Services Organizations: In the nonprofit sector, I never went through a review process. They didn't have one. Employees hadn't received raises in a couple of years. I don't think that there is an internal desire to motivate people to achieve their goals. I don't think that there is a synergy among the company, goals, and the individual.

Mirvis and Hackett (1983) observe that nonprofit rewards are intrinsic: employees receive satisfaction from the variety and the challenge of the work itself. Wages are less salient, in the nonprofit sector, because nonprofit organizations are nonmonetary in orientation. Emanuele (1997) documented that there is a 20 percent wage differential between the profit and nonprofit sectors which favors the corporate manager. This is consistent with the view that salaries are the salient rewards for corporate employees (Mirvis and Hackett, 1983). Etzioni (1975) similarly maintains that utilitarian organizations depend on remunerative rewards to secure calculative commitment, echoed by one career changer now working in a housing organization:

The reward system in the corporate sector is a formalized, rational, and predictable process. Money is the primary reward. In the nonprofit sector, approval from testimonials and letters of appreciation are the most reliable rewards.

In these examples, we see that the scholarly literature parallels the empirical experiences of career changers who were once in the corporate world and now work in nonprofit organizations. Many career changers found that "psychic" or intrinsic rewards are more prevalent in the nonprofit sector. A healthcare career changer illustrates:

There's a psychic difference. In the nonprofit sector, you feel good about what you are doing. In the corporate sector you feel like your work goes to the bottom line and at the end of the day it doesn't make a difference in people's lives. In the nonprofit sector, senior management is more appreciative; there is more positive feedback on your performance. In the corporate sector, there are rewards for working long hours and doing a good job, but the rewards are monetary and advancement oriented.

An educational career changer also talks about the differences in psychic and monetary rewards:

> You have immediate satisfaction and gratification that you are working toward a goal in the nonprofit sector. In a corporation, it's hard to focus on what contribution you have made. You're a small cog in a huge wheel. Rewards are salary based and given at the end of the year.

A second educational career changer concurs:

> The rewards in the nonprofit sector are largely psychic. There is the feeling that I make my own job and I give it definition. I'm not just a person who sits behind a desk so if I left the desk I could be replaced. I have a unique role. The rewards are being around nicer people and being committed to a mission and ideals.
>
> In my corporation, there was a lot more money. I ate at fine restaurants. I don't even take lunch now.

A career changer working in the human services field gave up the monetary rewards of the corporate sector for the intrinsic rewards of the nonprofit sector:

> I've given up some monetary rewards to be back on the nonprofit side because what I am looking for in life revolve more around what I want to contribute to society as opposed to how well-off I and my family are. There are all different kinds of rewards .... It all comes down to what you are looking for. If you want to get lots of money, cars, or real estate, then you subjugate yourself to making money in the corporate sector. If you want to do more with your life, in terms of making a contribution to society, then you forgo some of the finer things in life. The true rewards in the nonprofit sector come from what you have accomplished, how you have improved people's lives, and improved society.

Another human services career changer believes the cut in salary is well worth it:

> My starting salary was one-third of my last salary in the corporate sector. But for the first time in 13 or 14 years, or maybe for the first time in my career, I want to get up in the morning and go to work. I want to learn my craft and want to do as much as I can to be successful in my position. I've just never had that attitude before .... It's been 10 years since my salary has been this low, but I've never been happier.

This human services career changer also distinguishes the sector reward systems:

> Don't go to work in the nonprofit sector if you want money. There's no such thing as a bonus; only small increases in salary. However, the nonprofit sector is more relaxed; you don't have people breathing down

your neck. In the corporate sector, there is more money and bonuses, overtime, etc.

Another career changer working in a university maintains that while there are fewer monetary rewards in the nonprofit sector, there are non-monetary rewards such as flexible hours and free tuition.

Differences in Governance and Leadership

Governance

Hodgkin (1993) found that corporate boards are dominated by "insiders and senior managers who are responsible for executing policy" (p. 420). Since most career changers interviewed for this study were at a middle management level in their corporate jobs, they did not have direct experience working with their boards. The lack of involvement with boards in the corporate sector, contrasts with the career changers' interaction with their nonprofit boards:

> *Career Changer, Nonprofit Association*: I have to admit that my for-profit involvement with the board was fleeting. I'm much closer to the board in both the nonprofits I've worked in because these nonprofits are smaller [than was the corporation]. Nevertheless, the boards are entirely differ-ent. The association board is made up of professionals. Most of these pro-fessionals have never managed a nonprofit organization and they feel that serving on this board was a way to further their careers. I found them hard to deal with because they just didn't understand the problems of managers and why you need staff who are professional managers. They [board of the association] didn't understand a lot of the issues because there were there only part time.

This career changer's experiences with his association board are consis-tent with Hodgkin's study, which maintains that since nonprofit board mem-bers are outsiders, "they have a poor understanding of their role and are not trained to address the problems of the organization" (pp. 424–425).

Another career changer maintains that his nonprofit board does indeed understand its role. "Their role is essential because they raise money—they are the life and breath of our organization."

The "life and breath" which this career changer talks about is also dis-cussed by Drucker (1990) who views the board of nonprofit organizations as the guardians of the organization. They are responsible for raising money and making decisions which affect policy (e.g., mission).

Leadership

Corporations need instrumental leadership skilled in deciding matters concerning ends and means, rather than on values or commitments, because they have utilitarian or rational goals. Since nonprofits (normative organizations) have cultural goals, it is functional to have expressive elites—people whose expertise is oriented around values and mission (e.g., teachers, ministers, professors, and doctors)—dominate the organization (Etzioni, 1975). Since expressive leaders rarely have superiors who set defined goals for them, there is a possibility that the expressive leaders will not have clear objectives (Drucker, 1990).

In distinguishing the difference between corporate and nonprofit leadership styles, a university career changer maintains that a corporate leader must be "an expert in something, while a nonprofit leader must know how to deal with people." A healthcare career changer concurred that nonprofit leaders have "more of a caring approach and are interested in the total person, not just what they produce 9-to-5, five days a week." Another healthcare career changer maintains that corporate leaders are authoritarian in their style of management and nonprofit leaders tend to include the entire group in the leadership process. A banker-turned-fundraiser speaks in more detail about the differences in the styles of leadership:

> The for-profit sector tends to be dictatorial, which is not to say that it can't be done this way in the nonprofit sector. Nonprofit leaders are usually more sensitive to the needs and feelings of individuals so their leadership style tends to be more of actually leading, as opposed to pushing and shoving. In the nonprofit sector, there is a tendency not to beat up on everyone if the deadline is not met. There is more of a tendency in trying to figure out how to get the work done. In the corporate sector, not only are they unhappy if you don't meet deadlines, but you might be [fired] if it were to happen again.

Differences in Decision-Making Processes and Language

Decision-Making Processes

Many nonprofit organizations, as opposed to corporations, make their decisions by consensus. The reason for this, as Hodgkin (1993) explains, is that decisions are often made to resolve issues of organizational values and conflicting constituencies' impressions of those values (e.g., board, staff, donors, press, vendors, customers, volunteers). Several career changers talk about this difference in orientation:

> *Career Changer, University*: I found that nonprofit organizations engage much more in consensus building, particularly those that have a strong volunteer segment. Even in the university, because we have a fairly strong and independent board, I find that there is a lot more need for consensus-building. In the for-profit sector, you have to build consensus because

you never have control of all the resources. There is still a lot less. In the private sector, you can work with a few people or a small group and get things done. In both the professional association I worked in and at the university, I spend a lot more time building relationships and building consensus in order to get things done.

Career Changer, Educational Organization: I have found that decisions are made through collaborative efforts, joint consensus. In the private sector, the opposite is true.

Career Changer, Healthcare Organization: In the corporate sector, decisions are made from the top down. In the nonprofit sector, decisions are more consensual. Consensus is where the feelings of the entire group are taken into consideration.

Career Changer, Arts Organization: In the nonprofit sector, there is more of a team approach and a lot of volunteer input in making decisions. In the for-profit sector, there is a top-down approach to making decisions. One has say but not as much.

Career Changer, Human Services Organization: Decision-making in the nonprofit sector is an inclusive process. It is done by committee and it is more satisfying because you feel you are a part of what is going on. In the business world, decisions are made by a group of senior people who are always making decisions for everything. As a result of their decisions, you are told what to do.

In addition to these observations, a career changer now working for a human services organization maintains that there are "more meetings, more consensus building, and more analysis before making decisions in the nonprofit sector." A career changer working for a university agrees that corporate decisions are made faster than nonprofit decisions. "In the corporate sector, you have to sell a product so you talk to your advisor and make a decision. In the nonprofit sector, you want to develop interrelations with others in order to be involved with the community."

Language

Normative or nonprofit organizations are more likely to have expressive language (e.g., expressions of praise or acceptance). In corporate or utilitarian organizations, the language is technical or instrumental (Etzioni, 1975). Etzioni argues that expressive communication in corporations depends on peer relationships and the extent to which employees are members of the same external organizations (e.g., church, union, volunteer organizations). "Nonprofits," states a healthcare career changer, speak the "language of the mission whereas corporations have bottom-line language." A career changer working for a cultural organization observes that nonprofit organizations use instrumental language, but it differs from the corporate sector. For example, nonprofit organizations use instrumental words like "funding, fundraising, or development." These words are not used in the corporate sector. A career changer working for a university says that nonprofit managers have language that "is oriented toward 'agreement' and is 'not necessarily black and white'". A career changer working in a school observes that nonprofit language is "more politically correct and more sensitive to other human beings. Corporations, on the other hand, are more apt to use a language conveying orders and commands." While cursing and foul language would never be used in one career changer's human services organization, she notes that this practice was common in her prior organizational culture.

Appearance: Diversity and Dress Code

Diversity

The Independent Sector (1993) found nonprofit organizations to have more older workers, people of color, and women than the profit sector. Career changers, on the whole, also observe there to be more diversity in the nonprofit than in the profit sector.

> *Career Changer, Healthcare Organization*: I think that there are more women in the nonprofit sector. A black man is supervising me in my current non-profit organization. This was not the case in my corporate experience.

> *Career Changer, Human Services Organization*: There are lots more women in key positions in the nonprofit sector. In the corporate sector, men hold most senior positions. It takes women and minorities three times as long to move ahead in the corporate sector.

> *Career Changer, Nonprofit Consultant*: There seem to be more women at the higher levels in the nonprofit sector than in the profit sector. They are more accepted [in the nonprofit sector], perhaps because they are not get-ting paid a heck of a lot. ... Since they are on the same pay scale [as their male counterparts], they are more easily accepted.

> *Career Changer, Arts Organization*: Nonprofits are very tolerant of people of color and older workers. There are many retired people working in the nonprofit sector. This wouldn't be the case in the corporate world.

> *Career Changer, Educational Organization*: My school serves urban minor-ity children. They have a full tolerance of everything here, which is simi-lar to my own approach. In the corporate sector, they had considerably less tolerance. They didn't even tolerate women.

One career changer believes that minorities are underrepresented in the nonprofit sector:

> Interestingly enough, in the nonprofit sector, I saw a big difference in the diversity of the managers and the people they were serving. For instance, if we were serving a minority community, I didn't see many minorities represented, as managers, in the organization serving these minority communities. I do believe that nonprofit organizations are tolerant of diversity. I just don't know if they have the desire to bring minorities into their organizations.

Not all of the career changers observe there to be a tolerance for older workers in their nonprofit organizations:

> *Career Changer, Healthcare Organization:* There are very few who are of senior age in my nonprofit organization. I think that it's difficult for older people to fundraise, given the nature of the work.

> *Career Changer, Human Services Organization:* While there are more older workers here than in the corporate world, early retirement was offered so that they were happy to push out people who had been here a long time.

Dress Code

Stone (1962) asserts that "appearance is the phase of social transaction which establishes identifications of the participants" (p. 90). It is through one's appearance that one learns the values of others. Most career changers report that the nonprofit sector has a more "relaxed dress code" than does the corporate sector. A healthcare career changer maintains that there is no need to wear a suit and tie "unless you [are meeting with] a client." In this career changer's human services organization the computer technicians come in "jeans everyday." And, a university career changer reveals that while the managers are expected to wear formal business attire, "the faculty has more freedom" in what they wear. He also believes that the dress code is associated with the organization's degree of professionalism. It is, of course, this professional style of dress which is valued in this career changer's prior corporation, thus distinguishing him from those who are "less professional." A healthcare career changer, on the other hand, defends the difference by saying that "since people earn less money in the nonprofit sector, there is less of an expectation to dress up." A human services career changer describes the casualness of nonprofit sector dress as compared to the rigid guidelines imposed in her former corporation. She admits, "women who wore pants were frowned upon." It may be assumed here that through dress, her corporation was able to maintain its gender boundaries (Epstein, 1970, 1981, 1988, 1995; Lorber, 1984; Walsh, 1977).

The Cultures Are Similar

A small proportion of career changers and "career nonprofit managers"[1] observe similarities between the profit and nonprofit sectors. Two career managers and one career changer provided this exchange before dislocated corporate managers during a training class:

> *Career Manager, Human Services Organization:* How do profits differ from nonprofits? Some have said that there is less pressure, less stress, and that it is more relaxed than the profit sector, and that we rest on our lofty, noble achievements. I have never worked there!

> *Career Changer (worked in nonprofit, corporate, and government sectors):* Whichever sector you work in, leadership is leadership. You make decisions and develop a vision for what you believe in and you do that in any organization. Skills are transferable from one sector to another. There may be different jargon or different reasons for doing things, but management is the same.

> *Career Manager, Human Services Organization:* One of the things that may not be obvious to those in the corporate sector is that we are no longer selling cookies to make organizations run. We are large and dynamic and are being run with greater efficiency. We are not so far from the corporate world.

The following career changers also agree that there is little difference in the areas of measuring results, leadership, work style, and support of their avocations. A healthcare career changer believes that like corporations, nonprofit results are also measured quantitatively (e.g., how many people are served, how much money is raised for the organization, how many additional communities are served). A consultant to the nonprofit sector asserts that since nonprofit organizations do not have a lot of money to spend on marketing, they are more likely to measure the results of their direct mail campaign (e.g., response rate). With regard to leadership, one human services career changer believes that her nonprofit leadership style is similar to the leadership style she used in her prior corporation. Both styles operated on a "level-headed even keel." In an effort to equate the value of work within the nonprofit sector with the value of work within the corporate sector, one "career" manager tells the dislocated corporate managers [within the training session] that they will work harder when they make the transition into the nonprofit sector:

> *Career Manager, Community Foundation:* Just because the sector is called nonprofit doesn't mean that "nonwork" is implied. They work harder, putting in 12- or 14-hour workdays and weekends. Many times there is no separation between their professional and personal lives.

In the area of support for an employee's avocations, it is observed that there are corporate environments which support volunteer activities, though one career changer questioned the self-interested motives of her corporation:

> *Career Changer, Human Services Organization*: There is a self-serving reason for the support of volunteerism within a corporation. Employees volunteer because the chairman supports it and because it makes [the employee] look good. In the nonprofit sector, there aren't as many tangible rewards for volunteering. We do it because we want to.

Another career changer was expected to become involved with the community as part of his job and the self-interest of the corporation: "Most bank lending officers have written into their job description that they participate actively in community affairs, become a board member of an organization, work for the benefit of the community, develop a reputation, and do networking so that you benefit the reputation of the bank."

NONPROFIT PROBLEMS AND CHALLENGES

Despite the ongoing debate of whether the sectors are more different than alike or more alike than different, there appears to be a consensus among nonprofit managers that they are facing deeply troubling and challenging times. "Career nonprofit managers" as well as career changers are honest in the assessment of their sector's deficiencies: a tarnished public image; a need for strategic advocacy and accountability; increasing numbers of mergers; reduced government funding and an attrition of donors and members; and a lack of management skills.

A Tarnished Public Image

Below two nonprofit managers speak about their sector's tarnished public image:

> *Career Manager, Human Services Organization*: We're in trouble and it's centered on our mission: the distinction between self-interest and altruism. Some nonprofits are using their missions to advance their self-interests. The public, as a consequence, has a misperception of what we are about. I call this private interest approach "mission creep." As a result of mission creep, the IRS is now looking at the executive compensation levels of nonprofit hospitals and universities to determine if their salaries are excessive. Mission creep has created a situation in which some states are threatening to take the nonprofit's property tax exemption away. There is a growing mistrust of nonprofits.
>
> Whose responsibility is this mission creep? In the two cases I am thinking of, it was the board who allowed the problems to occur. Nonprofits must teach people to be good board members. There must be

curriculum developed, which teaches board people to be good members. New York State is interested in board training because it is the board that establishes the mission. The board must maintain the mission as a North Star to guide the organization. They must check what's going on against the mission. In fulfilling the mission, they must be concerned with the outcome. Fulfilling the mission goes beyond financial accountability. The board is the moral owner of a nonprofit. They are trustees for the public and manage the assets of the nonprofit on behalf of the public.

Career Manager, Human Services Organization: There's less trust toward nonprofit managers and we've earned it. Nonprofit managers have become "me centered" instead of organization and value centered.

A Need for Strategic Advocacy and Accountability

To combat the tarnished image, the nonprofit sector must create strategies of strategic advocacy and public accountability according to this career nonprofit manager:

Career Manager, Service Organization: While nonprofits are good about their organizational issues, few can talk about the sector as a whole.

We become tongue-tied when we are attacked and feel the bottom is being pulled out from under us. As a sector, we need to work on a strategy that will help volunteers, staff, and board members talk passionately about this sector—about its role, its issues, and problems.

We also need to develop performance measures that prove the difference our sector is making. I believe there is a danger that in the absence of these performance measures, the government creates them for us.

Coping with Uncertainty: Mergers, Government Reduction, Attrition of Donors, Members, and Organizations

Nonprofit organizations are entering an era of uncertainty that is threatening the sector's existence. Within this era of uncertainty, mergers between organizations are becoming more and more commonplace, government funding is being cut, there is an attrition of donors, members, and organizations, and there is increasing competition from the corporate sector. This career nonprofit manager discusses the impact mergers are having on the hospital industry: "The biggest problem we face are the shifting sands. We don't know who's merging with whom. Donors ask us if we'll be here two years from now."

Two nonprofit managers discuss the devastating impact reduced government funding will have on nonprofit organizations, which for years have counted on government funding as the most stable source of funding:

Career Changer, Nonprofit Management Consulting Firm: The biggest challenge is that small and medium nonprofits have been living on government money and suddenly it has been reduced. Before this occurred, they didn't have the need to raise money. They are not ready. They don't have a fundraising budget, a fundraising staff, or a plan that will identify a donor constituency.

Career Changer, University: Higher education is facing a financial crisis because there is less government money available to support tuition. We have a tuition-driven budget and a small endowment. We don't receive many outside donations and less than 10 percent of our alumni give. Since we are a commuter school, it's hard to generate the school spirit that would influence donations.

In addition to reduced government funding, there is a growing attrition of individual and corporate donors, patrons, and nonprofit organizations:

Career Manager, Ballet Company: People who have always been philanthropic are getting older, passing away, and the younger people aren't replacing them. Sources of support are disappearing.

Career Manager, Theater: Our greatest challenge is our dwindling audiences. Our audience has aged, or they've passed away, or they are disenchanted. How do we get the families with young kids who don't have the time to commit to us? How do we diversify our audience?

Corporate Funder: There are corporations trying to walk away from their roles in philanthropy. ... Making money is more important than social responsibility. Social responsibility is an investment in the community. Businesses survive and do better in a community that has a quality of life.

Community Foundation Manager: These are not business as usual times. We have observed from the proposals we are receiving that there is attrition in the field. We aren't getting proposals from new organizations. Organizations have skeletal staffs.

Finally, the increasing competition for market share from the corporate sector places additional burdens on the nonprofit sector:

Career Changer, Nonprofit Service Organization: The registration fees to our conference were down this year because a for-profit organization ran a competing conference. They even stole our brochure layout. Since they were fueled by a bank and were able to hire some celebrities, they were able to outsell us.

A Lack of Bottom-Line Management Skills

Some career nonprofit managers argue that deficiencies in their management practices are in fact making it difficult to survive amid these growing threats:

Arts managers don't come in with the training needed to deal with people. They have no sense of how to motivate people, to reinvent an organization, or to move it forward. They choose staffs who are unwilling to take risks.

They don't understand finance or technology. They are ten years behind the times in terms of technology. Many box offices are still run manually, or, in others, the last computer was bought in 1985. Arts organizations need managers who can bring in what they learned in their corporations.

Several career changers observe deficiencies in decision-making processes chained to consensual methods:

Career Changer, Human Services Organization: It takes so long to make decisions and people are afraid to move. Because nonprofits have smaller budgets, they have to look at things from every single side and probably don't want to take the risks that go with making a decision without consulting others in the organization. In the corporate sector, if I had an idea and explained it to the partner, he made the decision right on the spot.

Career Changer, Cultural Organization: In the corporate sector, I didn't have to run around and ask for a million opinions and approval. Sometimes, I think there is the tendency at my organization to micromanage things, as opposed to giving people the latitude to get things done.

Career Changer, University: Nonprofit decision-making is much more cumbersome. More things are done by committee instead of executive decision. In the corporate sector, decisions are made quicker, especially if they involve the bottom line. People are usually given decision-making authority.

Another career manager comments on the deficiency in technology within her own nonprofit organization, as well as the need for strong nonprofit management due to public scrutiny and limited resources: "With regard to computers, we are retarded! With increasing public scrutiny and limited resources, nonprofits have to be smarter about the way they manage. There is a need for MIS skills as well as the need to train nonprofits how to use the technology. Foundations are asking nonprofits to display good management. Now we are scrutinizing their audits and 990s, where we didn't before."

Smith and Lipsky (1993) report that public funders are requesting that nonprofit organizations place greater emphasis on organizational management and fiscal responsibility. It appears as though private funders are following their lead. A service organization representing a regional consortium of 200 funders is working on making the collaboration between nonprofits and private funders operational. The executive director, who is also a "career manager," believes that corporate managers can help her shape and implement this goal: "We need to think strategically about how funders and nonprofits can work together. Who do we share in terms of our neighbors and constituents? Nonprofits are trying to think this way. Businesspeople bring an expanded sense of what we should be thinking about."

Another funder echoes this view and shares it with the dislocated corporate managers:

> Those people coming from outside the nonprofit field can help nonprofits think outside the box. They realize that they have to break their old ways, but don't know how to do it. Don't be shy about your perspective. They need to address greater board involvement, the tightening of the "give or get"[2] board policy, the sharing of resources, collaborating with others in the sharing of space, staff, and materials.
>
> Many executive directors came out of direct services and they have either had to acquire the business skills or had to rely on people like you.

CULTURE CHANGE: THE NEED FOR CORPORATE MANAGERS

According to several informants, the severe problems encountered in the nonprofit sector require a change in the way nonprofit organizations are managing their businesses. It requires the adoption of a rational model as a means of saving the "sacred" values of the sector (Rosow, 1965, p. 42). Rosow found that change within a system did not necessarily have to affect the core values of the system. Social change that requires rational or business solutions can be instituted without challenging the basic values of the system. It can be argued then that career changers, while respecting the core values of a nonprofit organization, are able to bring "rational solutions" to nonprofit organizations that do not affect their raison d'être (p. 42).

Here are descriptions of the ways in which "rational solutions" such as advocacy, staff development, cutting costs, and diversifying funding bases are being applied without changing core mission values:

> *Community Foundation Manager*: As nonprofit organizations are failing, others are taking over their work. The strong are surviving and getting stronger. What are they doing that the weak ones aren't? They are repositioning themselves. They are organizations that are involved in advocacy. They are taking staff development more seriously. They are paying attention to their middle managers. They are managing more efficiently by cutting costs, diversifying their funding bases, and they have become aggressive in securing private and public support.
>
> Since the resources from the government and foundations aren't endless, nonprofits are looking for other ways to generate money. They have become more entrepreneurial.

The previous passage is an indicator that it is through the allocation and execution of rational solutions that nonprofit organizations are surviving. It is important to note that it is the change in management style, not in mission, that is allowing for the survival of the nonprofits described above. Of course, an ongoing debate is centered on whether a different management style will actually harm or destroy the core values of nonprofit organizations. Culture change, therefore, in the cases outlined by the community foundation manager, is a change in attitudes and behaviors toward management style, rather than value orientation.

The Corporate Model

Career nonprofit managers as well as career changers of nonprofit organizations use the corporate jargon of restructuring, reengineering, and reinventing to indicate that they are finding it necessary to change the cultures in their nonprofit organizations. Examples of this are found in a human services organization, a small college, a university, a cultural organization, and a healthcare organization that have gone or are going through culture changes using the corporate model. This human services manager reveals how her organization changed its managerial leadership, processes of raising money, and definition of its constituency:

> *Career Changer, Human Services Organization*: Six years ago, we merged with another organization. We went through a process of justifying our mission. Were we a fundraising organization? Were we a service organization? Our vision statement made it clear: we are responsible for the human care needs of New York City. For us, the way in which we would implement our mission would drive whom we would serve. We began to identify new partners: new sources of funds from government and individuals. We reorganized. Our customers were our agencies, foundations, and the government. We developed the expertise of our staff. A new president was brought in to make changes. He was an MBA and we were social workers. I remember that when he used the word "customer" there was almost a riot! People were so upset. We needed a revolution or we wouldn't survive. Today, no one gets excited when the word "customer" is used. We are interested in outcome measures.

In producing change, Schein (1990) reports by bringing in people from the outside, the organization attempts to "unfreeze" the present system (p. 117). In the next example, culture change has been oriented around the need to establish a professional development department in order to save a college from a management regime that threatened its survival. The college's mission remained unchanged throughout the crisis:

> *President, College (Career Manager)*: The college owns riverfront property. Many of the buildings are not tailored for educational use. In the 1980s,

we had a president who was a high-risk taker. The board believed in the president and the board was not philanthropic. At that time, the president believed he could sell the expensive riverfront property, build a campus with state-of-the-art facilities, and turn a $40 million profit into an endowment. He wanted to build this campus in a city that was voted the worst city in which to live. The net result was that the alumni screamed that the college belonged in its present location. Meanwhile, the real estate industry collapsed. It would now cost more to build the new campus than the property was worth. The college would never realize a profit of $40 million. This [miscalculation] ended up costing the college $15 million. The president was forced to resign.

Now we need to create a vision to build a group of donors—of stakeholders. We spent four years battling the issue of where we would be located. Many of our properties were run down and had inappropriate use. We tightened the budget and refinanced our debt. We purchased two new buildings and sold off some. We wired the campus. We created a new image. We reshaped the board leadership. We found a new Chair who was a national figure and had expertise raising money. We hired a new development officer. For the first time, we conducted a national search for the development officer. We hired someone who is entrepreneurial and will look for nontraditional ways to raise funds. He's building a team. The new message is "invest in us."

This nonprofit career manager also speaks about becoming more corporate-like:

> *Communications Manager, Healthcare Organization*: My organization has been going through a reorganization. We have to become more business-like, and we are getting more and more like the profit sector. We now have business managers who are responsible for business plans for each of our strategic directions (e.g., health education or community-based services). We also will begin to go after large private donations.

The managers, up until this point, have addressed changing the management styles of their organizations as opposed to changing the mission of their organizations. The next two organizational representatives from a university and cultural organization talk about changing their organizational missions. The university, founded as a religious institution, is embracing a new mission with the utilitarian goals of helping more students use education as a means of finding work. The cultural organization is changing its musical orientation in order replace the audience it has lost.

> *Career Changer, University*: We are implementing an image-building strategy which is targeted at changing our image from a religious based organization to an organization which deals with the major issues facing our students. (e.g., Will I be able to get a job after graduation?)

Career Changer, Service Organization: A cultural organization had lost its audience and so had come to the conclusion that it was necessary to redefine themselves. They realized that up until this point, they had been perceived by the community as an elite organization. When they held focus groups with different ethnic groups, they discovered that they could remake themselves by producing programs that corresponded to the interests of these various ethnic groups. The strategy worked.

Why is change necessary? The human services organization, the university, the college, and the cultural organization all needed to be more sensitive to their constituencies or customers if they were to survive. Mission, in its present or changed form, can only continue to flourish if the human services organization is more donor-oriented; the university is more student-sensitive; the college is able to bring in new stakeholders; the cultural organization produces events oriented to the interests of the changing community.

Ott (1989) argues that "what has worked repeatedly for one organization may not work for another" (p. 3). In other words, business practices do not always work in the nonprofit sector (Bush, 1992). While the corporate model may be helping some nonprofit organizations survive, the outcome is not always positive, especially when the core values regarded as sacred are replaced with rational utilitarian goals as has happened in the hospital sector:

Development Manager, Hospital: While there are many good business practices in the profit sector that can be applied to the nonprofit world, there is every indication that total adoption of the private sector model for healthcare institutions does not work.

Healthcare institutions can and should recognize the patient and their families as clients and treat them as such, but healthcare management cannot use staff reduction and reduction of services as a good business model. Healthcare staff is the deliverers of vital services, and the "face" to the client. They can make a difference between a good experience in a difficult situation, and an overall bad experience. At some point, staff reduction will result in the inability to provide quality care and can ultimately result in an inability to fulfill the primary mission.

Nonprofit management has the overall responsibility to filter, sort, and adopt the best business practices for their organization. To take what can work best from the profit sector and adapt it to the nonprofit, and to reject those practices that will negatively impact on their ability to provide quality service is the goal.

Only then will the best business practices be successfully married to excellence in healthcare.

It is of course the particular consequence of "eliminating the core values," or mission of a nonprofit organization, which frightens nonprofit managers and influences their hiring processes and biases within their selection processes.

HIRING PROCESSES AND BIASES IN THE NONPROFIT SECTOR

Corporate Managers Experience Bias

In making the transition into the nonprofit sector, corporate managers identify two particular types of "discrimination" based on their occupational background and to a lesser degree based on their age. Occupational stereotyping involves a "preconceived attitude about a particular occupation, about people who are employed in that occupation, or about one's own suitability for that occupation" (Shinar, 1975, in Lipton et al., 1991, p. 129). Occupational stereotyping allows the insider group (nonprofit organizations) to create employment boundaries that prevent those with different occupational backgrounds (corporate managers) from entering. Mechanisms of exclusion are very evident within the recruitment process. The preeminent trade publication in the nonprofit sector, *The Chronicle on Philanthropy* (2001, pp. 51–63) lists advertisements for nonprofit managerial jobs which typically include the following language: "Broad knowledge of the principles and practices of major gift fundraising, preferably with a large university"; "Prefer candidates with experience in a nonprofit organization"; "Management experience in a nonprofit membership association is preferred." All three of these requirements exclude applicants from the corporate sector.

Career changers interviewed for this study on career transition experienced intense occupational stereotyping. Despite Jim's 15-year record of volunteering and raising money for various nonprofit organizations, he found it difficult to "convince others why he wanted to switch":

> I've been poking around the nonprofit sector for four months. I need to determine if I am experiencing lip service from nonprofits. They tell you that they need business skills, yet they want financial managers with 8–10 years of experience in the field or fundraisers with experience in the field. Is there a built-in bias against us?

Michelle also found that her volunteer experience did not quite count as work experience:

> I believe that one reason I did not get hired was because there were so many qualified people who were looking for work. If it were between choosing someone with five years of experience and me who didn't have nonprofit work experience, they would hire the person with the experience.
>
> I once was interviewed for a job and I thought I would be hired. At first, they said I was in the running and they liked me. Then someone who already worked for the organization was hired instead of me. She got the job because of her experience. If the difference is between hiring someone

with real experience and someone with volunteer experience, they will
hire the person with real experience. My [real] experience is in publishing.

Though statistically, according to Lynn Burbridge (1994) and the
Independent Sector (1993), nonprofit organizations do hire more older workers than the corporate sector, career changers still maintain that there is discrimination based on age during the hiring process. David, who transitioned
from a Wall Street firm to a human services organization, considered age
discrimination a "real concern." He maintains that "retooling oneself can be
viewed skeptically by the nonprofit sector. People are very much aware of age
when they see people starting out again. Let's say it was subtle."

Kevin, a career changer now working for a human services organization,
believes that the nonprofit sector has trouble "accepting people over 45."

Why do some corporate managers experience bias when they are seeking
employment in the nonprofit sector? One career nonprofit manager from a
service organization believes that there are three reasons. First, corporate
managers are perceived as having different values from nonprofit managers.
Second, corporate managers are viewed as being unable to adapt in a culture
with scarce resources. Third, nonprofit managers question the corporate manager's motivation for making the transition in the first place. These biases are
explained in detail below.

1. *"There is a perception that you're not one of us, and you don't understand
our mission."*

> You are perceived as good hardheaded managers. We in the nonprofit sec-
> tor believe that you believe that we are soft-headed and that we don't
> know how to manage. That irritates us. We believe that you are hard-
> headed and tougher. You are perceived as being able to handle compli-
> cated financial transactions. You can get the job done. Nonprofits, on the
> other hand, are great at talking, but not as effective on delivering.
>
> On the minus side, you're not one of us. You're perceived as not
> understanding our culture. We are progressives; we are Democrats; we are
> pro-gay and lesbian lifestyle; we are 60s people. You are not part of that.
> You don't have an awareness of understanding our work. You are not
> musicians or artists. You didn't go to social work school.

The phrase "you're not one of us" corresponds to ways in which nonprofit
organizations have historically selected their leaders. One "career" human services manager, for example, reveals that her sector is "slow to look at people on
the corporate side, and that most people in the human services field have
human services (e.g., social work) backgrounds." Many nonprofit managers
believe that only managers with nonprofit backgrounds can understand nonprofit cultures and missions. In other words, only insiders are able to understand the culture of an organization: "one must be one to understand one"
(Merton, 1972, p. 15). This "insider doctrine" which Merton described, argues,

for example, that only African-Americans can understand and teach African-American history; that only male lawyers can understand male clients (Epstein, 1981, 1995); and that female doctors should only select specialties focusing on women and the family (Lorber, 1984; Walsh, 1977). This sense of "forced specialization" or the typing of jobs by race, gender (Epstein in Lamont and Fournier, 1992; Milkman, 1987), and occupation is echoed by a "career" human resources manager of an educational organization. She maintains that "it matters whether you did direct mail in a department store or for a direct mail company because we want to know if you will understand our environment."

Of course the "insider doctrine is fallacious," states Merton because we "are all insiders and outsiders" (Merton, 1972, p. 24). We do not inhabit just a single status such as a corporate manager, but inhabit several interrelated statuses (e.g., volunteer, board member, financial lender to nonprofit organizations, philanthropist, consultant to nonprofit organizations). "Differing situations," says Merton, "activate different statuses" (1972, p. 25). One can be a community leader in the evening and a stockbroker during the day. The "boundaries between insider and outsider are not fixed" (p. 28). There may be an overlap between statuses. The individual may have attributes in common with other statuses. There is "variation within a category" (Schur, 1984, p. 29). Despite the stereotype that corporate managers care nothing for the nonprofit sector, there are many corporate managers who have long been involved with the nonprofit sector. Corporate managers who volunteer share that status with nonprofit managers who volunteer. This sharing of status proves critical to piercing the insider doctrine. Many nonprofit managers want corporate managers to understand that while they need their business skills, they need them without losing the "heart" or the core mission of the organization.

2. *"Corporate managers can't handle a culture with scarce resources and a different reward system."*

Some nonprofit managers perceive that corporate managers would think it beneath them to play a dual role of "chief cook and bottle washer" and to take a cut in salary as well. In other words, the culture shock (Hughes, 1981) or the gap between what is anticipated and what is actually expected in the role would be so intense that the individual would not be able to conform and adapt in this new organizational culture. A "career" executive director of a service organization speaks about these fears:

> We are afraid that corporate executives come in with expectations of a support system that isn't there. You must understand that there is a need to pitch in at every level (e.g., word processing and so forth). We know that this isn't necessarily the most efficient way to run an organization and we fear if we bring in a corporate person, they will have different expectations.

Similarly, a nonprofit financial manager who comes from the banking industry believes that one nonprofit organization did not hire him because they could not offer him an expense account that could compete with his former position. After continuously finding it difficult to convince nonprofit employers that she was willing to take a pay cut from her previous corporate position, another former banker realized that she needed to eliminate discussion of her prior salary from all future salary negotiations.

3. *"Corporate managers' motivation for making the transition may be questioned."*

A successful career changer warns one cohort of corporate managers that nonprofit organizations will question the dislocated corporate manager's rationale for making the transition, fearing that the corporate manager is only interested in the job because he has been downsized from his previous position. Another career changer believes that there is a perception in nonprofit organizations that people in the profit sector are "not as concerned as they are [about the mission of the organization]. They are also suspicious that you want to work for them because you can't get a job in the corporate sector." Nonprofit employers question the motivation behind changing one's career and worry what prevents the corporate manager from changing his mind and returning to the corporate world.

The benefits and social relations acquired in an occupation give that individual his identity (Trice and Beyer, 1993). Rosow (1974) writes about the difficulty of withdrawing from a role that has defined an individual's identity and self-image. It is, therefore, understandable that the nonprofit manager questions whether or not the corporate manager is able, given the investment of time in building a reward and social network system around his corporate occupational identity, to relinquish this identity for another.

Of course those corporate managers who maintain their corporate identities through the use of a corporate résumé perpetuate the biases and stereotypes mentioned above. Paul, a former banker, admits that his résumé "didn't talk to the values and considerations for which the nonprofit organization was looking." In making a transition to the nonprofit sector, he sees a need to "fit oneself, to reinvent, to shape oneself into a mode of thinking and behaving which is more comfortable for those working within the nonprofit culture." Ron, a former retailer turned fundraiser, did not realize that his experience as the president of a nonprofit organization was important to include in his nonprofit résumé. He remarks, "I thought that I didn't have the background and experience, but when I looked closer, I realized that I did have volunteer experience. I didn't know how to package myself to include volunteering. My résumé was a for-profit résumé so the employer probably didn't understand how I might fit."

The inability to package oneself, to reinvent oneself makes it difficult to penetrate biases and barriers maintained by nonprofit employers. In addition, the lack of peer networks also serves as a barrier to employment.

Lack of Peer Networks

When an individual becomes a member of a group, he quickly learns what is expected with regard to behaviors and attitudes (Merton, 1968). Peers are instrumental in socializing new recruits as to these expectations (Becker et al., 1961; Brim and Wheeler, 1966; Elkin and Handel, 1984). Peers may also serve as mentors guiding the recruit's career path or as reference groups in determining the recruit's credibility or ability to conform and perform within the new environment. The majority of the career changers interviewed emphasize that their initial lack of peer networks in the nonprofit sector was an enormous barrier in seeking a new career.

Since his prior reference group or his corporate occupational network reinforced the corporate manager's identity, there was little need to create a new occupational network of nonprofit peers. It is this cost of commitment (Blau, 1964) or the loyalty to one's profession that prevents one from establishing differing networks of peers. An individual's peer networks tend to be homogeneous and found exclusively within his occupation (Golden-Biddle and Linduff, 1994; Lorber, 1994; Waldinger, 1992). Fred, now working for a university, had always been able to find former members of his corporation in almost every corporate culture. As he struggled to make a career transition, he found there were "some but far fewer" of his corporate colleagues in the nonprofit sector. Pat, now raising money for a human services organization, admits that finding the "initial contacts," in the nonprofit sector, was hard. John, who moved from financial services to a human services organization, began his nonprofit search "without knowing anyone" in the field. Karl, now also working for a human services organization, "didn't know where to look and believed that it would be very hard to get into major organizations [without the support of a peer network]."

Chapter 4 introduces the Nonprofit Management and Communications Program, a training program designed to help resocialize corporate managers for careers in the nonprofit sector by exposing them to nonprofit managers (peer networks) within a classroom setting. After briefly describing the structure of the program (a more in-depth description is presented in Chapter 5), Chapter 4 uncovers the profile of the applicant, his previous occupational background, and motivation for making the transition to the nonprofit sector. The applicant selection process for entry into the Nonprofit Management and Communications Program is also presented in detail.

Notes

1. The career nonprofit manager is a manager who has spent his entire career in the non-profit sector.
2. "Give or get" typically means that a board member of a nonprofit organization is expected to give or get donations for the nonprofit organization with which he is affiliated.

Chapter 4

The Nonprofit Management and Communications Program

INTRODUCTION

Millions of employees have been displaced over the last decade, and many of these have been corporate professionals and managers. Unfortunately, government agencies have not deemed it necessary to create career transition programs for white-collar displaced managers. Only one program—the Nonprofit Management and Communications Program[1] (Program)—emerged to address this particular stratum, and it did so with the special intention of building a bridge to the nonprofit work world. It therefore provides a unique resource for research concerning the adult resocialization of corporate managers. Other managers have made this transition alone, but by studying the Program I could follow many managers all encountering similar problems and observe the range of responses and adaptations. No other setting that I am aware of would have provided such a research opportunity.

DESCRIPTION AND STRUCTURE OF THE PROGRAM

Offered over a 5-week period, two nights or mornings a week, for 2- to 3-hour sessions within a classroom setting, the Program introduced 10–15 dislocated corporate managers, at a time, to the nonprofit sector—its trends and culture.[2] More importantly, it helped these corporate managers create new occupational identities based on the expectations of nonprofit managers. Sessions within the Program were designed to help the corporate manager learn these expectations. Orchestrated around Goffman's (1959) metaphor of dramaturgy, the Program's five-component curriculum ("the introduction," "the assessment," "the résumé," "the dress rehearsal," and "the mock interview") concentrated on helping the corporate manager learn the role he was expected to play both during the interview and on-the-job. This was accomplished by exposing the corporate managers to nonprofit managers who would act as peer socializers, focusing on the attitudes and behaviors necessary to succeed in the nonprofit sector. In the early sessions of the Program, these attitudes and behaviors were first learned and practiced by the corporate managers "backstage"[3] (Goffman, 1959, p. 112; without an audience of nonprofit managers) with the help of a trainer, and in front of other members in the group who were also looking to change careers. It was during these backstage sessions that the corporate manager learned to create verbal and written impressions that would favorably engage the nonprofit manager during an interview or during social interaction with members of the nonprofit sector. Methods used backstage included an interactive exercise called the "assessment" in which the trainer helped the corporate manager learn to tell his occupational story or "biography" (Goffman, 1963, p. 62) in such a way that a nonprofit manager would find it compelling. Another method rehearsed backstage included helping the corporate manager design short (one minute) introductions. These introductions were used to create first impressions when the corporate managers were introduced to 16 to 20 different nonprofit managers from the human services, arts, healthcare, and educational subsectors of the nonprofit sector over a period of ten sessions. As the Program progressed, the corporate managers were socialized by this nonprofit peer reference group regarding the career paths of nonprofit managers; nonprofit culture and its difference from corporate culture; managerial and volunteer roles; problems within the nonprofit sector; the need for corporate expertise and culture change within the sector; the hiring processes and biases of nonprofit managers; the methods of changing careers; adaptation and culture shock of career changers within nonprofit cultures. This peer socialization was accomplished through lectures developed by the trainer and nonprofit panelists, discussions between the nonprofit manager and the corporate manager concerning nonprofit cultural and role expectations, verbal and written feedback given by nonprofit managers on the corporate managers' mock interviews, newly crafted résumés, and classroom verbal introductions.

It was within this socializing process that the corporate managers determined whether or not they wanted to adopt the behaviors and attitudes of this new "reference group." If the corporate manager were indeed motivated to change identities and this process of peer socialization succeeded, there would be a distinct change in the verbal and written presentation of "self" as the course proceeded. This would be detectable in the introductions performed "on-stage," before the nonprofit managers, in the third and fourth sessions of the 10-session Program, and in the "new résumé" oriented around the managerial needs of nonprofit organizations. The identity change would also be apparent in the backstage "dress rehearsal" session where the corporate manager prepared, with the help of the trainer and the participation of his group, for a "mock interview" with a nonprofit interviewer in the classroom. This nonprofit interviewer would be either a career manager with exclusive credentials in the nonprofit sector, or a career changer who had an understanding of the profit and nonprofit perspectives. Merton (1972) calls an individual like this who has multiple perspectives a "free-floating" individual, thereby having the abilities to understand the worlds of both the insider and outsider, and to help these groups understand each other (p. 29). Having played the parts of both the corporate manager eager to change his occupational identity (outsider), and the corporate manager who had been socialized by the nonprofit sector (insider), the successful career changer (free-floating individual) is able to help both insiders and outsiders understand each other.

During these latter sessions of the Program, a few corporate managers were unable to make a break from their previous roles, or needed additional socialization before they could successfully interact with nonprofit managers.

APPLICANT OCCUPATIONAL BACKGROUNDS

The dislocated corporate managers who applied and were interviewed for the Program had generally worked for large Fortune 500 companies for a period of more than 10 years, and had been earning a median salary of between $60,000 and $100,000 before they were terminated from their corporate positions. The majority of these managers were white and aged 45–60; 60 percent were women and 40 percent were men. They worked for companies which once had taken care of them: all the dislocated corporate managers interviewed remembered a time when their jobs were quite satisfying. When asked "what they liked most about their old jobs," the managers emphasized the following values: "autonomy and the freedom to think and create"; "the money"; "the ability to support one's peers and to cooperate with others"; "the opportunity to be a maverick in a bureaucratic company"; "the chance to work for a company who cared about the individual."

The majority of the middle- and senior-level managers interviewed remembered a time, before the mid-1980s, when their company was paternalistic and took care of them and their families. In return, they played by the rules of the game. Profiled below are excerpts from interviews with 19 dislocated managers who describe their corporations before their cultures changed.

Betty[4] believes that her company, a large consumer goods company, was definitely a company that cared about the employee and his immediate family. When Betty's husband, a long-term employee of this same company, died, the company hired Betty. She believes that this company, was "loyal to me as his widow" and that they "helped me get through his death." During the time immediately following her husband's death, this company would have "paid me just to lay on the floor." Betty rose through the ranks during her 15-year stint with the consumer goods company. She remembered a time in the early 1980s when she was able to begin and market a program to universities, including Harvard and the City University of New York. She was given "carte blanche to do anything" and it was through her work that she was able to "bridge the corporate and academic fields."

Jim's tenure with a financial services company lasted 30 years. Before the culture changed in the 1980s, he remembered, "There used to be a collegial attitude in my company. It was very social. They used to care about people, you felt good about being there, you had a certain pride. It used to be a meritocracy and promotion was [given] by performance and merit."

Gary worked 10 years for a financial services company where he "enjoyed the money and the good friends I made there." He went on to say that the corporation was "family-oriented and until the mid-1980s they had picnics for the families of employees."

It became obvious that while the corporate managers appeared to have enjoyed many aspects of their corporate cultures, they were doing so while adhering to what Jackall (1988) calls the "moral rules" (p. 4). Jackall believes that employees who follow the rules make great sacrifices in exchange for the possibility of achieving status and power within the organization. Jackall claims that these rules include neglecting family responsibilities for the sake of the company, separating conscience from actions, showing loyalty to your boss, and never contradicting him. In accepting the rules of the corporation and the benefits that accrue through adherence, the employees are essentially allowing the corporation to closely control their actions within the organization, through the use of benefits including paternalism, monetary rewards, autonomy, authority, creativity, and the opportunity for the accumulation of good friendship networks.

The dislocated managers discussed the costs attached to following these "moral rules." Sean worked on Wall Street for 25 years and felt that there was great pressure placed on the individual to "make the deal" at any cost, including sacrificing one's personal life:

> Wall Street is not very kind; they will take everything from you, and try to ring out more. There's no empathy. Your so-called friends will screw you. It was very high pressure and this pressure comes from getting there first and getting the trade done. My personal life and work life were unbalanced and I didn't do those other [personal] things. I spent all of my time climbing the corporate ladder. It's all bullshit. I would do it differently and wouldn't be so one-sided.

Other rules reported by the dislocated managers are reminiscent of those described by Jackall. They include: "management doesn't like to hear bad news," "meritocracy is based on who can promote himself best," "allow your manager to take credit for your work," "you must deal with the politics or you're not part of the group," "perceptions are created by your network alliances," "if you attach yourself to a fallen angel, you're in trouble," "if it's traceable take the heat and don't blame your boss," and "staying up working all night is a rite of passage."

Another set of rules determines the gender and race of the manager who has senior status within an organization. Both the women and men who were interviewed recognized the small proportions of women and people of color holding senior managerial positions within their corporate cultures. Jackie remarked, "Of the 32 vice presidents in my company, I was the only female vice president in the room." Minnah revealed that "it was nearly impossible for a woman to become a vice president within my industry." Still another woman named Terry admitted that she was hired because she was a woman, and she carried that "stigma" around with her. It was her impression that "men ran the show" and that her work was "always typed last" because of her gendered status in the company.

Keeping your mouth shut within an environment where men ran the show was an apparent rule for some women. One female manager was sexually harassed for a period of a year. When she approached a female attorney within the same company for some advice, she was advised to keep quiet. Dislocated managers observed that people of color were not treated any better. The vice president of operations asked an Asian manager whom a colleague had brought into his company if he spoke English. Another white female manager, from a different company, observed a white male manager telling a black female worker, "we have a systems guy coming in and giving a presentation, you won't understand it, but try to listen up."

The categories of gender and race create insiders and outsiders within workplace cultures (Blalock, 1982; Epstein, 1970, 1981, 1988, 1995; Merton, 1972). These distinctions also exist for Americans who work for foreign-owned companies operating in the United States. Here are some examples of how American managers were made to feel like outsiders within their foreign-owned companies:

> Americans were used. For ten years, I worked for a company that showed no respect for Americans. The message was clear: you're not one of us. We were considered outsiders. The non-Americans made the real decisions. They made the decisions for us. There was an atmosphere of stress and fear. Eventually you would adjust, but you were scared to death. One time I went out of my way to create a long-range plan for the department. My manager [non-American] came into my office holding the plan and threw it into the garbage saying, "I did not understand this." I was devastated. I felt like shit for the next two months.

Another manager reported:

> Non-Americans ran the company at the top. They didn't mingle much
> with the Americans. I had one non-American friend who had an American
> wife and he was looked down on; they were treated like outsiders. The
> company once sent me to Japan and I wanted to mingle with the locals
> and to get to know them. Did the company accept that? NO. The non-
> Americans had a club in Japan; they all went there together and hung out
> together. They didn't want to mix with the locals.

Despite the harshness of these rules, managers seemed to conform. The
manager who had his plan thrown in the garbage wrote a resignation letter
that day, never delivered it, and managed to discover it 4 years later when he
was forced out. The woman who was sexually harassed for a year and lost
many "good assignments" kept quiet. Why? First, the benefits of long-term
employment for many of these managers outweighed the costs incurred. Long-
term employment benefits included healthy salaries, social and workplace networks, authority, autonomy, and status within the workplace and community
(Trice and Beyer, 1993). Another reason for their willingness to stay was that,
for the most part, these managers were employed during the economic recession of the early 1980s and during the late 1980s when the elimination of
managerial positions continued to occur. People "just like them" were losing
their jobs. When there are fewer external opportunities within their industries,
workers will tend to have greater dependence on the organization with which
they are affiliated (Rosow, 1965). Managers perceive limited opportunities
within their own industries and outside their industries as well. Since most
occupational networks of managers with rates of low mobility (e.g., long-term
employed and/or unemployed) consist of within-industry contacts (Blau,
1964; Granovetter, 1995; Trice and Beyer, 1993), there are fewer opportunities
to receive informal leads to jobs outside of an employee's chosen industry.

Thus, the reduction of jobs within the corporate sector and the likeli-
hood that these long-term managers had not formed occupational networks
outside of their industries compounded the anxiety and insecurity this group
of managers faced as their corporate cultures began to change.

Almost all the displaced managers described a process whereby the old
companies they liked underwent changes turning into very different places
before these managers were eventually let go. Thus, we consider briefly the
issue of organizations and culture change.

Schein's (1990) article on organizational culture describes seven stages
frequently employed for producing change within an organization:

> 1) highlight threats to the organization 2) articulate a new direction
> 3) fill key positions with new incumbents who may be brought in from
> outside 4) reward adoption of new direction and punish adherence to the

old direction 5) create scandals to discredit those who try to preserve dysfunctional traditions 6) create new emotionally charged rituals around the new assumptions 7) seduce or coerce organizational members into adopting new behaviors. (p. 117)

During their interviews the dislocated managers revealed in detail the extent to which their corporate cultures had changed. These changes conformed to Schein's schema. For example, Sarah recalled when change occurred in her company:

> The industry really changed in the mid-1980s and got worse. My company and others cleaned house. We consolidated; everyone was brought to central headquarters. We had a massive reorganization and the new people had all of their own people; I didn't have entree to the new people. Then they started to offer lucrative early retirement packages and many people left. In recent years they have just been letting people go by the tens of thousands. There is a leaner, meaner environment today. The objective is to reduce costs and the best way to do this is to reduce the workforce. You keep the younger workforce without families, medical problems, and pensions.

Culture change in this environment was characterized by articulating a new direction that emphasized the reduction of expenses. In this case, a new group of role models were brought in to execute this new direction. New role models were recruited from outside the corporation in order to impose a new direction. Established managers were believed to embrace the old culture and were viewed as a problem.

In the examples below, we see more examples of culture change and its effects on the long-term manager. Richard was coerced through a sense of fear into working on Saturdays, Mary was seduced into training her replacement, and Sam's boss was strongly advised to discredit his subordinates. Older people or long-term employees within these corporate cultures were made to feel undervalued and in some cases were harassed until they left (as Jim reports), or just thrown out without any notice or reason (as was Bob's case). In each circumstance, the old assumptions and the managers who represented them were displaced.

For Richard's company, restructuring began in 1995:

> They brought in new management and started laying people off. It was an inside takeover with new reporting lines and new people. The new people made it clear that they were interested in getting rid of the old people. The hours of work got longer—forcibly longer. People were working weekends because you were expected to. People were coming in Saturdays so that everyone would know that they were there, it was a show. Maybe they didn't do squat, but everyone knew they were there. I came in one Saturday, I guess out of fear, and they didn't have their act together so I left; they gave

me a hassle about it. I stopped getting bonuses, stopped getting reviews—
it was corporate punishment.

Richard went on to describe the way his company's efforts to change the
culture affected company morale and his own mental health:

> There were a series of downsizes, it happened over time, you would hear
> about departments being wiped out. But you never knew, people were liv-
> ing day to day; there was uncertainty all the time. The last few years were
> terrible; I felt like an outsider. I wasn't sleeping at night, but I became
> resigned to being a second-class citizen; I lost all my drive. One day I
> went to my computer and it was turned off. The guy who fired me didn't
> even shake my hand. He just said something like "we feel we should have
> a parting of the ways; Dave in personnel will take care of you."

The same impersonal severing of a long-term employee is revealed in
Bob's story:

> In my case two firms merged and since I was the oldest, I was an easy tar-
> get. I went home for the holidays on Friday, said goodbye to my boss, and
> he didn't say anything. They called me on Monday and told me not to
> come in. I was fired over the phone; they read me a legal statement. They
> told me my personal things would be shipped to me.

Mary worked for a large technology company for 15 years, and found she
was expected to help reengineer her out of a job in 1993:

> They brought in 50 financial consultants who started to change every-
> thing. They made all of these cuts. These consultants are young and you
> have to train them. You train these people and then most of the existing
> people are cut, the consultants leave, and you're left to pick up the pieces.
> It's true that my company needed new systems; they were using stuff that
> was 15 years old. If you had successfully turned over a system, you were
> no longer needed. I thought that there was so much work that I was
> pretty safe. I had helped with the implementation and then I was told that
> a consultant was taking over my job. One of the personnel people came
> to my office and told me I was cut.

Both Mary and Sam revealed that their bosses tried to save their jobs but
the die had already been cast. Sam, who spent 35 years in the financial services industry, remembered:

> We went through a big downsizing called "Fix '94," in 1994. They tried
> to identify all the ways the company could become more efficient.
> They cut all the people over 45. Forty to fifty percent were laid off. It was
> terrible for morale; it was devastating. They wanted to replace us with
> people they could hire for half as much. We got all new people. My boss
> was summarily fired, probably because he refused to give me a bad
> review. As part of "Fix '94," the company tried to build a case against

people so they wouldn't be taken to court when they cut people. My boss was told that if he refused to give me a bad review it would go into his file.

When corporations began to change the corporate culture, managers reported experiencing a reduction in status including a loss of authority, lack of communication, disrespect, and even humiliation. Jim recited one example:

> They try to make the older people miserable so they'll leave, people in their 40s and 50s. They will harass you, give you lousy reports. They initiated internal on-line monitoring of monthly sales. They watch the number of calls you make, the number of prospects, who you talk to—it's all counted. Everyone is ranked by sales and there are imposed quotas. They circulate the daily numbers stating who brought in the most business. People are ranked with a zero after their name. It's humiliating to suffer that crap. Everyone comes down on the non-producer.

After long-term employees are terminated, they exist in a liminal state (Newman, 1988). They are no longer corporate managers, and they no longer enjoy the rewards their status once offered them. On the other hand, they have not entered a new workplace status so their occupational status is ambiguous (Douglas, 1966; Newman, 1988). Rosow (1974) notes that the ambiguous state derived from role loss deprives the worker of his social identity. Without an occupational role, the worker has no authority, no responsibility, no rewards, and no membership within a group. Trice and Beyer (1993) maintain that when a worker is forced to go through a withdrawal from his organizational culture, he often experiences an "organizational death." A study on dislocated workers, conducted by Harrison and Sutton (1986, in Trice and Beyer, 1993), found that 23 out of 44 informants believed that forced withdrawal from work was "worse than a serious illness" and 9 out of 44 felt that it was "worse than divorce or the death of a spouse" (p. 170).

These feelings affect the dislocated manager in a variety of ways: Some become ill. Sam spoke of colleagues having heart attacks. Many are angry. Mary believed her company took away her identity and self-value. Richard promised himself that he would never be loyal to another company. He won't "kill himself for another organization. He won't be loyal to a group who won't be loyal to him."

Vicky believed that "people are so insecure that they are grabbing jobs they don't really want, and they are not committed to it." She reasoned that since the job one takes may be gone in 2 years, it was not likely that a commitment would be made. Jim was also certain that this mass dislocation of long-term employees would have negative effects on employee loyalty and commitment in the corporate sector:

> They've destroyed any sense of loyalty in any corporation. No one feels safe today; everyone is looking over his shoulder and has three other jobs

lined up in case he needs to leave. So the costs of all this may be greater than what they thought they were going to save by cutting back. I don't think any employee today is going to really believe anything that management says today. Nothing is taken at face value today.

Still others like Sarah clung to their former identities since there appeared to be no replacement for what had been lost: "I was used to being in a position where people were always returning my phone calls. I was always able to identify with my job in the private sector. There's a comfort level being in a corporate environment. I understand corporate speak."

Not only does the dislocation of long-term employees cause a loss of workforce identity, self-value, loyalty, and commitment to those corporations which betrayed them, but many of these workers face major difficulties reentering the workforce and are in fact forced to take undesirable jobs just to stay afloat. These are the managers Newman (1988) categorizes as "downwardly mobile" (p. 95).

Karen, a former advertising manager, spoke about this new status:

> I hear so many of my peers today saying they don't understand what's going on. We all saved money and thought we were going to be OK. The money we saved is gone. We have to start over again. We can't believe it. There's no social consciousness today, just profit consciousness. You don't feel safe. You have to do more with less. I want to feel necessary, like my life isn't over. Now I make art out of ripped-up rejection letters.

Sean is on the verge of bankruptcy and can't even find work in a department store as a sales clerk: "I went to a job fair a while ago. There were three lines and they were three blocks long. I stood there for 5 hours and never got into the fair. I tried to get an entry-level job at a department store and someone said they've decided not to hire anyone over 35."

In sum, corporate managers who applied to enter the Nonprofit Management and Communications Program were cast aside by their workforce cultures and for the most part had determined that it was unlikely that they would find work in their chosen fields again. It was precisely this shrinking pool of opportunities that caused these corporate managers to think about alternative careers.

Josh believes that his age will prevent him from finding work in his old field:

> The most drastic thing for me was that after working for my company for 30 years, where would the opportunities be for me at age 52? I knew that trying to break back into another corporation, particularly into a highly competitive field like technology, would be difficult.
>
> The main thing was that after 30 years with the same company, I didn't think that I could do it again. It's not that I didn't think that I had

the constitution, but I didn't think that I would be accepted. The technology world is very oriented to younger people and so too, as you get older, rightly or wrongly, people view you as being less and less in touch with technology. I don't think it is true. But I think that is the perception. I realized that I wouldn't get a fair shake in that industry.

Cindy also feels her industry limits its employment to those of a certain age: "It was my perception that, at age 50, it would be hard for me to get a job in the corporate sector. I don't know if this is true or not, but that was my perception. I thought that it was less likely that I would be discriminated against in the nonprofit sector."

In the final analysis, Josh's and Cindy's companies have indeed reduced the role of the older worker, and so these employees conclude that their work commitments need to focus elsewhere.

Carole's decision to seek work in the nonprofit sector came after her chairman and all of his allies (including Carole) were eliminated:

> I had gotten very close to the chairman. The next thing you know, the chairman was axed and all of the people he liked were axed, as well. This really woke me up. I have family obligations and I really didn't want to get back into the same type of competitive and very difficult environment—and for what? To move up to the next level? After this happened, I became more active in looking at the nonprofit sector and trying to determine where I could fit.

Finally, Ron's decision to make a transition to the nonprofit sector was influenced by diminishing opportunities in his industry and the fact that so many people are competing for the same positions:

> I thought that it would be a lot easier to find a job in the retail industry. I found that the industry was changing and that everyone was downsizing. I was coming out of middle management, where all of the downsizing was occurring and I was looking for a job at the same time as half the people in the industry. The competition was fierce.

While limited opportunities in one's field might be a motivation for changing careers, the selection process for entering the Nonprofit Management and Communications Program required that other motivations be present as well. The selection of students, therefore, was based on carefully analyzing the motivations of the candidates.

THE SELECTION OF STUDENTS: DETERMINING MOTIVATIONS

In ascertaining whether or not the candidate was appropriate for the Nonprofit Management and Communications Program, the director of the

Program (who also served as trainer) looked for "the real motivation" behind the career change. This focus on discovering the "real motivation" was critical in determining whether the candidate was willing to accept the anticipatory socialization processes within the classroom setting. Brim and Wheeler (1966) and Schein (1990) maintain that any individual must be highly motivated to accept socialization processes; otherwise socialization will fail.

In changing careers, the dislocated manager has to be motivated to change his reference group from the corporate to the nonprofit sector. Rosow (1974) maintains that in order for a successful transition to occur, there must be a shift in the actor's reference group: the group of people he looks to for affirmation, identity, and norms. Transitioning from one role to another requires breaking one's identification with a prior role and ceasing to conform to old standards. It demands identification with new norms. It is through role distancing and the selecting of one reference group over the other that an actor is able to avoid possible role conflicts (Rosow, 1974).

In ascertaining whether the corporate manager would leave his prior role behind, the trainer asked a series of questions concerning his motivation for changing careers. These questions, asked during an intake process, were aimed at uncovering the extent to which the manager was ready to acquire a new group identity, his history of volunteerism within the nonprofit sector, and his willingness to internalize the values of a nonprofit culture.

A Need for Group Identity

In addition to shrinking opportunities within an occupation or industry, what is the primary motivator influencing a decision to change careers? The answers were as follows:

"I like to be around nonprofit people"; "Many of my friends are social workers"; "I want to find meaningful work and service has always been important to me"; "I want to work in a nurturing environment"; "Collaboration and the goals of nonprofits have always been important to me"; "I'm now in a position to give up the income I'm used to making": "I need to feel a passion and I used to feel that"; "I've been isolated for too long and I want to be part of a team"; "The corporate culture is cold and stale and I believe I would like the team spirit of a nonprofit"; "I have no desire to work around the clock any more; I can't find any work in my industry and I believe nonprofits care less about age"; "I need to work."

For many of these workers the primary motivation is to be part of an organization which cares about them as individuals. The majority of them are more likely to focus on being motivated by the collaborative and team-oriented activities of organizational life than the money they made in the profit sector.

Corporate managers who are in a liminal state are insecure and struggle to reorient themselves around new organizations which will help them gain the rewards they have lost—the main reward being a sense of self-worth and renewal which come from being a part of an organizational community.

A History of Volunteerism

While this group of dislocated managers was obviously eager to be part of an organizational community, it was important to determine if they indeed viewed the nonprofit sector as their next reference group. Their history of, or commitment to, volunteerism and their desire to internalize the values of nonprofit cultures were used to assess this.

In evaluating their commitment to becoming employees within the nonprofit sector, the trainer asked questions concerning their history of volunteerism. Did they have a passion for a specific cause, within the nonprofit community, whether it was arts in education, or bringing computers to inner-city kids, or bridging the communications gap between blacks and whites in South Africa? If so, what had his involvement been in the nonprofit sector? Was the manager willing to continue volunteering during his career search? Since so many nonprofit employers view volunteer experience as an important indicator of commitment to the nonprofit sector, the degree to which applicants answered these questions favorably demonstrated their motivation to transform their occupational identities and accept the process of socialization into a new organizational culture.

Many of the managers have a long history of community service and volunteerism. For example, Pat's volunteer work has included raising money and lending her financial expertise to a variety of Jewish philanthropic organizations. Her observations are as follows:

> There's very little difference [between the nonprofit and corporate sector] in terms of management style. People are focused, dedicated, and hard working. A good number of my friends are involved with the nonprofit sector, maybe 30–40 percent. I'm getting to know people who seem interested in my skills because I bring a lot to the table. I'm finding people very receptive and they're very open for informational interviews. I don't really see barriers; I think I'll land something if I wait long enough.

Sam has extensive volunteer experience as a board member and as president of a civic association, as president of a trade association, and as president of an alumni association. In addition to his pro bono work, he has worked with nonprofit managers as part of his corporate job. His depiction of nonprofit organizations is based on working with community-based nonprofit organizations since the beginning of his corporate career:

> I have many relationships with nonprofit groups. There is less trust in the business world than there is in the nonprofit sector. Nonprofit managers take on more work and more responsibility [than corporate managers

do]. They tend to take on more work themselves than they should; they should learn to use more volunteers, do more fundraising. I see the non-profit sector as change agents that are necessary for the well-being of communities and civilization. Government is getting out of funding services and there will be more need for the nonprofit sector. New or younger nonprofits haven't developed their management styles; they think things will just happen for them. When I asked one group how they were going to manage their debts, they said, "God will provide." Many of these people are well trained in the arts or service, but not in business. Many groups that should do well don't get off the ground because they don't have the management; then people get discouraged, resources get used up, and the whole thing falls flat. Then nonprofits get a bad rap.

Though Michael has only been volunteering for 2 years, he has immersed himself in many different volunteer activities within his nonprofit organization including fundraiser, board member, and staff attorney. Here is what he learned:

The sense of mission and purpose appeal to me. This organization attracts a different sort of person: kinder and gentler, and that appeals to me. I don't want to work the insane hours I worked before. They make a strong effort to involve volunteers, people who are not employees. But otherwise I think this organization is run similar to a corporation. Nonprofits seem not as pressure-packed, but things do get done. They seemed thrilled to have me and I think that I've had enough volunteer experience that people can see I'm serious about it [making the transition].

Bob's 30-year experience as a board member resulted in these impressions:

It's not true that nonprofits have a slower pace of work; it's just different. Some people work seven days a week. You're not going to sit back and relax. They have a lot of managerial problems. They've never looked at things from a business point of view. The new director at the organization where I volunteer is better. He's a manager. He's organized and understands control and business. In the past, we didn't select good people to run it and it was micromanaged by the trustees. Our board is huge and unworkable. They have to change this; they have to be able to ask inactive people to resign.

In contrast, those with little or no volunteer experience are less willing to leave their corporate roles behind. Allen's contact with the nonprofit sector has been "very limited," and when he did volunteer he felt that he was "always an outsider and not very welcome." For this reason, "it was easy for [him] to walk away." He believes that nonprofit organizations will regard him as a "know-it-all."

Jeff believes that nonprofit organizations are less efficient than corporations. He also believes that nonprofit organizations view him as an outsider because he does not have any volunteer experience. He admits that not having this experience has probably hurt him and that "putting it [volunteer work] off was probably a mistake."

Even though Keith has not been exposed to many nonprofit organizations, he is "not convinced that everyone in nonprofits is out to do good." After having an interview with a human services organization he remarks that "nonprofit people seem flighty—different from businesspeople." He complains that the "environment was very distressing, it was all under construction, and they said that 'it had been like that forever.'" Keith adds, "[He] would have a hard time working in an environment like that." While he has begun to volunteer, he does not understand why the lack of volunteer work should hurt him. He also admits that he may not be getting better responses to his résumé because he tends to send nonprofit organizations his "corporate résumé."

When comparing the responses of dislocated workers without volunteer experience with the responses of those with volunteer experience, it becomes apparent that those without experience are more likely to use generalized categories or stereotypes. Examples of these include: "less efficient," "saintly," or "flaky." When using these stereotypes, corporate managers are less likely to justify or give concrete examples of these behaviors. Many dislocated workers have a view of the nonprofit sector that is based on their limited exposure to the sector and its managers. Deaux and Lewis (1984) write that in the absence of behavioral evidence, beliefs may be implicated and this process of belief implication is called stereotyping. Of course, stereotyping results from the "need for coherence, simplicity, and predictability in the face of an inherently complex social environment" (Bodenhausen and Wyer, 1985, cite Tajfel, 1981, p. 267). Wilder (1984) determined that "persons expect differences between groups and homogeneity within groups" (p. 178).

For those who cling to their old corporate statuses or are debilitated by their unemployed or downwardly mobile statuses, stereotyping the nonprofit manager as "less efficient" or "saintly" serves to distance themselves, in a positive manner, from those who work for nonprofit organizations. Rosow (1974) found that downwardly mobile workers tend to "deny failure and strive for success, asserting and reinforcing the values of their former position" (p. 131). Through the process of stereotyping and the creation of insider and outsider boundaries between the profit and nonprofit cultures, dislocated workers try to sustain the belief that they are part of the elite insider group (Merton, 1972).

Those with volunteer experience are more likely to give examples of nonprofit behaviors as distinct from stereotypes. Those who volunteer have an understanding of the relationships that exist between nonprofit employees and between board and staff. Through volunteering, there is an opportunity to learn and adopt the behaviors and attitudes that predominate in nonprofit organizations and, in essence, become an accepted member of the organizational culture.

Within the intake process, it is observed that some dislocated workers appear to be committed to leaving their former occupational statuses behind and view nonprofit organizations as their next reference group, composed of individuals, they wish to emulate. Nevertheless, the limited contact with the nonprofit sector affects the way in which these workers view the nonprofit sector, creating barriers for entry as well. After a long career on Wall Street, Sean, who had almost no volunteer experience with nonprofit organizations, had this to say:

> I don't see any real differences between the private and nonprofit sectors; they're all about making sales. But in the nonprofit sector, they're backward in terms of finance, management, and investment policy. There are two types of nonprofits: those who have built up an endowment over the years and provide a real service; the others are the ragtags that are dependent on the state. The nonprofits are probably more committed than the private sector is. What they're lacking is an understanding of private sector ideas and techniques.

Though priority was given to those who had previous experience volunteering, students such as Sean who were genuinely interested in the nonprofit sector and expressed a willingness to volunteer were accepted into the Program as well.

Internalizing Values

According to Trice and Beyer (1993), it is likely that the corporate manager will bring the attitudes and behaviors he has acquired from one organizational culture into the other. This being the case, it was important, during intake, to assess the extent to which these attitudes and behaviors would be rewarded by the nonprofit culture, the extent to which there would be a conflict in values, and the extent to which there would be a willingness, on the part of the corporate manager, to internalize new organizational values. For example, did the candidate enjoy working on his own, or working as part of a team? What types of processes were used to complete work tasks: motivating subordinates or getting the job done at the expense of others? Would a different pace of work frustrate the corporate manager? What stereotypes did the corporate manager have of managers working in the nonprofit sector? How much emphasis was placed on maintaining the reward and status structure of the corporate manager's prior organization?

Candidates who emphasized the enjoyment of working on their own to the exclusion of organizational goals, as well as getting the job done at any cost were not accepted into the Program. Furthermore, those who were committed to a specific pace of work and had little tolerance for adapting or changing within new organizational cultures were also unsuitable candidates for the Program. Mary, for example, confided that she really didn't have any particular commitment toward a cause and that maybe her values are different.

She asserts:

> I don't necessarily have the strong commitment. Nonprofits stress mission and commitment. Maybe the skills I value highly are not as valued in the nonprofit sector: I like good, solid management and fiscal accountability. I think that maybe they need more accountability, could improve their efficiency, and tighten up their business practices. Then, maybe they would have more money to do what they need to do.

Since many nonprofit organizations will not be able to match the displaced manager's prior compensation, it was important to assess how strongly each displaced manager identified with the corporate reward system. Did he realize that the majority of nonprofit organizations offered salaries far below the salaries offered in the corporate sector? Was he really ready to give these rewards up? Did he believe that this career change was "a step down"? What was it about the corporate culture before it changed that really motivated the corporate manager—the money or the sense of workplace community?

Some corporate managers said they couldn't go below a certain salary range because of family obligations. After discussing the realities of nonprofit salary ranges, which fall approximately 20 percent below corporate salary ranges (Preston, 1989, in Emanuele, 1997), the candidate and the trainer determined if the candidate could realistically achieve his salary goals. Others were definitely unwilling to take a salary outside of their subjective predetermined range. For some, this was "a step down." This was an indication that the candidate was tied to his prior status and reward system and unwilling to work within the reward system of a new organizational culture. If the candidate's expected nonprofit salary range was by nonprofit industry standards unrealistic, the trainer usually recommended that the candidate not take the Program. The ideal candidate responded that he was flexible with regard to salary and would work within the reward structure of the new reference group.

Van Maanen (1976) suggests that the tendency to be motivated by monetary values is rooted in the influence of the larger society. Within the United States, industries that provide great monetary rewards are held in high esteem. Trice and Beyer (1993) maintain that the "American culture places extraordinary emphasis on the individual ... and the execution of individual goals, rather than entities pursuing collective goals" (p. 57). To illustrate this point, Waldinger (1992) found that municipal workers left government managerial positions in the early 1980s when opportunities and greater monetary rewards arose in the corporate sector. More recently, nonprofit employees with computer experience have been moving to the corporate sector for higher salaries (Sommerfeld, 2000).

A proportion of dislocated managers interviewed do not identify nonprofit organizations as their new reference group because they still identify with the monetary values of the corporate sector. Sarah admits that she has become both "elitist and snobbish" about her former corporate status and she does not know if she has "a burning desire to work in the nonprofit sector." She still very much identifies with her old industry and at this time is "not shifting her energies in the direction of nonprofits."

Vicky is having a difficult time deciding if the nonprofit sector is the right next move. She is "overwhelmed by the [difference in] jargon." She does not understand how the nonprofit she interviewed with will be able to find someone to work for "$25,000 a year." Furthermore, she does not know if she "would be challenged" if she entered this new world of work. She knows that in order to do that, she will have to transform her occupational identity. This concept of "remaking" herself "scared" her.

Maggie believes that because she has associated herself with the consumer products industry for 20 years, it will be difficult to focus on "identity change and transformation." In fact, she reveals that the "psychological transition" is "harder than the search itself."

Finally, after the Program was explained to the candidate during intake, a series of questions were asked to determine whether the candidate was willing to make a commitment to the class itself and to the subsequent job search: How much time was the manager willing to give to this career search? Was he willing to do the necessary research and arrange a significant number of informational interviews? Did the manager understand it would take between 6 and 8 months to land a job? Was the manager willing to learn what motivated others in a new organizational culture or was he convinced that "he knew it all and his way was the best way?" Was the manager willing to try to understand why some nonprofit managers had a hiring bias toward corporate managers?

For those who had severe financial concerns, the 6 to 8 months it would take to change careers must have seemed like an eternity. Even some without financial concerns found this time-consuming commitment to be problematic since "being in transition" or "unemployed" for so many in our society induces a stigma that one is not worthy of employment (Newman, 1988). The stress that this stigma places on the self-esteem of these managers prevented some of them from continuing their nonprofit search. If the candidate had a volunteer history, workplace values that were oriented toward the nonprofit sector, and was willing to invest time in learning the nonprofit culture through conducting the appropriate research and necessary networking, the candidate was encouraged to join the Program despite concerns about the time commitment.

Each candidate admitted to the Program, accepted the spot, already having been oriented toward the nonprofit sector by the trainer. This orientation or induction stressed the importance of peer socialization through volunteerism, the cultural differences in workplace values, biases against hiring outsiders, and the importance of investing time in research and networking within the new reference group.

THE FIRST DAY: SETTING THE STAGE

When each corporate manager entered the training room ("the stage"), the trainer was there to greet the manager by name, to introduce the manager to the others who had arrived, to show the manager where to hang his coat, to inform the manager where the restrooms were, and to show the manager to his seat. Each corporate manager who arrived was seated with other newcomers around a large oval table. In addition, the trainer invited each manager to partake in some coffee, tea, and cookies with the other managers who had arrived before them. It was through this initial orientation process that the managers learned that they were respected participants in the eyes of the trainer and that they began to informally identify with the shared experiences and expectations of the other members in the group. The managers were noticeably excited about the class and the interaction that took place among the managers was almost immediate.

For the most part, the corporate managers came to the class dressed in formal business attire: the men wore suits or pants and a sweater; the women wore dresses, suits, or slacks and a blouse. A few managers did not observe this "unofficial" dress code. It was unofficial because the trainer did not indicate at any time what to wear to the class. The trainer expected that since the corporate managers understood they would be meeting potential employers in the class, the managers would want to dress in an appropriate fashion and give their best appearance. This was not always the case and it was interesting to watch. Deviant cases included a former manager who wore a hot pink T-shirt and short outfit; a high-level government manager who wore jeans and a flannel shirt; a former marketing manager of an advertising firm who wore farmer jeans with a tank top; another advertising manager who wore workout sweats.

Since the purpose of the first class was to help these managers regain some of the self-esteem that had been lost as a result of their being dislocated, the trainer deliberately avoided correcting this behavior. In addition, this deviant behavior was observed to be self-correcting. As Gregory Stone (1962) notes in an article on appearance and self, appearance corresponds to the "reflected image of others back on the self" (p. 86). Since the majority of these managers were interested in aligning themselves with both the corporate managers and the nonprofit employers, they usually conformed to the "unofficial" dress code by mirroring what the "others" were wearing in subsequent classes.

The most important function of the class was to provide the dislocated corporate managers a structure for forming their new identities. From starting on time, to learning what to wear, from the kinds of questions asked, to the tone of concern and respect, corporate exiles were being socialized into patterns appropriate to the nonprofit world.

In the next chapter, I will describe five major steps which each cohort undertook, each of which had a practical purpose, but was also a way of molding or transforming the self.

Notes

1. In the fall of 1991, Tom Cracovia, director of Continuing Studies at the City University of New York's (CUNY) Baruch College, invited me to test a classroom training concept which would help dislocated corporate managers move, as employees, into the nonprofit sector (see Appendix C: Recruitment of Applicants). In the spring of 1995, through the efforts of Drs. Paul Attewell, professor of sociology at CUNY Graduate Center, and Bert Flugman, director of the Center for Advanced Study in Education (CASE) at the CUNY Graduate Center, this experiment became a bonafide program of CASE called the Nonprofit Management and Communications Program. As the creator of the Program, I also served as the Program's director and chief trainer.

   In 1995 and 1996 the Nonprofit Management and Communications Program received funding from the Consortium for Worker Education which exceeded $300,000. The Federation Employment and Guidance Service (FEGS), a large human services agency, provided the Program with in kind classroom, administrative, and office services. This unique collaboration among CUNY, the Consortium for Worker Education, and FEGS is the setting for this ethnography.

2. Since the success of the Program depended on interactions between employed nonprofit managers and the dislocated corporate managers, and required extensive attention given to each corporate manager by the trainer, the class group was kept small and members were carefully selected. Usually, the trainer interviewed 40 candidates in order to achieve the optimum class size of between 10 and 15. The people selected for the Program were typically mid- or senior-level managers with expertise in a functional area which would be useful to the nonprofit sector such as marketing, finance, computers, human resources, press relations, or law.

3. In Goffman's *Presentation of Self in Everyday Life* (1959, p. 112), he uses the concept "back-stage" to describe activities that the audience does not see or participate in. Nonprofit managers are never in the classroom when "backstage" activities with corporate managers are occurring.

4. I have changed the names of people and organizations used in this study.

Chapter 5

The Program Components

INTRODUCTION

In this chapter, I will describe the important steps or five components of the Nonprofit Management and Communications Program that displaced managers experienced. These components are called: The Introduction, The Résumé (and Cover Letter), The Assessment, The Dress Rehearsal, and The Mock Interview. Some of these will seem, on the first impression, to be mundane and practical things such as one's introduction of self, reworking of the résumé, and preparation for an interview. They are indeed practical skills, but for our theoretical purposes, they are also important markers or evidence about peoples' sense of self, self-confidence, or lack of ability to adopt another world-view.

When I describe these components, I will begin by showing how unsocialized managers still shaken up from their displacement and still committed to their corporate sense of self do these mundane activities. Then I will show how they undertake the same activities after their socialization and sense of self have changed. This chapter therefore provides the ethnographic proof of the extent to which these individuals change and become resocialized.

The Introduction

Early Introductions

When the dislocated corporate managers first entered the class and had assembled around the large oval table, they were each asked, by the trainer, to go around the table, one by one, and introduce themselves stating their background, area of expertise, and involvement with the nonprofit sector. These initial introductions were performed as a "backstage" exercise, or without an audience of nonprofit managers. Even this ordinary activity provides a window into how these managers initially viewed themselves:

I Am My Industry

Bill: I did marketing for a bank and for an advertising company. I volunteer for a clinic where children are waiting to be adopted.

Larry: I worked in real estate for 15 years where our objective was to make money. Before that, I worked for the government where I wrote a manual that taught nonprofits how to get money from the federal government.

Mark: I was an accounting and systems manager for a financial services company and while there I volunteered with nonprofits [in my spare time].

My Company No Longer Needed Me

David: I was the head of human resources for a financial services company where I was asked to downsize the organization and I was downsized as well. My area of expertise is downsizing.

Margaret: I spent 6 years in retail as a planner and analyst. I was the by-product of a merger. I want to take my volunteer experience and turn it into a full-time job.

Here's a Sentence about My Nonprofit Life

Cara: I started my career in art museums doing publicity and public relations. For the past 15 years, I have been an executive in a family business where I did everything from managing people to sales and finance. When the business closed, I thought about what I wanted to do. I want my own passion. I bring a lot to the nonprofit sector.

Ralph: I've spent my career doing commercial real estate and I've also been involved in a financial capacity on the board of a nonprofit which provides affordable housing. I'd like to marry my commercial real estate background with my interest in affordable housing.

Ed: I've been messing around with the federal debt [class laughs]. For the last 4 years, I've been the treasurer of an organization dedicated to feeding the homeless. This has given me the greatest pleasure.

I Want to Make a Difference

Michael: I am a lawyer and I practiced law with a large firm. I now have the opportunity to think about what I want to do when I grow up. Nonprofits make a difference and I never had that feeling when I worked for the firm. I can use my legal skills in the nonprofit sector and I want to figure out what else I can do.

Eve: I'm a fashion designer and for over 20 years I've had great success doing that. I love my work. For 4 years I've been out of a job. I've been able to spend more time with family and friends. I have found that I am a social being. I began my career in the nonprofit sector and have clung to the memories of what work can be when it is meaningful. I want to give to others what my industry has given to me.

Lee: I also worked for a financial services company and took the buyout. I'm tired of financial services [class laughs]. I want to do something with the elderly.

The Nonprofit Sector Is My Career Goal
Jim: I seized the opportunity to take early retirement from my financial services company because I have been involved with the nonprofit sector for the past 15 years and want to spend the rest of my working career as a fundraiser or financial person of a nonprofit organization.
Sam: I'm an ex-financial services manager and I'm liberated! I have extensive nonprofit experience and I want to play a leadership role in strategic marketing, management training, and budgeting. I have a deep interest in nonprofits and I serve on the boards of several nonprofit organizations. I helped establish a nonprofit consulting firm. I want to offer the nonprofit sector my expertise and hope that they will allow me to assist them.
Martha: I was with a financial services company for 13 years and did their marketing and communications. Since leaving, I have been volunteering at two human services organizations in order to gain experience in fundraising. I am also volunteering for a large agency that needs communications because of its complexity.

These early introductions usually follow a pattern. First, an introduction begins with the identification of a specific industry whether it be banking, financial services, or advertising. Second, the introduction continues with an explanation of the person's current situation (e.g., in early retirement or recently downsized). Third, those with nonprofit volunteer experience tend to mention it, usually as an afterthought, at the end of the introduction, or as a lead-in to their more significant work history within the corporate sector. Fourth, while many talk about a need for "greater satisfaction" or "to make a difference," these concepts are not linked to any specific career-goal or role within a specific type of nonprofit organization.

This pattern is not surprising given the fact that these managers have been socialized in the corporate sector and still identify themselves as members of this particular reference group. A select few have begun to withdraw from their prior role and do have a specific goal that they are able to articulate, even at this early stage.

After the corporate managers introduced themselves before the group and the trainer for the first time, the trainer helped the corporate manager understand the purpose of the introduction as well as recommendations for reshaping it:

> The objective of the introduction is to show the nonprofit manager that you have an understanding of their world and that you want to support their mission or goal through your skills and resources.

You want to build a bridge of communication between you and the nonprofit manager through telling brief, targeted, and compelling, as well as passionate stories that relate to them.

You build a bridge of communication using concepts that the nonprofit manager can and will relate to. Be careful in selecting your choice of words. If you choose to label yourself as "unemployed" or that "you have taken early retirement" and you do not have the opportunity, in a short introduction, to express or define what you mean by those words, the listener may form his impression based on his own interpretation of these labels. I suggest that instead of forming an impression based on the usage of these concepts, you define yourself based on what the listener is interested in hearing. Here is what I mean:

1. Stress your present and past relationships with the nonprofit sector as a volunteer, philanthropist, trustee, or employee. Be succinct about your role and the type of organization in which you did nonprofit work. In other words, what did you do and for whom did you do it? Here are some examples: I've worked for the United Nations in helping to resettle Filipino refugees, and I'm now helping a housing organization which supports patients with AIDS create a fundraising plan; I've supported the management of nonprofit organizations through directing a corporate giving program; I'm volunteering my legal expertise to a Jewish philanthropic organization.
2. State your expertise (e.g., the Internet, management information systems, telemarketing, fundraising, finance, and knowledge of the nonprofit sector's accounting rules).
3. State your objective as concretely as possible: Using this expertise, I want to be the executive director of a small educational nonprofit.
4. What do you want to learn from the nonprofit managers who visit you in this classroom? Some of you might want to know where you fit in; or how the nonprofit organization uses computers; or about the relationship between the financial officer and the development officer; or the need for advocacy; or the need for publications, and so forth.
5. Don't forget to smile and maintain eye contact!
6. You should be able to make a dynamic impression in 15 seconds. The outline for reconstructing your introductions should follow this format: skills (e.g., marketing, finance); passion (e.g., for a particular cause(s)); volunteer experience (e.g., name an accomplishment of which you are most proud); goal (e.g., to support the marketing needs of a community development organization).

Based on some of your backgrounds and occupational goals, I have constructed three examples of how you might transform your occupational identities:

The transformation of a banker to a development officer:

Trainer: I've spent the last 10 years developing the nonprofit market for my company. My clients included: [name them]. In order to be able to build this client base, I spent the majority of my time learning about the financial and investment needs of nonprofit organizations. I know how to help nonprofit organizations maximize their income and have helped universities like [name them] increase their capital goal by 150 percent. I would now like to do this full time for a nonprofit organization as a development officer.

The transformation of a partner in a law firm to a community activist and leader:

> *Trainer*: For over 30 years, I have had experience facilitating the crusade for the empowerment of victims, children, and communities in the United States and abroad through law, teaching, and community work. My leadership experience includes working with diverse socio-economic groups in challenging health-related, housing, and educational situations. My skills embrace mediation and conflict resolution, facilitation and team building, strategic planning and board development, as well as fundraising. I am seeking a leadership position with an organization that serves as a catalyst in community and individual empowerment.

The transformation of an investment banker to a development officer:

> *Trainer*: I want to work for an educational school of higher learning which is specifically aimed at offering all kids of all economic levels a good education. I am a product of Jesuit schools so I understand their commitment to children of all socioeconomic backgrounds. I have spent my career cultivating and retaining high-net-worth individuals and would like to help a Jesuit school of higher learning do the same.

This initial "backstage" exercise pushes the corporate managers to present themselves as managers who have an understanding of and respect for the nonprofit world. The managers worked on their introductions at home. These introductions were later performed before 16 to 20 different nonprofit managers throughout the ten-session Program. As the sessions progressed over time, the corporate managers' introductions continued to be restructured as they were influenced by the nonprofit manager's attitudes toward them.[1] Since the corporate managers also respected each other as peers, they also tended to influence the transformation of each other's introductions prior to interacting with their audience of nonprofit managers. Here, one corporate colleague advises another:

> *Teresa*: I am a financial manager with 16 years of experience in planning, budgeting, and auditing. I also have 7 years of experience in a nonprofit educational and training organization.
> *Gary*: Why don't you mention your nonprofit experience up front. You're too general in talking about that part of your career. You need to be more specific so nonprofit managers can zero right in on you. I don't

remember anything you just said, but when I first met you, you said that you had spent the first part of your career helping children. That stuck. That's nonprofit to me. All this corporate stuff doesn't sink in. Seven years of nonprofit work sinks in.

Thus, among the corporate peer group, there appears to be an effort to support each other's struggle in creating a good impression before the audience of nonprofit managers arrives in the classroom.[2]

New Introductions

As the corporate managers listen to the panels of nonprofit managers lecture about their workplace experiences, they work to restructure and refine their own presentations of self in the final sessions of the class. They are not just working on a presentation, they are working on an identity change or a "change of soul" (Caplow, 1964, in Van Maanen, 1976, p. 101).

Here are some examples of introductions that are given in the latter third portion of the class before a group of nonprofit employers:

Ralph: I have a background in finance and administration. I have a passion for affordable housing and was recently appointed president of a housing organization.

Cindy: Nice to meet you [class laughs].

Pam: I am a creative professional involved with the arts and children. I want to use my marketing skills to support the educational needs of children. I volunteer with an international children's organization and I have created cause-related marketing projects to help them raise money.

Craig: I work as a volunteer for a fledgling nonprofit that raises money for the public schools. After being an attorney for 18 years, I want to help grow this organization so that they can hire me.

Kevin: I have a passion for an organization that raises money for nonprofits. I am now volunteering for that type of nonprofit. I managed a special event for them that raised $100,000 for five nonprofits. I want to use my experience in special events, planning, and research to help support the educational needs of children.

Ed: I, too, like everyone else in this room felt that I had to make a difference in the life of someone else. I work with homeless children. I now have a nonprofit client and I'm using my skills to help them launch a national donor campaign.

Mel: My presentation is a work in progress [class laughs]. It's constantly changing and expanding. Everyone that I'm meeting [in this classroom] influences me. I want to serve the planning giving and major gift needs of a human services organization. I've been in the investment field. I've taught business and economics at the college level. I'm interested in being involved with an organization that conveys a broad positive feeling. Where the journey takes me, it remains to be seen.

Transforming the Corporate Résumé

Early Résumés

When the corporate managers first describe their occupational identities, they typically gloss over their volunteer experience, and the rationale or motivation for wanting to make the career change is not fully developed. The reason for this may lie in the fact that in the corporate sector, volunteer experiences, as well as the desire and motivation to change careers, are not greatly valued. The same situation holds true for the résumé. Within the corporate sector, a corporate manager is expected to have a résumé that reveals an appropriate career path including company names, educational credentials, jargon, and accomplishments considered suitable within his particular industry. Here are some examples of "professional summaries" that begin corporate résumés:

> *Michael*: Skilled corporate attorney with broad experience, including large and small mergers and acquisitions, insurance regulatory matters, trademark, employment, securities, loan, and licensing matters.
>
> *Sam*: Manager in the international and domestic retail banking field with in-depth experience in operations, loans, and financial audits.

In addition to the "corporate résumé summary," the full corporate résumé begins by listing the last corporate employer. The last corporate employer for the majority of these managers was a large financial or consumer product corporation. Underneath each corporate position held is a list of accomplishments written in the language of that particular corporate culture:

> *Martha's Corporate Résumé*
> The Bank
> Vice President, Marketing
> Established marketing communications objectives to meet the changing needs of the dynamic corporate finance industry.
>
> *Mark's Corporate Résumé*
> The Accounting Firm
> Associate
> Participated in the divestiture of a $100 million subsidiary of a conglomerate.
>
> *Michael's Corporate Résumé*
> The Law Firm
> Associate
> Worked on corporate-owned life insurance matters, tender offers, management buyouts, stock, and asset transactions (including stock-for-stock mergers).

Since these descriptions were written with the expectations of corporate employers and their industries in mind, there is little or no attempt to relate these descriptions to a different industry of employers. A nonprofit attorney, for example, would probably not be involved in "stock-for-stock mergers," since there are no shareholders in a nonprofit corporation. It is unlikely that a nonprofit organization would be involved in the divestiture of a $100 million subsidiary except perhaps in the case of a nonprofit hospital. A corporate communications manager's résumé emphasized that the communications plan was specifically developed for the financial industry with no mention of its applicability in other industries.

In these corporate résumés, the language and listed skills are different from the language used in a nonprofit résumé. As such, the "corporate résumé" becomes a barrier to entering a nonprofit organization. What then does the corporate manager do to restructure his occupational identity within the framework of a résumé? Within the classroom, the trainer gave corporate managers advice on restructuring their identities within the context of a résumé. First, there was the arduous task in selecting the résumé structure. Should the manager use a chronological or functional résumé? The trainer explains:

> There is no one model for getting a job. You are being exposed to many different employers in this class who will have different opinions concerning the proper résumé format. There are those nonprofit employers who believe that résumés are a screening device used to exclude people from dissimilar backgrounds so that if you can avoid using the résumé as a representation of your "first impression" you are better off.
>
> If the nonprofit organization demands a résumé, the situation and comfort level will dictate which résumé to use. A functional résumé is often used when making career transitions because it focuses on the skills and achievements that can be transferred to any industry. This type of résumé presents you as a manager with a skill set, rather than a manager raised and groomed within a specific industry. It is designed to help you come across as a marketer or a financial manager rather than a banker or a retailer.
>
> Chronological résumés, or a chronological listing of employment, are more likely to be used when seeking jobs within the same industry. A career changer, using a chronological résumé, is more likely to have positive results if there is a personal connection between the employer and the candidate, or if the employer is also a career changer and can identify with your motivation to change careers as well as how your skills will support the skill requirements of the position.
>
> Executive recruiters and human resource people function as screeners for their clients or employers and are more likely to request a chronological résumé because many have expressed that functional résumés are

"often used to hide something." Make sure your functional résumés also have a chronological listing of employment, and when submitting résumés to executive recruiters or human resource personnel, ask permission to submit both types of résumés.

The trainer also helped the ex-corporate managers think about using the nonprofit organization's language within the fabric of their résumé:

Before submitting a résumé, please try to read the annual report of the nonprofit organization. The résumé should reflect the language of the annual report as well as the language in the job description itself.

The trainer then provides sample formats of functional and chronological résumés. In the class, each of the corporate managers was asked to compose both a functional and a chronological résumé which would be presented to a nonprofit manager, before engaging in a mock interview during the closing sessions of the Program.

Format of a Functional Résumé

Job Objective: To serve the mission and leadership of a (select one) healthcare, cultural, or educational organization through a well-developed skill base encompassing administration, communications, direct and data base marketing, finance, systems, and fundraising skills.

or:

Summary of Qualifications: Seasoned communications professional serving the healthcare, educational, and insurance sectors with a well-developed skill base including finance, systems (list other functions).

Primary List of Accomplishments
(list the skill first, then list three work and/or volunteer accomplishments in both profit and nonprofit organizations under each skill; emphasize in each accomplishment how you saved or made money and/or what the results of your actions were; in order to reveal your networks and access to resources (e.g., money), work in the names of your clients if you are able.

Administration
- accomplishment
- accomplishment
- accomplishment

Communications
- accomplishment
- accomplishment
- accomplishment

Direct and Data Base Marketing
• accomplishment
• accomplishment
• accomplishment

Chronological Listing of Employment
(list your last job first: company, title, and dates only)

Community Service
(list your volunteer and board affiliations: organization, title, and dates)

Professional Memberships
(list organizations and dates of membership)

Education
(list the names of your schools and degrees)

Since these managers already had experience developing chronological résumés, the trainer emphasizes how to make these chronological résumés more "nonprofit":

> First, eliminate all of the jargon your industry uses. Next, begin your chronological résumé with your current volunteer work, listing your achievements underneath. After you list your corporate jobs, accomplishments under each job, and the years at each job, make sure there is a category of "Community Service" which indicates a chronological listing of your volunteer work.

Next, the trainer told the class that this exercise of written identity reconstruction would be easier if the corporate managers were first able to verbally express their new identities and in essence reorganize their career stories or biographies,[3] by emphasizing their skills and volunteer experience. The story was more detailed than the classroom introduction. The trainer, once again, helped the corporate managers structure a story by giving them the outline of the story:

> What are your functional skills? Identify yourself as a marketer, human resource, financial, public relations manager, or manager of information systems.
> What have your significant accomplishments been in the profit and the nonprofit sectors? How did you help your organization save or make money? How did you change and/or help improve the systems of the organization? What types of improvements/innovations did you bring or make?
> What is your management style? Do you enjoy making decisions as part of a team? What is your knowledge of managers in the nonprofit world in terms of how they make decisions; how they perform their roles, and how they will interact with you? Have you worked with all levels of the organization? How do you build relationships with other workers

within an organization? How would you do it within a nonprofit organization (board, staff, and volunteers)?

What types of resources can you bring to the nonprofit organization? Who do you know within the corporate, foundation, and funding community? Can you recruit board members and volunteers? What types of donated services could you cultivate?

What has your commitment been to the nonprofit sector? Where have you volunteered? What types of projects have you been involved with, and what happened as a result of your participation?

The Assessment

With the help of this outline, and an in-class "backstage" exercise called "the assessment," the corporate managers began to reconstruct their occupational verbal identities with the help of the trainer. These assessments were conducted one-on-one between the corporate managers and the trainer in front of the class. Here are some examples of the process:

Trainer: Tell me about your background.

Manager: (reads it off a sheet of paper) I am a computer services professional. I began as an engineer and worked my way up to manager.

Trainer: Do you know what you did?

Manager: Yes.

Trainer: So why are you reading it?

Manager: I'm nervous. I also worked at saving my company $2 million a year.

Trainer: How did you save the company $2 million a year? Here's the challenge. You need to be able to tell a nontechnical manager how you did it. For example, how did you work with your users? How did you help to assess their needs?

Manager: I went to departments within the company and reviewed their business processes. Then, I determined which business practices were costing too much money and set up a team to solve the problem.

Trainer: I understand that some of your clients were nonprofit organizations. I want you to take your background and relate it to a nonprofit organization.

Manager: For the past 5 years, I have been helping foster inner-city kids aged 8–12 years learn the computer.

Trainer: What do you want to do next?

Manager: I want to help public school systems become computerized.

In the early part of the class, corporate managers had not yet formulated how their career story or biography could be used to manage the impressions of a nonprofit manager. This particular exercise helped the corporate manager think about the different selves encased within his biography. This particular manager being "assessed" is not just a computer person, but a computer person who has helped inner-city kids learn computers. In managing the impressions of public school officials, he could create a biography which stresses his inner-city-kid self.

Here is an assessment conducted with an advertising manager:

> *Trainer*: Why do you want to work in healthcare?
>
> *Manager*: With my remaining years...
>
> *Trainer*: I don't mean to interrupt, but is this the language you really want to use to communicate your first impression to an employer?
>
> *Manager*: I'm interested in working in the health field, specifically for an AIDS-related organization. I currently volunteer for an AIDS unit of a hospital.
>
> *Trainer*: Why is this field compelling to you?
>
> *Manager*: I have firsthand experience working with AIDS patients. I have an understanding of direct service and I want to support this type of organization with my financial and operations skills.
>
> *Trainer*: When I asked you "why" you wanted to work in this field, I was really asking what is motivating you to move from advertising to working for an AIDS-related organization? The "why" in your case is about the organization's mission, not about you. Your understanding of the organization's direct services is motivating you. It may be assumed that the nonprofit employer of this type of organization may also be motivated by the organization's mission. Through your understanding of their process, you are identifying with the values of the listener. Through your skills you will be able to support their mission.

If the listener is meeting this manager for the first time and she begins her story with "in my remaining years" several assumptions could be made on the part of the listener. First, this person plans on disengaging herself from the workforce in a few years. And if this is the case, she may not be motivated to give 100 percent of herself to the mission of the organization. Therefore, she is deadwood. Of course, as the trainer digs a little deeper, she finds that this is not the case at all. This manager has a great deal to offer an AIDS-related organization. Her biography should intentionally reveal her commitment to this type of organization at the beginning of her oral and written presentation.

Another assessment was conducted with a marketing manager:

> *Trainer*: Tell me about your background.
>
> *Manager*: I've done communications, public relations, and documentaries. I've worked with nonprofits on diverse issues.
>
> *Trainer*: You gave me a skeleton. What types of media? What types of issues? Who did you work with in the media? Drop some names. What types of publications covered your work? Who were your clients?
>
> *Manager*: I produced a documentary on public television. It was an educational documentary on an organization that supports incarcerated women.

Another Manager: Nonprofits will want you. In this case, bring your corporate life with you—they want it.

Trainer: You need to relate your corporate accomplishments to your nonprofit audience. You do know nonprofit employers, and you do understand at least one nonprofit culture. You're not just any marketing manager—you're a marketing manager who understands the nonprofit world.

Manager: As a volunteer, I developed a communications plan for this nonprofit which they can use to develop their media and funding relationships. I created a newsletter for them, which is directed at publicizing their educational programs.

Trainer: What are your goals?

Manager: My goals are fuzzy. This volunteer work is more rewarding and more meaningful than my work in the corporate sector.

Trainer: What does that mean?

Manager: Creating media campaigns for this organization is more meaningful than dealing with the SEC or insider trading.

In this case, the corporate manager has the components of a good nonprofit biography. As the manager is probed, she becomes more detailed in describing her nonprofit behaviors and attitudes, demonstrating her knowledge and understanding of the sector, its managerial relationships, and decision-making processes regarding communications, education, and fundraising. Her motivation for selecting this reference group over a corporation is specifically defined. It's not just that nonprofit organizations give meaning to her life, but that creating media campaigns to reveal the horror of incarcerated women is more meaningful than constructing a media campaign about insider trading. And, yes, this corporate manager's peer is right. This biography must stress the prior corporate culture and positive consequences, which arise from the interdependence between the profit and nonprofit cultures.

The following assessment was done with a lender from a financial services corporation.

Trainer: Tell me about your background.

Manager: I have been an adjunct professor in business for over 20 years.

Trainer: I like that introduction. It conveys that you have been working in the nonprofit sector for a long time. Defining yourself as a teacher is very different from defining yourself as a financial services manager.

Manager: As a result of being involved as an adjunct, I was able to assist the dean of the Business School in creating a graduate summer institute in financial management.

Trainer: You created this institute with the dean?

Manager: Yes, and with the chairman of my corporation.

Trainer: You forged a public–private partnership?

Manager: Yes, it ran for 8 years. I helped plan the curriculum and recruitment.

Trainer: Of students?

Manager: And faculty. Every financial services corporation in the area participated.

Trainer: Is this in your résumé?

Manager: No.

Trainer: Please make sure this accomplishment is in your résumé.

Manager: It will go to six pages!

Trainer: These are great nonprofit accomplishments. You developed programs for a university. You built relationships between academics and businesspeople. You raised grant money from financial institutions, and you earned tuition from students.

This corporate manager is able to portray himself as a nonprofit person with the ability to create interdependent relationships between the corporate and nonprofit sectors. However, as was discussed before, many corporate managers do not place their "nonprofit selves" on their corporate résumés because it cannot be used to create a favorable impression before the corporate managerial audience. If this corporate manager eliminates the financial industry jargon and accomplishments, which do not relate to his nonprofit audience, he will not have a six-page résumé!

The New Nonprofit Résumé

In the classroom, the corporate managers learned that the majority of nonprofit human resource managers desire a chronological résumé:

Human Resource Manager, Educational Organization: When I see a résumé that is not chronological, I wonder what they are trying to hide. I want to see a summary of qualifications up top, the dates of employment, and accomplishments. Volunteer activities are important to list.

Human Resource Manager, Cultural Organization: I want a chronological résumé. I want to know where you did it and for how many years. I don't like to see that you have jumped around.

Again, there are always exceptions:

Human Resource Manager, Human Services Organization: I don't care if you send me a functional or a chronological résumé. If it's functional, make sure there is a chronological listing of employment. There should also be an objective statement up on top of the résumé that tells me what type of job you're looking for.

The following is a discussion between corporate managers and a nonprofit human resource manager concerning whether to submit a chronological or a functional résumé:

> *Human Resource Manager*: I prefer the chronological résumé from people who have eclectic backgrounds. I welcome a cover letter that helps me make sense of it.
>
> *Corporate Manager*: What about submitting both (a functional and a chronological résumé)?
>
> *Human Resource Manager*: Since we are screening for our organizations, we need to make sure that people aren't selling us a bill of goods. Submit the chronological résumé.

Regardless of the debate among human resource professionals around whether or not to submit a functional or a chronological résumé, corporate managers were expected to prepare functional and chronological résumés, as a requirement of the class. The rationale behind this is centered around the belief that even if the corporate manager submits a chronological résumé, he must be able to convey in both the cover letter and the interview the set of functional skills which he will bring to the organization. It is in knowing these functional skills that corporate managers are able to shed their prior industrial statuses of "banker" and "insurance broker," and take on functional statuses, which relate to nonprofit organizations such as marketing, management information systems, human resource, and financial managers. One can be a corporate or a nonprofit manager and share the same functional status. In addition, since résumés would be reviewed and critiqued by a nonprofit manager during a mock interview in class, the corporate manager was advised to relate and orient the résumé around the mission, language, and objectives of the organization with which he was interviewing.

In the earlier portion of this chapter, examples of "corporate résumés" were presented as indicators of "corporate selves and identities." Here are some examples of the newly crafted nonprofit résumés (biographies). The job objectives or summary of qualifications and accomplishments give a different presentation of self, utilizing the mission-oriented language and skills needed by nonprofit organizations:

Objectives/Summaries

Mark: Hands-on accounting manager with accomplishments and expertise in profit and nonprofit accounting and accounting operations, financial systems design, development of managerial policies, financial and MIS procedures, and financial and operational audits.

Sam: To support the development activities of a nonprofit institution, utilizing over 30 years of multifaceted leadership experience as a new business developer, fundraiser, board member, and corporate planner.

Pam: To support the development efforts of a cultural organization utilizing expertise in special events, direct mail, corporate solicitation, organizational management, budget planning, and research.

Martha: To support the fundraising and marketing efforts of a human
services organization, utilizing expertise in new business development,
marketing and fundraising, financial management, and managerial and
organizational leadership.

Joan: To contribute to the mission and effectiveness of a community-
based organization. To support its leadership with over 17 years of
nonprofit, corporate, and agency marketing communications experience in developing and executing programs that link issues and results
among diverse constituencies.

Within these functional résumés, here are examples of how corporate
managers selected functions relevant to nonprofit organizations, highlighting
the accomplishments conducted in both their profit and nonprofit work and
volunteer lives.

Richard's Nonprofit Résumé

Fundraising and Project Management
• Volunteered and provided musical talent to create an audiocassette that
will be sold statewide to raise funds for a religious organization.
• During special assignment with company affiliate, collaborated and
negotiated with foreign management to achieve settlement of long-over-
due funds totaling $2.1 million.

Michael's Nonprofit Résumé

Legal
• Volunteer with the general counsel of a nonprofit human services
organization working on a variety of legal issues.
• Served as law clerk to associate justice of the Supreme Court of
New York.
• Closed or nearly closed many large and small transactions (ranging
from $2 million to $300 million in value), such as tender offers and
asset purchases.
• Served as editor of *University Law Review*.

Pat's Nonprofit Résumé

Finance
• Performed financial analyses for companies with sales ranging from
$30 million to $12 billion for an investment bank. Efforts involved
critiquing projections and recommending cost-saving measures.
Presented recommendations to board of directors of clients.
• Served on budget committee of religious organization. Duties included
preparing annual projections for the nearly $2 million annual budget
and comparing the budget to the actual results. Recommended cost-
saving measures and revenue enhancements totaling $50,000.

Ron's Nonprofit Résumé

New Business Development, Marketing, and Fundraising
- At a large retail store, increased national sales from $2 to $3.5 million in 540 stores.
- As president of a human services organization, planned annual Toy Drive/Christmas Party to collect 170 toys for distribution to the Harlem Hospital Orphanage Unit and the Single Parent Resource Center.

Sam's Nonprofit Résumé

Managerial and Organizational Leadership
- Established annual fundraising record of $80,000 as past president of a 650-member volunteer organization, which raises money for charities.
- Created high-performance, 12-member team for the bank, delivering average annual net earnings increases of 16 percent over budget of $2.5 million.

Finally, corporate managers were encouraged to begin their chronological résumés with their current nonprofit volunteer activities. Here is an example:

Martha's Nonprofit Résumé

Nonprofit Communications Consultant
- Advising social services agencies regarding opportunities to increase visibility and distinguish their broad range of services.
- As a volunteer for a human services organization, plan and execute fundraising campaigns for 10 accounts. Initiate setup meeting, train campaign captains, address employee groups, and provide all appropriate support to assure positive results.
- Develop and implement plan to improve marketing and revenue opportunities for a human services organization.
- Consulted on Annual Report and communications opportunities for a human services organization.

The Cover Letter

Learning the language, values, belief systems, management styles, and goals of an organization, prior to sending in a résumé and a cover letter, may appear obvious to the midcareer manager. "But," states one human resource manager, "you'd be surprised at the garbage people will send. The cover letter should have some indication that you understand what we do. People tell us they want to work for a museum and we don't have one!" Another human services human resource manager tells one cohort that people confuse her human services organization with an airline that bears part of the same name.

Within the classroom, nonprofit managers tell the corporate managers that cover letters are used to explain both your skills and motivations for wanting to make the transition. One nonprofit educational manager states that a cover letter must reveal: "What is compelling you to make this transition? Tell me in your cover letter. Someone who really wants to work for a social services agency won't stay here long and won't be good for our organization over the long term."

Another nonprofit financial manager suggests that "a good cover letter is more important than a good résumé. The cover letter gets you reading the résumé. The résumé is presented in a restricted format. The cover letter can answer all questions up front. It makes your reasons for making the transition clear. It shows you really thought about the job."

Cover letters should be succinct and explain any inconsistencies in the résumé as this human resource manager explains: "I like a succinct cover letter, which highlights your accomplishments. If there is a break in your employment, tell me why in the cover letter. For example, we are about to make an offer to someone who explained that for the past 5 years, he had been out of the workforce taking care of his children, while his wife worked."

Process for Submitting the Résumé and Cover Letter

Presentation of self extends to the written document or résumé, the processes of submitting the résumé, and the cover letter. With regard to process, many human resource managers of large organizations reveal that they do not take kindly to cold calls from anxious job seekers. One manager of a foundation tells the class that she receives 8000 résumés a year and many calls from people who "think she has a few minutes." Another warns that she does not like people who "bug her to death" because she does not have "the staff to answer calls." She maintains that if unsolicited résumés are received and there is a position, she will be in touch. Of course there are always exceptions to this rule. Another human resource manager of a large nonprofit human services organization encourages phone calls from overly persistent job seekers because she "knows you're interested."

Few nonprofit organizations use executive recruiting firms or "head-hunters" unless they are hiring a senior executive due to expense. Instead they use advertising, the Internet, and alumni associations in order to recruit managers. One human resource manager from a university describes their selection process:

> You can't network yourself into a university. It isn't like a corporation. Every job is posted and we are required to advertise all jobs so that any applicant can apply. You must meet the minimum qualifications. I post the jobs on our home page. In addition to using the Internet to post jobs, we use *The Chronicle of Higher Education* for jobs that require academic experience and *The New York Times* for financial and technical jobs.

The recruitment process varies from one organization to another. Another human resource manager informs the class that because she works for a well-known nonprofit; there is no need to advertise because she is "deluged with résumés."

The Nonprofit Interview: Achieving the Right Chemistry

In class, the corporate managers learned that the nonprofit interviewer expects that the corporate manager not only come armed with a set of appropriate skills and volunteer experience, but also be passionate about and motivated toward the mission of the organization. Aspiring employees need to anticipate the nonprofit manager's expectations concerning appearance, attitude, and commitment. It is only by anticipating and adhering to the expectations of the interviewer that "the right chemistry" or identification with the other occurs.

Having "the right chemistry" is essentially a managed interaction where the expectations of both the audience and performer are met. A nonprofit communications manager gives the class her definition of chemistry:

> Everybody has a style with which they are comfortable. Through the interaction between the two of us, I get to feel if the chemistry is right. The way you speak, your ability to listen and pay attention, your appearance, your handshake, your eye contact, your efforts to learn about our organization, and your enthusiasm about our organization will affect the chemistry between us.

A career changer who is now the executive director of a nonprofit organization tells the class why chemistry is important: "The chemistry must be based on how well the candidate knows my organization, and how well I think his personality will fit within this culture. Since my organization is small, you can't afford to have one person in there who irritates the others."

The Rules for Achieving Chemistry

Human resource and nonprofit managers suggest the following rules for achieving the right chemistry in an interview:

Watch Your Attitude during the Interview

In achieving the "right chemistry" one human resource manager warns against bullying:

> I won't be bullied. People from corporations may have the attitude that they are so superior because they were with a big corporation for 30 years.

Well, that's great. But, if you want to be here, you had better think about presenting yourself in a different way.

People make big mistakes walking into a nonprofit assuming they know what we know. They know nothing about the backgrounds of the people they will be working with. For all they know, their old boss from a bank may be working for the organization they are interviewing with. Why assume things? There's a fine line between offering your expertise and assuming that the people you are talking to have no idea what you are talking about.

Another human resource manager wanted to make sure that career changers who are out of work are prepared to take a reduction in salary: "If a career changer was making $75,000 a year and now he is out of work, he can't expect to make $85,000 in his new career because he isn't making $75,000 any more. You must be prepared to go down because of the reality of the economy, or because you are making an investment in yourself in order to change careers."

Learn the Culture and Where You Fit

One human resource manager from a cultural organization maintains that the corporate manager's presentation of self must incorporate the culture of the organization with which he is interviewing: "People in transition must present themselves in a fresh way to each organization, learning as much about the organization as possible beforehand. You must learn about the culture before you interview. We have to believe that you'll fit in and give to us."

Another human resource manager comments:

> We look to see that you have made a commitment to our industry, that you have an understanding of what we do. If someone has made the effort to learn the human services sector, that gets my attention. If you know where you might fit, that impresses me.
>
> Our culture is paternalistic and we nurture our employees to a great degree. We do less of pushing people out and try to counsel people back in. We need to know what your supervisory style is like and what you're comfortable with regarding your work environment. It's important that you have a good feeling about [us] and that you are comfortable in [our organization], or you won't like us.

In learning where to fit in, a human resource manager of a foundation advises that corporate managers think about "taking a job of lower status and then transforming the function and operation of the whole organization."

Volunteer

The executive director of a service organization advises corporate managers to volunteer so that they can learn the culture and be perceived as a member of the culture: "It is through volunteering that you learn the underlying substance of the work. It is also through volunteering that you will be perceived as having learned it. They will think of you as one of them."

Once inside a culture, it is possible for a corporate manager to form a cognitive map of the organization so that links with significant individuals are formed and their expectations, in order of importance, may be learned (Van Maanen, 1977). A community foundation manager believes that volunteering is "the best training ground for understanding what the sector is about." The volunteer experience may lead to a position within the organization. A human resource manager tells the class the reason why: "A volunteer who has been with us for 6 years is now looking for a job inside the organization. He'll be taken seriously because he knows important people in the organization and has learned the culture."

Listen to Your Interviewer

It is important not only that the corporate manager have the skills and expertise, but also that he understand how those particular skills and expertise can help solve organizational problems. One human resource manager points out that one manager she interviewed did not understand who his "audience" was:

> I just interviewed someone for an information technology job who didn't listen to anything I was saying. He didn't watch my body language. I told him that I wasn't always a satisfied user of computers—that there were a number of us who had concerns from the user point of view.
> Well, this was his opportunity to ask me what my problems were. He said nothing. When you're interviewing, everything is a conversation. I'm your audience.

Preparing for the Mock Interview: The Dress Rehearsal

During the first session of the Program, the trainer asked the corporate managers to select one nonprofit organization from a list of four nonprofit organizations (designated by the trainer). Consequently, all assignments, including the résumés and mock interview, were based on the nonprofit organization the corporate manager selected. In preparation for their mock interview with a nonprofit manager, the trainer coordinated an exercise, during session #8, called "the dress rehearsal." This interactive exercise, between each corporate manager in the class and the trainer, helped each corporate manager "learn his lines." Before the interactive exercise between the trainer and the class commenced, the corporate managers broke up into four different groups, based on the organization they had selected, and were charged with figuring out how they could each "make a difference" in the organization they had selected. After about 15–20 minutes, the trainer asked the four groups to reassemble around the large table and to present their ideas, collectively and individually, before the group and before the trainer, who played the role of the nonprofit manager. The trainer then critiqued each corporate manager's presentation. This exercise forced the corporate manager to revisit the expectations of nonprofit managers and project an understanding or empathy toward the nonprofit culture. Empathy, according to Reuben (1976) (in Gudykunst and Kim, 1984), involves "a display of respect, responding to others in a non-judgmental way, initiating and terminating interaction based on the needs and desires of others" (p. 198). "People who empathize with others don't use the perspective of their own culture when interpreting other cultures" (Gudykunst and Kim, 1984, p. 196).

In "making a difference" the manager was challenged to demonstrate empathy by linking his motivation with the mission of the organization. Here are some examples of the dress rehearsal responses to "making a difference" within several nonprofit organizations:

Human Services Organization

> *Sam*: I know, from reading your annual report, that you want to create a donor-oriented program. With my background in strategic planning, I could help you evaluate the process, evaluate the strengths and weaknesses of the process, and segment the donor market. I would conduct in-depth interviews with segments of the donor market. I would then take the results of the interviews and map them against the mission of the organization.

> *Trainer*: I want to see you going through the process. How will you make this happen? I see your path: step 1, step 2, step 3. What are you doing in between those steps? How would you go about segmenting the donor market? Who do you think these donors are? How would you get to them? What would be discussed in the interviews?

> *Mark*: I know that you are responsible to donors and the agencies in which you deliver funds. I know you are also looking at ways to cut costs. I can assist you in becoming more efficient and economical. I can help you determine which services can be consolidated. My budgeting background could assist me in analyzing how your agencies use their funds, whether they are using their funds, and where the shortfalls are.

> *Trainer*: I can see the big picture. You're a big-picture person. I still need to see you doing it. I need to see you in action. How would you go about determining if there is a duplication of services among agencies? When senior-level nonprofit managers make these kinds of inquiries, employees "freak out." It may mean that you will get rid of people. How do you handle the sensitivity of that situation? Effectiveness in the corporate and nonprofit sector may mean different things. Within

this particular nonprofit, do you understand the criteria for success and how to measure it? Most nonprofit organizations are lean to begin with, and there is no room to cut. What words can you use to convey that you are sensitive? You want to help them in using "their money effectively." If there is, in fact, a duplication of services, you want to be able to develop systems that encourage collaboration and cooperation among agencies. These are positive words.

Healthcare Organization

Pat: I believe that I may be able to assist you in identifying new sources of funds. I have been effective in making links and raising new sources of income. I can also assist you in recruiting volunteers.

Trainer: Give life to your ideas. Let the interviewer know the kinds of funding sources you will be able to approach. What is your strategy for helping them attract volunteers? What types of volunteers would you go after? What would they look like? The more specific you are; the greater impression you will make.

You will come across better when you give concrete examples of what you mean and when you believe that you actually can make a difference. More importantly, the interviewer has to believe you. A former student of mine who just made a transition said that he got the job because "they believed me. They believed that I wanted to be there and to raise money for them." You must believe this yourself or they will not. OK, now how can you make a difference, Ron?

Ron: One of your major challenges is that you want to fund research. I know that you want to create an awareness about your cause. I can help you by creating special events.

Trainer: Fill in the blanks. Dream. What type of event would you do? If you come up with an event that is really "special," it will separate you from the rest of the applicants.

Cultural Organization

Pam: I want to help reduce the deficit by creating an event.
Trainer: What kind of event?
Pam: An event with great musicians.
Trainer: For example? Come up with an event!
Pam: I know you're facing a deficit. I can produce a direct mail campaign for you that would be segmented—getting the right message to the right person. In developing the mailing list, I would use the lists of other cultural organizations.
Trainer: Which organizations?
Pam: The Metropolitan Opera, museums, *Art News,* and *The New York Times.*

Trainer: Let the interviewer know that you know the kinds of lists you would need to launch an effective direct mail campaign. Tell the interviewer that you have a feel for their audience, that your dad is a musician.

Community Development Organization

Martha: When I visited your organization, I had the pleasure of meeting your executive director and he told me that you are developing a new strategic plan. I understand that its purpose is to build a broad communications program targeted at your constituencies: the board, funding sources, and government agencies.

Trainer: What would your message be?

Martha: They are the social, economic, and cultural anchors of their community.

Joan: I believe that in order to raise funds, you need a comprehensive marketing and communications plan. You need a strategy that encompasses the execution of materials, brochures, and advertising.

Trainer: Be careful in assuming that they need this! You might begin with, "I understand from reading your literature that you are engaged in developing a new strategic plan. I may be able to help." OK, now be specific, what would you do?

Joan: I would create, produce, and narrate a public service announcement to help create a wider awareness for your goals, mission, and needs.

Trainer: What has to be communicated within this public service announcement? What is the angle? What would you stress? What would make it sexy?

Think about a campaign. Start to dream. If you got in the door, what would you do to show them off to their constituencies? What about creating a video that brings people to tears?

The Mock Interview

By the end of the 5-week Program, the corporate managers were at different stages in the development of their identities and this became apparent in the one-on-one mock interviews between the corporate managers and the nonprofit interviewers. During these mock interviews, each corporate manager had a 5-minute back-and-forth dialogue with a nonprofit manager. The interviewer was either a career changer or a career manager from the nonprofit sector. Of course, "in real life," the corporate manager might encounter either type of nonprofit manager. The purpose of including career changers in this exercise is that it is likely that he both identifies with the struggle of the corporate manager and understands the expectations of the new organizational culture. The career changer is in a position to help the corporate manager anticipate, learn, and adapt within his organization. The nonprofit "career" managers, on the other hand, are interested in assessing whether the corporate manager is ready to become an organizational member in a new sector.

I first focus on interviews that indicate that additional anticipatory socialization, such as volunteering or interning, is required:

Human Services Organization (Career Nonprofit Manager)

Nonprofit Manager: I've looked at your résumé. It seems that your expertise is in marketing and public relations. How do you think your skills translate from profit to nonprofit?

Beth: I worked for a small corporation and when I started, I was making $100 a week. When I left, I was making $100,000 a year. I increased their sales from $1 to $5 million with no advertising budget and lots of press.

Nonprofit Manager: You mentioned salary [class laughs]. If you worked for us, you'd be working long hours for less pay. What is it about the nonprofit sector that interests you? Where does your interest in us come from?

Beth: Last year, I began volunteering. I love it. They appreciate me.

Nonprofit Manager: You've had volunteer experience and exposure to non-profits?

Beth: Yes, I get clothing manufacturers to donate clothing to this organization, and then they receive donations for the clothing.

Nonprofit Manager: Volunteering has given you a taste of nonprofits. Volunteers are essential to us. They provide the oversight; they own the organization. If you were given a position in the nonprofit sector, you would be working with volunteers. What is your understanding of the role of the professional manager vis-à-vis the volunteer who would be working with the professional manager?

Beth: I don't understand what you mean?

(At this point, it was clear that the corporate manager was having difficulty understanding the language and the role relationships of the nonprofit sector.)

Nonprofit Manager: Nonprofits have professional managers and volunteers working together. The board members volunteer their time, give money, expertise, and skills. The professional manager is hired by the board to run the day-to-day operations. Any manager who gets a job with a nonprofit organization will be working with volunteers and with volunteer committees. The public relations committee is composed of volunteers. You are considered staff. It is likely in an interview that you will be asked about your staff role in working with volunteers. In fact, it may be the question on which your interview turns.

Many professional managers fail because they don't have an effective working relationship with their volunteers. The volunteers own the organization. In every field, there is jargon (e.g., the role of the professional manager versus the role of the volunteer or board member and how they interact). It's better you hear this now.

Beth: I have never gotten a job through a résumé. People hire me because they like me.

Nonprofit Manager: When you work in a nonprofit organization, you have to be people-oriented. The fact that you are a people person suggests that you like working with people. That gives me a positive impression that you will have the ability to meet with people and that they will like you. If someone were to ask you how do you work with volunteers, you might say: "I'm a people person and I love working effectively with all types of people."

If you really are interested in working in the nonprofit sector, give examples of your interest during the interview such as other volunteer experiences.

Beth: I will be working with two other human services organizations.

Nonprofit Manager: Bring that out in the interview. Do you want the job because you're interested in the nonprofit sector or because you want a job? Are you committed and involved? I suggest that you bring it out. I always look for that. I've seen hundreds of résumés. I look for people who have been involved with the nonprofit sector. The nonprofit sector must be part of your personality and thinking.

This corporate manager needs additional anticipatory socialization because the nonprofit manager is not convinced that the corporate manager understands the culture, language, and role relationship between the nonprofit manager and the volunteer. The nonprofit manager wants to see evidence that the corporate manager has a nonprofit self. Perhaps, the volunteer experiences would help shape the expected identity.

The following manager also had problems exposing his nonprofit self:

Human Services Organization (Career Changer)

Nonprofit Manager: I'm curious, what position did you report to and how did your boss's job differ from yours?

Allen: I reported to the controller. He was the head of budgeting systems.

Nonprofit Manager: Were you one of a number of assistant controllers?

Allen: Yes.

Nonprofit Manager: What information did you provide?

Allen: Financial reports and procedures.

Nonprofit Manager: Do you see your transition into nonprofit as a challenge?

Allen: The cultures are different. I've been having lots of informational interviews. In my corporate job, I never went home feeling satisfied. I hope to feel that way working for a nonprofit.

The nonprofit manager critiqued the corporate manager's interview:

Nonprofit Manager: You want to be prepared to offer more. You need to get me to think that you really want to be in the nonprofit sector. Relate your experience to the nonprofit world. Take advantage of opportunities in the interview. The interviewer has a list of questions. The interviewer will stop you if you're taking too much of their time. You were forthcoming and I appreciated that. There was no appearance of being overly cocky.

The human services interviewer is looking for the corporate manager to talk more about the nonprofit sector because it would be an indication that he understands how the nonprofit world works. The interviewer also indicates that the tone of voice used in communicating knowledge or the avoidance of appearing "cocky" is appreciated. Thus, the way in which one presents oneself becomes as important as the knowledge itself. Here is an example of a corporate manager who still has this lesson to learn:

Healthcare Organization (Career Changer)

Nonprofit Manager: Why do you want to work for a nonprofit?

Earl: Over the years, I have worked in both profit and nonprofit and frankly, I sleep better when I work in nonprofit. It's more satisfying. I'm not motivated by profit. The nonprofit world is the real world. There's more emotional satisfaction, more emotional profit in nonprofit.

Nonprofit Manager: Tell me about your position in local government. How did you jump right in?

Earl: I didn't jump in. It jumped on me! I've always been a political volunteer. After moving to my community I was asked to run and I did.

Nonprofit Manager: And you served for 6 years?

Earl: Seven years total. I was instrumental in changing the old form of government into a new form of government where the people would elect the officials directly. They first elected me by committee and when we changed the government, I became the first elected official.

Nonprofit Manager: What is it about your skills and experience that is propelling you into the nonprofit sector?

Earl: I'm a good communicator. I have won over 100 awards for my writing skills. I'm a good manager and spokesperson.

I've done every form of communication: strategic planning in government, nonprofit, and business. I have good skills as a writer. I've written a novel, a screenplay, and articles. I'm a good manager. Most managers can't create, and most creative people can't manage. I'd like to think I can do both well.

The interviewer then critiqued Earl's interview:

Nonprofit Manager: You come on strong. You might come on a little heavy. I wanted to know more about your skills and how they can be applied to our organization.

Mental Health Organization (Career Changer)

Nonprofit Manager: Please tell me about yourself and your strengths.

Elaine: My specialty is people and fundraising. I've also been doing organization development for 20 years, since I was 5 [laughs]. The organization development work combines systems theory and psychoanalytic theory. In other words, what motivates people to think and how can they move organizations forward? The area I'm interested in is mergers and creating new corporate cultures. I've been working with a bank that merged with another bank. You're dealing with two [organizational] cultures. I've also worked in South Africa helping the black townships achieve financial viability working together with the whites. I've built a strategy in which the local radio stations are working with the local nongovernmental agencies and they are working with the local corporations and foundations. It's community development work.

Nonprofit Manager: How did you develop the strategy?

Elaine: In South Africa or in general?

Nonprofit Manager: Either one.

Elaine: It varies depending on the corporation. There's no formula. I see that your organization is about to merge with another nonprofit.

Nonprofit Manager: How did you know?

Elaine: I did my homework. With mergers, systems get thrown in the air. Important things get stirred up. After the merger, it doesn't go away. I look at the issues in defining a new structure and a new culture.

Nonprofit Manager: I notice that you have raised money. Please elaborate.

Elaine: Yes, I raised money to promote a literacy campaign in 200 cities throughout the world. I'm well connected with corporations and foundations throughout the country. I sold what I believed in. Your organization is so large that the tendency may be to swallow up the organization you are merging with and it just becomes a program. This is a disservice to you. Their culture could be expansive to you. You need to create a compelling vision that the entire organization will buy into. If you don't you'll be in trouble.

The nonprofit manager critiqued Elaine's interview:

Nonprofit Manager: You have great credentials and I like the way you presented yourself. You are articulate. There's one problem. You have two areas of expertise. It's hard to consider you because it's difficult for me to determine what it is you do. Focus on either organization development or fundraising.

Elaine: What should I have focused on with you?

Nonprofit Manager: We need both of the things you have. Select one thing and stick with it.

In this particular case, the nonprofit manager wants the corporate manager to define the role she wants to play in terms of a singular function. This, of course, is not always the case. There are organizations with scarce resources that may need to recruit managers to assume multiple tasks. There are other organizations which are interested in understanding all of the possible tasks the applicant can perform before directing him to the appropriate department managers within the organization for more extensive interviews. It's difficult to anticipate what the expectations of an interviewer might be. This corporate manager might have asked the nonprofit manager, up front, what the organization's greatest challenges were regarding both organization development and fundraising and after learning these expectations, focused on the manager's greatest area of concern. It's important to engage the interviewer so that the corporate manager can build a biography filled with nonprofit selves based on the expectations of the interviewer.

The Successful Mock Interview

Successful mock interviews occur when a corporate manager meets the expectations of the nonprofit manager. The corporate manager, in each of these cases, is able to engage the interviewer through the use of a nonprofit biography that portrays an empathetic nonprofit self, sharing a similarity of experience and status with the nonprofit interviewer. Here are some examples:

Human Services Organization (Career Changer)

Nonprofit Manager: Please tell me about your background.
George: I've spent most of my career doing product marketing, specifically to the $20 million a year African-American market. Before that, I sold holiday items that generated $3.5 million a year for the company.

I wanted to interview with you because 3 weeks ago, I read your ad and learned that you help 5000 people every month and that all of these people got a second chance at happiness. I thought wow, if I could work for an organization that gives that much to people, well … I have something in mind.

As a volunteer, I have created events for nonprofits. I know that every year you do [a large special] event. I want to be an events planner and plan an event which would complement your event. In the spring, I would bring together the manufacturers, retailers, and designers of the home-care industry. Their contributions would benefit the homeless and we would call it "Homeward Bound."

The nonprofit interviewer has this to say about George's interview:

You were excellent. You have the passion. You found the fit, the angle—the link. You gave me a specific example that I valued right away. You know a lot about us. You did your homework.

Hospital (Career Manager)

Nonprofit Manager: I don't know how much you know about hospitals.

Michael: You know something, I read your annual report!

Nonprofit Manager: Then you know that we're in the midst of a capital campaign, and we are building a donor base to support us beyond the campaign. I'm interested to know what is motivating you to move to the nonprofit sector?

Michael: That's a fair question. The last couple of years, I've been volunteering for a nonprofit human services organization. I have found my passion. I realize that I like being involved in a cause which benefits society. I don't get the same feeling when I'm drafting merger agreements. I realize that I have a commitment to this organization because I believe in what they're doing. My belief in them has caused me to experience fundamental career happiness. It's not too late to change careers.

Nonprofit Manager: What skills do you bring?

Michael: As a corporate lawyer, I bring analytical skills. I have some knowledge of the healthcare field, but it is not my area of expertise. I have a smattering of experience as a fundraiser. As a volunteer, I have been successful in soliciting donations from others. Before I asked people for donations, I found that it was important to listen to what was going on in their lives. The donor has needs and most successful fundraising builds on those needs.

Nonprofit Manager: Did you like asking for money?

Michael: Yes, I did. For me soliciting face-to-face makes a difference. Connections aren't made over the phone. My strength is in developing relationships.

Nonprofit Manager: You could initiate a planned giving program. Do you have experience in planned giving?

Michael: No. But I have received some materials on planned giving.

Nonprofit Manager: It wouldn't take you long to learn.

Michael: When I worked for a law firm, I organized a fundraising campaign for this organization with which I'm now volunteering. Colleagues wanted to know why they should commit their money and devote their time to this organization. I was able to answer their questions.

Nonprofit Manager: What type of organization do you want to work for?

Michael: I'd like to work for a healthcare organization and I'm not just saying that [class laughs]. I was a biology major in college and once entertained notions of going to medical school. I volunteered for a hospital between my sophomore and junior years in college. Recently, personal family experiences have led to interactions with hospitals, and I recognize the importance of total healthcare, of caring for the individual, and not just the disease.

Michael's interview was critiqued by the nonprofit manager:

Nonprofit Manager: If I could get my boss to sign off on my hiring an assistant, I would hire you tomorrow.

Michael: I'd start tomorrow!

This hospital manager also interviewed a corporate systems manager:

Nonprofit Manager: I see that you have an extensive background in accounting. Why do you want to move to a hospital?

Mark: It's a two-step decision. The first decision was to work in the non-profit arena. I've been involved with nonprofits for 25 years and I know the difference between an organization that earns a profit and an organization that cares about people. I'm an accountant and a systems analyst. I bring the skills of financial control and systems building. I understand that hospitals are on the cutting edge of technology and have gleaned that they are investing in managed care.

I'm uniquely qualified to help hospitals identify cost savings within their present systems and processes and to help them build cost-effective systems and processes.

Nonprofit Manager: I like that a lot. Hospitals are behind in their infra-structure. They need technology to run the hospital.

Mark: It's good to hear that there's a need. I've been taking courses in healthcare management. I have a certificate in healthcare management.

Nonprofit Manager: Do you have recent experience in nonprofit management?

Mark: Yes, I've done consulting for a human services organization.

The hospital manager critiqued Mark's interview:

Nonprofit Manager: I'd be happy to pass your résumé along within my organization. I'd be more aggressive in stating your skills up front.

Cultural Organization (Career Manager)

Nonprofit Manager: I see that you have nonprofit clients. Why do you want to make the shift from profit to nonprofit?

Pam: I spend a lot of time on the job.

Nonprofit Manager: This will not change!

Pam: If I spend time working advertising toothpaste, it means nothing. I volunteer for an organization that saves homeless kids and I know I want to work for a nonprofit.

Nonprofit Manager: Define direct response.

Pam: If a television commercial has a phone number at the end, that's direct response. If a radio announcement has a phone number in it, that's direct response.

Nonprofit Manager: Why do you want to work for us?

Pam: I'm the only "suit" in my family. Everyone in my family is a classical musician and has played at jazz clubs in Harlem. I like the marketing area. I would like to market something I believe in.

Nonprofit Manager: You must put your soul into your fundraising pitch. You must believe in what you're doing. You know when someone's trying to sell you something they don't believe in.

The cultural manager critiqued Pam's interview:

Nonprofit Manager: Your skills are transferable. I love the story about your family. We are looking for someone with marketing skills. Please keep in touch.

Community-Based Organization (Career Changer)

Nonprofit Board Member: Please give me a 2-minute overview of yourself.

Martha: I've been working as a volunteer fundraiser. I am learning how nonprofit agencies work in the Bronx and in Brooklyn. I also do pro bono marketing work for another human services agency. Prior to these two experiences, I did marketing and communications for a financial services organization.

Nonprofit Board Member: What position are you interested in?

Martha: A group of us visited your organization and we discovered that you are developing new directions for the organization. I would be interested in creating a strategic communications plan that would reach all of your constituencies.

Nonprofit Board Member: We are in the midst of change. We are moving toward economic development as the underpinning of our organization. We support other nonprofit services. We need to find a way to sustain these nonprofit services. There's not enough public funding. We need to look for a way to augment the funding of this organization. We believe that it can be done through economic development.

Martha: I understand from visiting your organization that you're developing moderately affordable housing. Tell me more.

Nonprofit Board Member: Over the years, our neighborhood has suffered economically. We now see a change. The middle class is coming back. How can we convince younger people to come back? They won't come unless we can provide services so that they feel something is happening. If you come to work with us, what is your salary range?

Martha: I'm flexible. It depends on the job responsibilities. I'm anxious to continue my nonprofit career.

Nonprofit Board Member: Why do you want to make a transition?

Martha: For the last 2 years, the corporate sector hasn't excited me. I've been active in the nonprofit sector, to some extent, all of my life. I want to give back.

Her interviewer critiqued Martha's interview:

You did a great thing that surprised me. You came out to see our organization. I wasn't prepared for the amount of knowledge you had about us. It was a very comfortable interview. There is a possibility that if we were looking for a strategic communications person, you'd be a serious candidate. You were very direct. You curried me. You became involved. The question you asked me strengthened my impression of you.

All five of the corporate managers interviewed in this section are now working for nonprofit organizations because they learned to anticipate the cultural expectations of the interviewer. They learned to anticipate the interviewer's expectations through observing and networking with the nonprofit manager in and outside of the classroom. It is through the process of networking with nonprofit employers that career changers ultimately find employment in the nonprofit sector.

Networking

Granovetter (1995) notes that when career changers have few professional ties in occupations other than their own, they must build new professional ties through voluntary groups in order to build a new occupational network. It is only through joining a new group that the career changer will be able to shorten the information chain between himself and the employer. The shorter the information chain between the recruit and the employer, the more likely it is that the recruit will be hired. According to Granovetter, the best information chain is the zero information chain, where the employer and the recruit know each other. A chain length of two indicates that there are two intermediaries between the employer and the recruit. An employer looks to an intermediary's network of contacts, if the employer does not have the likely candidate as part of the original applicant pool.

Within the classroom and in interviews with 35 additional career changers, I found that the majority of these career changers find their jobs through contacts either with the employer or with an intermediary of the employer. In other words, the majority of the career changers find their jobs through networking. A smaller percentage find their jobs through formal means (e.g., advertisements in newspapers, employment agencies).

Within the classroom, corporate managers learned about and engaged in the process of networking. Successful graduates of the Program told the class how important networking is in finding jobs in the nonprofit sector:

> Pat: The most direct link to employment was through this class. A person from my organization came to speak to the class and he referred me to his colleague. The colleague introduced me to my future boss. It took a long time for me to find a job and it's all in the timing. Circle back to the people you interview with. People leave and retire. Persistence pays off. Think of excuses to write to people. Send them articles. Send them thank-you notes. Zero in on what they think is important.

> Darlene: A direct personal contact gets you the job faster than reading the paper. I heard about this position through the class.

Sam: I immersed myself in networking. I did lots of informational interviewing and then had a regimen where I followed up. Even people I
didn't think I should call, I did. Be persistent. Go back to those you
interview with. Volunteering in the community helps you network.

Here is an example of the networking process within the classroom
between a corporate manager and a nonprofit manager:

Corporate Manager: If you were hiring a development person and got a
résumé from someone who didn't have the typical development back-
ground, what would make you invite this person in for an interview?
Development Manager: It would depend on the level of the job.
Corporate Manager: I haven't been a development manager, but I can raise
money. I recently raised $300,000 for a community development project.
Development Manager: That sounds like fundraising to me.
Corporate Manager: I raised $1 million in advertising for a national
literacy campaign.
Development Manager: Please see me after class.

It is within this chapter that we see the extent to which the corporate
manager's identity is tied to his prior corporate world-view. The Program and
each of its components are an effort to help the manager relinquish the many
ingrained habits that have become "second nature" to the long-term corporate
manager. It is within each of these steps that the corporate managers are able
to develop a greater sensitivity to the nonprofit sector.

In summary, a component in becoming fluent in the language and culture of the nonprofit sector is a result of learning these expectations from
established employees in the nonprofit world. Not only did the corporate
managers need to learn the facts and expectations from a nonprofit peer
group, but they needed to begin networking with this peer group as well. It
was through the various Program components that the managers were, in
fact, able to present their new nonprofit selves, network with nonprofit
employees, and learn their cultural expectations. The interactions (e.g., interviewing, feedback on résumé and introductions from nonprofit managers, discussions between the corporate and nonprofit managers during classroom
sessions on nonprofit role and cultural expectations) were intended to give
the corporate managers practice in dealing with nonprofit gatekeepers and to
gain access to employment opportunities within the nonprofit sector.

Notes

1. Burke (1980, in Demo, 1992) writes that the "self-image is a 'current working copy,' of
the identity .... It is subject to constant change, revision, editing, and updating as a function of variations in situations and situational demands" (p. 305). The identity is developed through a sequence of interactions with significant others such as employers and

peers. Identities are shaped through learning the requisite expectations of others including the appropriate values, knowledge, attitudes, behaviors, and motivations that correspond to a given situation. This process is called socialization (Brim and Wheeler, 1966; Elkin and Handel, 1984; Rosow, 1974; Van Maanen, 1976, 1977, 1983).

2. The importance of the peer group's support in maintaining both individual and collective good impressions is discussed in Becker and colleagues' (1961) study of medical school students, *Boys in White.*

3. In Goffman's *Stigma* (1963), he asserts that through the creation of a biography, the individual can sustain different selves and can to a degree claim to be no longer something he was.

Chapter 6

Transition from the Profit to the Nonprofit World

LEARNING CULTURAL EXPECTATIONS

Introduction

Nonprofit managers understand what is needed to succeed in their sector. Within the context of the classroom, many nonprofit managers came and talked to the displaced managers about their own careers. Instead of teaching in an abstract way, nonprofit managers related their own personal experiences as a way of showing the importance of certain roles and ideas. Their "moral tales" are in fact professional signposts, which describe the most important roles in the nonprofit sector.

From the corporate manager's perspective, these lectures by nonprofit managers informed them about the expectations held by people in the nonprofit world. However, the students have to separate out the personal details of the stories from the message: what is expected of them when they interview and when they get a job?

Within the classroom, the dislocated managers learned about the role expectations of key managerial positions as well as some of the values guiding behavior in nonprofit cultures. They learned that volunteerism is an essential socializing process both in learning the cultural expectations of nonprofit organizations and in substantiating their commitment to the sector. It is through peer socialization, or learning the expected attitudes and behaviors from this reference group of future peers, that the dislocated managers are able to continue reshaping their identities.

NONPROFIT MANAGERIAL CAREER PATHS

Dislocated managers learned nonprofit cultural expectations by hearing established nonprofit managers describe their own career paths. The Program arranged for two kinds of nonprofit managers to socialize the students: "career nonprofit managers" and those corporate managers who have successfully attained managerial positions in the nonprofit sector. This first section focuses on the career paths of those nonprofit career managers who have spent their entire career in the nonprofit sector.

Saul is a healthcare fundraiser who has spent his entire career in healthcare. He describes his career path this way:

> I knew when I was in college that I was committed to healthcare. I wanted to be involved in finding a cure for cancer! After college, I worked for a surgeon who was also a researcher and I was exposed to the medical side of a hospital. While working for this surgeon, the hospital paid for my MBA. I later learned that the development department was about to launch a huge capital campaign and was looking for an entry-level person to do foundation and corporate fundraising. The development department believed that they could train the right person to do development, but could not teach someone the hospital culture in such a short amount of time. It was a perfect melding of their needs and my background. I worked my way up in the development department. It was a great place to be trained and I spent 16 years with this institution.

What did corporate managers learn from this hospital fundraiser who was raised in a hospital culture since the beginning of his career? First, the nonprofit manager's biography indicates that he entered the field motivated by the mission of the organization. Second, the organization does not want to spend either the time or the money training a manager unfamiliar with the hospital culture. Third, though the hospital culture may not have been willing to invest its resources in the training of an outsider, it is willing to invest its resources in the staff development of a loyal and committed employee. Fourth, the investment results in the long-term career advancement of this employee within the organization. The lesson in Saul's biography is that nonprofit people wear their sense of mission on their sleeve, that they prefer promoting insiders. That once inside, demonstrating commitment, promotion opportunities follow.

Saul continues:

> The next logical career move was to go to a smaller institution for a bigger job. I was recruited by a smaller institution where I became the number two fundraiser. I'm now the chief fundraiser at another hospital.
>
> I think when you are starting out in the healthcare field, you should select a hospital where you are exposed to everything in a fundraising

department—capital campaigns, planned giving, and major donors. You
need to learn the big picture.

Here the corporate manager learns that if one begins as a generalist
working for a large institution, the next logical career move is to become a
more senior manager at a smaller or medium-sized institution.
Saul continues:

I now have a career changer working for me. He doesn't know development, but he has made it his mission to take on anything.

This was a hint that successful adaptation within a new organizational
culture requires the new recruit to be willing to "take on anything."
Frank, the president of a national arts organization, reveals his career
path:

When I was in college, my father wanted me to become a lawyer or a den-
tist. I went for the big money—I was an English major! After college, I
faced my first bold reality: all of the poet jobs were taken! I began substi-
tute teaching in junior high, which I believe every American should do.
Then I went into real estate for 3 years where I learned marketing,
accounting, and sales. I knew that I wanted to be involved with the arts
world. I knew that being an artist was not my calling. But I found a field
called arts administration where I could combine my creative impulses
with business management skills. I entered the field the traditional way
through an internship and eventually worked my way up to executive
director.

For the past 10 years, I have been the president of a national organization committed to the local arts agency movement. It's a growing movement. In 1965, there were 600 local arts organizations. Today, there are
3800 local arts organizations.

Peter Drucker (1990) claims that the first job "is a lottery ... and it takes a
few years to find out where you belong and to begin self-placement" (p. 195).
Similarly, in the case of this arts manager, it takes some time before he finds
the career sequence (Hughes, 1981) which will lead him to his present position. For many, the arts administration career sequence begins with an internship. Internships provide "trial periods for the learner" (Brim and Wheeler,
1966, p. 80). For this manager, the internship is a socializing process that pre-
pares him for leadership roles within his organization.

Both Saul and Frank have homogeneous career sequences. In other words,
they have moved exclusively within their own industries, and their networks
involve members of the same occupation. Rosow (1965) categorizes such managers as "socialized" (p. 37). A socialized member conforms to expectations
about the behaviors and values of his group. The more committed, the more
intense his effort is within the organization. A socialized member, according to

Rosow, conforms to the values of his organization on moral rather than utilitarian grounds. Saul's and Frank's self-image and identity are linked to their role within the occupation (Rosow, 1974; Trice and Beyer, 1993).

Corporate managers who change careers, or withdraw from their prior role, have a harder task than Saul and Frank. They must develop a new peer network of nonprofit practitioners who can socialize, mentor, and help them structure the next career sequence of their life cycle.

The Successful Career Changer's Sequence

Throughout the life cycle, an individual is engaged in a series of role changes and life transitions (George, 1993; Moen et al., 1992; Neugarten and Datan, 1973). An important part of the Nonprofit Management and Communications Program involved successful career changers discussing these role changes and life transitions with the corporate managers. Since some of them have been in the same situation as the displaced managers, their advice carries special weight, and their insights are often quite deep. Sam was a financial lender who began his own nonprofit organization:

> My career started as a commercial banker. Most loan officers have written into their job descriptions that they take a leadership role in the community. That means working with nonprofits and their boards. I did this for 25 years or longer. I had the responsibility for raising over $100 million for my community.
>
> I believe that you're best off getting a generalized background in development before you specialize. Most chief executives of decent size nonprofit agencies have a broad managerial background.

Sam was able to create a peer network of nonprofit managers through his work at his corporation. He is familiar with the role of fundraiser because he has practiced this role, under the "guardianship of peers," for over 25 years. Since he was socialized by this peer network and had acquired their values, he felt comfortable creating a nonprofit fundraising organization that helps nonprofit managers survive government reductions. It is also interesting to note that having been socialized by nonprofit managers, Sam takes their point of view with regard to the career sequence of fundraisers.

Utilization of Successful Anticipatory Socialization

In his various corporate and volunteer roles, Sam was exposed to anticipatory socialization processes that allowed him the opportunity to practice and learn the expected attitudes and behaviors from a reference group of future nonprofit peers. In understanding the importance of involving the peer or reference group in the anticipatory socialization process, Rosow (1974) maintains that "a peer group is a rich source of models. The authority group personifies the goals of socialization. The peer group provides many of the means of adaptation" (p. 94). Volunteerism is one role that allows Sam to interact with the nonprofit network of peers, and leads to his later employment within the nonprofit sector. This is not surprising. Moen et al. (1992) found that "any voluntary participation at any time in adulthood appears to promote multiple role occupancy in latter years" (p. 1633). Similarly, Granovetter (1995) asserts that it is through the contacts made in these voluntary organizations that one is able to develop the network of informal ties that lead to career change.

Since it is the peer group that provides direct exposure to the new reference group (Rosow, 1974), the Nonprofit Management and Communications Program was deliberately structured to provide the corporate managers with direct exposure to the nonprofit reference group as a means of achieving successful anticipatory socialization. Successful career changers who had gone through the Program were invited into several classes to discuss their ability to anticipate the expectations of the nonprofit interviewer.

Meredith, who transitioned from corporate law to hospital management, reveals:

> The class was very helpful in terms of learning about the nonprofit organization before the interview. I was able to gain knowledge about what nonprofits were doing by talking to nonprofit managers in the classroom. I also met career changers who had made the transition. I learned about the managerial issues of nonprofits: their mission, financial issues, and their new accounting systems.

Matthew, who moved from publishing to human services, also learned what to expect in an interview:

> I learned what the mindset of nonprofits are and what the culture is like. The organization chart may say something in words, but there is a feeling in the agency that has a lot to do with why they are there and why they exist. Without the class and the interaction with the nonprofit managers, I never would have been able to understand this. I never would have been able to translate what I had been through in business into something that made sense to someone in a nonprofit organization.

Fred, a career changer working for a university, concurs:

> Since I didn't have experience in the nonprofit sector, having the knowledge helped build my confidence. I learned about the many kinds of nonprofits [e.g., universities, trade and professional organizations, hospitals]. I learned how to think about their perspective [e.g., their motivation and what they were looking for]. I learned to figure out where they were coming from.

Carole, previously with a consumer products company, and who had found her new managerial position with a human services organization, believes that the nonprofit managers she met in the classroom gave her "a better view of nonprofits":

> We learned that they are driven by serving, rather than by private gain. We learned that different things needed to be stressed in a nonprofit interview and that our presentation must reflect their way.

Furthermore, Carole used the class as an opportunity to "make connections and open doors for networking purposes."

Stan, who moved from financial services into education, thinks that it was the "exposure to the nonprofit managers (reference group) that convinced him to persevere in his career search":

> Meeting the nonprofit managers in class made it real for me. I could touch [the new career] in an experimental phase. The course helps you eliminate some of the areas of nonprofit and to differentiate between nonprofits.

Finally, career changers report that they are better able to anticipate the ways in which nonprofit managers will behave and think on the job. Michael, who transitioned from a law firm to a human services organization, remembers: "You got insight into the personality profile and attitude profile of people who work in the nonprofit sector. Every person you met, you got a better feel for the nonprofit profile." Kevin, a certified public accountant turned fundraiser, believes that the class "prepared us for the consensual style of decision-making."

Nonprofit Roles

As a critical part of the anticipatory socialization process within the classroom, the corporate managers learned about nonprofit role expectations for specific kinds of jobs. Examples of peer socialization are found in the interactions between the nonprofit and corporate managers where the nonprofit managers are imparting the important expectations of various roles to the corporate managers. This section reviews the roles of executive director, financial manager, communications manager, fundraising manager, volunteer, board member, and the relationship between the funder and the development officer.

The Executive Director

Kathy, a career changer, spent more that 20 years in an insurance company before assuming the executive director role at a $2 million human services organization. She talks about her relationship with the program staff and the board of directors:

> I have to be the jack-of-all-trades. I have to be able to deal with the air conditioning and the personnel. In my case, a broad management background was ideal. You have to handle the administrative side of things and leave the program side to the professionals. As the leader of the organization, I can't tell the professionals how to do therapy, but I can ask a lot of questions. The staff must support the board. The nonprofit board helps us do fundraising, marketing, and government affairs. They help us make connections with foundations and individuals that can support the organization.

In Kathy's case, she was expected to bring her broad managerial expertise from the corporate sector into the nonprofit organization because the organization recognizes the "usefulness of the characteristics the individual already possesses" (Van Maanen, 1983, p. 255). She also learned that her instrumental or administrative role is quite distinct from the expressive role of the therapist. In order to avoid conflict, she respects the fact that the "dual leadership roles" of the administrator and the therapist ought to be kept separate. She understands that in this type of organization it is functional for the expressive leaders to dominate the organization since "they initiate and direct goal activities such as building up and sustaining the required value commitments" (Etzioni, 1975, p. 170). Within the context of her role as executive director, Kathy focuses on instrumental activities such as fundraising and board relations.

James, a manager from a human services organization, talks about the role of the chief professional officer (chief executive) in making the board of directors look good:

> In the nonprofit sector, you have a responsibility for volunteer leadership. Your role, as the chief professional officer, is to make the volunteers look good. The chair of the board doesn't write his speeches. Volunteers are not trained so you have to make them look good. If you come from a corporation where you're visible and now your role is to make others look good, that's a significant change.

This particular organizational culture does not tolerate the pursuit of individual goals over collective goals (e.g., personal visibility versus visibility of volunteers), but according to Etzioni (1975) and others this is a common feature in nonprofit organizations.

The Financial Manager

Marshall, a financial manager, made the transition from a communications corporation to a nonprofit that helps women form their own businesses.

He describes how the culture influenced his role:

> As you know, business enterprises are organized around profits and they employ operational accountability measures efficiently. Nonprofits don't always realize revenues as a result of economic activity. We do training and counseling and receive 10 percent of our revenue from these activities. We also get grants and contributions. Our revenue from these sources isn't directly connected with the services we provide. Nonprofit accounting has to reflect that. In nonprofits, dollar accountability and integrity is reflected in the mission.

Unlike corporations that are able to measure results based on calculating the rate of return for resources expended, nonprofits find it difficult to measure results because there are weak links between donor revenues and the beneficiaries served (Mirvis and Hackett, 1983). Many nonprofit organizations do not produce outcome measures that give an indication of how grants and contributions improve or change the lives of their donors or beneficiaries (Moore, 2000). Scholars such as Drucker (1990), Smith and Lipsky (1993), and Moore (2000) repeatedly urge nonprofit organizations to develop outcome measures to document their significance or value.

Marshall explains that he had to learn the new accounting rules of the nonprofit sector, and discusses these rules with a corporate manager:

> *Marshall*: Nonprofit financial managers now have to be familiar with Financial Accounting Standards Board (FASB) 116 and 117. Under these rules, unconditional promises or pledges to make contributions must now be recorded at the time of the pledge.
> *Corporate Manager*: In traditional nonprofit accounting, revenues were matched with expenses in the year they were received. Now, a pledge comes in and it must be recognized as revenue in the year it was pledged. The pledge may, in fact, be a revenue stream for a lot of years thereafter. People who want to give money are confused because based on this new system you may look like you're in better shape than you are.
> *Marshall*: Yes. That's the major drawback.

Next, Marshall discusses his role with the corporate manager and what he may expect:

> *Corporate Manager*: I have a question. You work four days. I understand that some nonprofits can't afford a full-time financial person so that the financial person may work two days for one organization and three days for the other. Is that true?
> *Marshall*: Yes, some nonprofits can't afford to pay someone full-time.
> *Corporate Manager*: I've also heard that nonprofit organizations are less concerned with a financial person's abilities to cut costs and efficiency and more concerned with their ability to help in the fundraising effort. Is there a dual focus?

Marshall: Not in our organization. I'm expected to make sure that our revenue is keeping up with expenses. I analyze all contracts with government agencies. I do the payroll twice a month. I pay our vendors. I do all of the reporting requirements to funders who give us money. I fill out the 990 tax form. I do all of the budgeting and cash flow projections. Cash flow is not always easy to predict. We may allocate money to hire people for a project and it is difficult to know when the money will come. Funders make grants as they see fit. It's difficult to plan.

Another Corporate Manager: What kinds of reports do you do for donors?

Marshall: If a donor sponsors a program, they want to know how many [people] came—the results. They want a comparison of budgeted to actual expenses.

The Communications Role

In Ott's (1989) ethnographic work on organizational culture, he argues that what works for one culture may not work for another. Similarly, Bush (1992) worries that conflict may arise if corporate values are imposed on nonprofit goals. In two cases that follow, however, it is apparent that what worked for a corporate marketing culture may indeed work for a nonprofit culture. Both the healthcare and foundation communications managers are using "corporate" marketing strategies such as segmentation, catalog marketing, and direct response in order to support nonprofit activities:

Corporate Manager: You all have different messages to get out to different constituencies. Who are your primary audiences and how do you reach them?

Communications Manager, Educational Foundation: Our Association has 22 market segments. I reach them through catalog marketing and the Internet. The messages I send are different depending on the group. One group is not interested in what another group is doing unless it relates to them. At the Foundation (within the Association), I work one-on-one with students and professors.

Communications Manager, Healthcare Organization: We don't do an education piece without a marketing hook. We put together educational pieces with coupons which people can send in for a free copy of our magazine. We capture a name and then they begin to get direct mail from us. Hopefully, they become members. Segmenting can't be carried too far.

Another nonprofit manager relates a more typical, and less corporate, way of reaching her constituency:

Communications Manager, Human Services Organization: We have a newsletter. We have a wide audience and we must touch all audiences. The newsletter goes to parents, the media, donors, and volunteers. We need to be able to relate how a particular service helped an individual family. The donors are interested in whether their money was used wisely. They want to know how much of their grant went to direct services versus administrative costs.

In the following discussion, the class learned about the close links between the communications and the development roles in nonprofit organizations:

Corporate Manager: What percentage of your job involves fundraising?

Communications Manager, Healthcare Organization: We are a fundraising organization and everything we do is promoting the fundraising machine. I direct a communications department that produces publicity for the fundraising department. We do the TV spots and their media campaign. The development department isn't set up for that.

I'm involved in raising money for my department. I had to find an underwriter for one of my magazines. I wrote the proposal and raised the money.

Communications Manager, Educational Foundation: I am involved with corporate fundraising. We do little direct mail solicitation of donors. We approach corporations directly for large gifts.

Finally, there was a discussion about "cause-related marketing"—an interdependent relationship between the corporate and nonprofit sectors. Note the corporate jargon the nonprofit manager uses below such as "customer," "broker," and "bottom line." Also note the need for the nonprofit organization to maintain its nonprofit ethics and integrity amid the corporate goals of profit and competitiveness:

Another Corporate Manager: What is cause-related marketing?

Communications Manager, Human Services Organization: You go after marketing rather than donation dollars from a corporation. For every product they sell, they will donate a certain portion to us. Cause-related marketing is a win-win. Both the corporation and the nonprofit organization have a stake in the same consumers. Corporations used to do social marketing—they would give money to feel good. There isn't that kind of money around any more. If they give us money, there has to be a bottom-line benefit for their customers.

I think that there's room for consultants who can broker large organizations like ours with corporations. We do have strict guidelines concerning which corporations may use our name.

Another Corporate Manager: Aren't you concerned with the amount of increased cynicism that may arise from having your name on scarves and shoes?

Communications Manager, Human Services Organization: There is an ethic to it. If we lend our name to a product, the product will have a tag about our organization that says: "for more information, please call us."

The Development Role

Development managers of a theater, a research organization, and a hospital spoke to the corporate managers about this very important role. Common themes that led the discussion included listening to donors, the need to have role relationships with organizational members, conflict between short-term and long-term goals, reduction of funding sources and the challenge to replace them, and fundraising methods:

> *Trainer*: Please describe your responsibilities as a fundraiser.
>
> *Development Manager, Hospital*: My current role is a challenging one. As the Director of Development, I have to worry, on a daily basis, how much money is being raised. I have to deal with follow-up. I have to make sure that the donor feels good about his donation, and I have to worry about my staff. When you get caught up in the day-to-day, sometimes you forget about raising money. It's easier to do that than to raise money! You need to manage your time and set priorities within the organization and for your staff. There are aspects of the job I hate. Working with your staff as a team can be fun or not so fun. There is an ongoing process of educating your board and staff about development.
>
> I have a passion for the hospital. I need to let other people see that passion. Donors want to know that you care about the organization. As a development person, you have to learn to listen to what the donor is saying. Donors can have different agendas, different reasons for giving.
>
> *Development Manager, Research Organization*: Development is so different than what I thought it was. I thought it was making cold calls. Development, in fact, draws on every skill you can imagine. You're in the middle of everything. It involves strategic planning, public relations, and marketing. You get to know everyone in an organization. You're involved in the major decisions of an organization. Your job is to know everything about what that organization does in terms of their relationships with donors, board members, and volunteers. You're never bored.
>
> It's hard to think about your long-term fundraising goals. Every day you're involved with volunteers and board members. You need a high tolerance for dealing with demanding people. You have to be the sort of person who doesn't need to be out in front all of the time.
>
> It's important to find out why people want to give to your organization. A donor may have a passion for one part of the organization. The more you listen to the donor, the more you're able to figure out what they want and the better it is for the donor and the organization.
>
> *Development Manager, Theater*: Yes, in development, you're at the heart of what goes on in programming and even building maintenance! You have to know everyone in the organization. You have to be able to interview the lighting designer so that the fundraising proposal to a foundation reveals why it is important to have upgraded lighting equipment.

Your effectiveness depends on how others in the organization do their jobs. You can't be expected to come in and save an organization. You are part of a team. When you're interviewing for a job, you have to assess if the organization has a clear sense of what it is doing. Look at the board and the leadership. Does the board have confidence in the executive director? If you are representing the organization to funders and there is no confidence in the executive director, you won't receive funding. Public confidence is important too. If people don't feel that you are properly managing your resources, they won't give you money.

Corporate Manager: Do you use telemarketing and the Internet to raise money?

Development Manager, Hospital: No way. You raise money from major donors one-on-one. We respect the privacy issues of wealthy donors and we only use public sources to conduct research on them.

Another Corporate Manager: How do you actually wrestle the funds?

Development Manager, Hospital: Wrestle is not a good word. You have to ask for the donation, no matter how much cultivation you do. You have to find a connection between the donor and the institution. That connection could be a doctor or a trustee. It's nice if the staff person is there in case someone falters and then you have to ask for the donation. The reality is that the person who asks for the donation should be a person the donor feels close to. In healthcare, it shouldn't be the doctor.

Development Manager, Research: The cultivation of a donation from a major donor usually happens over time. Over time, you are able to get to know the person, and you will have a sense of whether the person is interested in giving.

Development Manager, Hospital: If you are talking about a major donor, they expect to be asked. You don't make "the ask" in a letter. Foundations and corporations have established guidelines for making donations. They expect a written proposal. You never ask a major donor for a gift in writing.

In this case, the nonprofit manager is adamant about not imposing corporate strategies (e.g., telemarketing, Internet, wrestling) on nonprofit fundraising efforts. Fundraising from major donors is done face-to-face over a period of time. In this case, what works for one culture does not work for the other (Ott, 1989).

The Role of the Institutional Funder

Relationships in the nonprofit world between the institutional funder (e.g., foundation/corporation) and the development officer are important for corporate managers to learn:

Foundation Manager: Most people who approach us are making a difference in the city and they need our help. We don't have an application. We ask nonprofits to contact us through a letter of inquiry. If we feel the project has merit, we call them and ask them to submit a five-page letter with a budget. I often work through several re-writes of their letter before it is submitted to the funding committee. Most of our applicants don't have a background in proposal writing. I then bring the proposal to the staff and if the staff is favorable, it is submitted to the funding committee of our board. I rarely take anything to the board that is turned down [by the staff]. We don't like to be the sole funding source of an organization. We like to give declining support over two to three years.

Institutional funders, such as foundations and corporations, often have different goal orientations. Since a foundation is a nonprofit organization, its goals are cultural and are designed to change people's lives (Drucker, 1990; Etzioni, 1975). Since a corporation's goals are instrumental, their funding guidelines are "market oriented." In other words, grants and loans made to nonprofit organizations are made to improve the environment in which the corporation does business. If the environment is a fertile one, more money is made for the shareholders. Grants and loans to nonprofit organizations are viewed by corporations as a means to an end. The fundraiser has to keep the instrumental goals of the corporate funder in mind when submitting a proposal. This corporate funder stresses his corporation's goals and their relationship to the nonprofit sector:

Corporate Funder: This generation of nonprofit managers needs to understand that the market drives us. Those nonprofits that have political clout can provide credibility to the funder. We tie our giving to our business strategy: our products, services, and employees. We give to a business school that will provide us with the best people. We support charity dinners because we make business contacts at these dinners.

Corporate Manager: Is grant-making similar to lending money?

Corporate Funder: We have a revolving loan fund that supports the creation of jobs, housing, and so forth. The quality of the relationships we have with those receiving loans and grants are similar. Our motivation to invest in these organizations is similar.

Another Corporate Manager: Do you think that mergers between nonprofits offer opportunities?

Corporate Funder: It is possible that nonprofits can offer better service if there is an effort to streamline and consolidate.

Another Corporate Manager: How do you measure results?

Corporate Funder: All funders are human beings and they want to have a sense that they are touching people's lives. Beyond that, we do head counts, survey the number of jobs created, and the number of housing units built.

Another Corporate Manager: If the focus of giving has to do with the corporation's image, what does a small organization do if they can't compete and make the same banners as Lincoln Center?

Corporate Funder: Image is a broad term. We want to create the perception that we are good corporate citizens. We are concerned with the

> well-being of children and the organizations that serve children. We are
> influenced by the policies of our local community managers. If they are
> involved, we may get involved. There has to be some relationship
> between the organization and our company. Maybe we support an
> organization in a community where our employees live.
> *Another Corporate Manager:* How does your corporation view the corpo-
> rate matching gift program when it can't always control the outcome of
> whom the gift is made to?
> *Corporate Funder:* Most corporate matching gift programs are oriented to
> education. Others are broader. Some match dollar-for-dollar; others are
> a three-to-one match. We treat this program as a "corporate benefit." It
> shows the company cares about its employees. We go one step further:
> if the employee volunteers for 6 hours a month, we will give a donation,
> in the employee's name, to the nonprofit where he volunteers.

This corporate funder has instrumental goals that are "market driven,"
evaluated for quantitative results, and tied to its image or reputation. Philanthropy is tied to the corporation's business strategy and thus a nonprofit manager must link his funding proposal to the corporation's goals in order to
receive a contribution from this business. This corporation measures the
results of philanthropy in a quantitative fashion, which means that the nonprofit must be accountable for its funding (Smith and Lipsky, 1993). Finally,
the dislocated corporate managers learn that this particular funder, as a way
of enhancing its reputation and image among its employees, ties its philanthropy to the communities where its employees live and work.

The Volunteer and Board Member Roles

Corporate managers learn that the roles of the board members and volunteers are critical in understanding the accepted values and behaviors of nonprofit organizational members. In gaining access as volunteers, they learn that
their relevance in terms of the skills they provide is extremely important to the
nonprofit organization. In addition, they observe that the nonprofit volunteer
experience has to be relevant to the dislocated manager's own motivations
including learning new skills, anticipating behaviors and attitudes, meeting
potential employers, and building their self-esteem. The dislocated managers
also learn the extent to which nonprofit organizations use volunteerism as a
method in confirming the career changer's commitment to the sector.

Relevant Skills

Nonprofit organizations recruit board members and volunteers with
management skills that they identify as relevant to them. This board member

confirms this:

> *Board Member:* I'm a former banker and now I am a trustee for three boards. One organization has an annual budget of over $100 million, one is the equivalent of a mom-and-pop grocery store with a budget of $200,000, and one is a healthcare organization with a budget of $2 million. Your corporate skills are transferable. The contacts I made in business are useful. Investment skills, strategic planning, public relations, and financial planning are used as well.

When the individual enters a new culture, he must earn the respect of the insider group before he is allowed to participate (Wax, 1983). The open or closed structure of a group will also determine whether the outsider will have access to the group (Merton, 1968). This attorney is successful, as a volunteer, because the group is indeed open to learning new skills:

> I was with the first group of business development volunteers. We were pioneers. I was the only attorney in Central Europe. I developed connections throughout the region because people wanted to do foreign trade at the borders. The most difficult task was teaching contract negotiation and the two rules of contract negotiation: signing a contract is not a preliminary negotiation, and honor thy contract! Just to get that concept across was hard. These people had a thirst for basic knowledge. By the time I left, people knew what a letter of credit was.

A nonprofit manager speaks about the openness toward outsiders with business skills:

> *Nonprofit Manager:* We look for people with professional skills very much like you. We need people with marketing, computer, strategic planning, and financial skills. We recruit pro bono consultants and assign them to our nonprofit agencies. Increased cutbacks in government funding make life difficult for nonprofits. Nonprofits don't always have the money to hire someone to do something as simple as selecting the right telephone system or helping them through an RFP [request for proposal] process. These are daunting tasks for some nonprofits. We had 94 projects last year. We act as a broker in identifying consultants for these nonprofits.

Relevant Motivations

Learning New Skills

Reference groups play an important part in gaining acceptance into the group (Merton, 1968). The newcomer must view the values of the new group as being relevant to him. For this corporate manager, volunteering for a nonprofit would only be relevant if she was trained to learn fundraising skills:

> *Corporate Manager:* After being downsized, I wanted to use my skills for
> an organization with a mission dedicated to something other than mak-
> ing money. I went to the library and learned about this volunteer oppor-
> tunity. At first, I was hesitant. I wanted to volunteer for an organization
> where I would have hands-on experience. This particular organization
> told me they would train me so I would be able to raise money. I now
> volunteer with a group responsible for raising $2–3 million. I feel
> comfortable doing it because I was trained.

Rehearsing Roles

Volunteer roles serve as an important type of anticipatory socialization
process for the career changer in learning, as well as practicing, the expected
role requirements of a particular job. This corporate manager learned how to
raise money through workplace campaigns and is able to practice this skill as
a volunteer:

> *Corporate Manager:* Some organizations I contacted didn't want to run
> workplace campaigns. A lot of people who said no initially, now say yes.
> I am able to reach people I think because 20 years ago I needed help
> from this organization and they gave it to me. My speech comes from the
> heart. I tell people every day, you buy a cup of coffee for 75 cents. Once a
> week, give that money to an organization that helps so many.

Another volunteer, also previously from the corporate sector, decided to
move to the community where his organization was located to be closer to the
constituency they served. He speaks about his fundraising and advocacy roles:

> *Corporate Manager:* My organization provides housing for people infected
> with the AIDS virus. They had no history of reaching donors. I started
> their fundraising program. I took some courses in fundraising and I was
> able to raise $8000 from local corporations in the community. I also
> helped to create two community parks. Both of these spaces were previ-
> ously filled with garbage and crack vials. They are now maintained by a
> community organization that I helped found. People in the community
> now garden in these parks and raise their own vegetables and flowers.
> The city threatened to destroy one of the parks and I helped run a cam-
> paign to stop them. Now our organization contributes $2000 each year
> to help improve the park. I have a passion for helping this community
> through fundraising, organizing, and creating parks.

Building Self-Esteem

Volunteer work serves two purposes: it offers credentials and skills that
may impress a nonprofit employer. It also provides a way to create a new

identity for the displaced manager. When corporate managers take on non-profit roles, they are treated with respect as valued people: their values matter, not just their profitability. They feel wanted. They feel like insiders:

> *Michael*: I went on interviews with many law firms. They made me ill. Then I became a volunteer attorney with the organization I'm working for now. I gave them two days a week without pay. Last November, they hired me full-time. I'm much happier. I believe in what I'm doing.
>
> *George*: Throughout my corporate career, I stayed involved with the community. Through housing and social services organizations, I worked closely with the Latino and African-American communities. It is the other sides of you that propel you anywhere.
>
> *Mark*: I volunteered for a small agency that was a subagency of my current employer. When I met my "employer to be" he was impressed with the work that I had done for this subagency and he offered me a consulting job. When his budget ran out, I finished as a volunteer. A year later, I saw a job advertised with this agency and had the best interview I have ever had.
>
> *Martha*: Through my volunteer experience, I learned what fundraising was about. I didn't think of myself as a fundraiser. I was given ten accounts and I became a fundraiser. There is a link between fundraising and communications. We are all fundraisers. Whatever you do you will fundraise. As a volunteer, I always felt a part of the family, the organization. I never felt like an outsider.

Employment Opportunities

As corporate managers struggle "to become" nonprofit managers, many found that volunteerism helped them ease into a new identity which they believe will ultimately lead to employment opportunities:

> *Transitional Manager and Volunteer*: My career is a work in progress. I'm an attorney. I chose my volunteer organization as a steppingstone. I will do community service for 2 years. I have chosen an organization in central Harlem and I have chosen to live in Harlem to live close to the community. Living close to the community gives me a chance to know people.
>
> My impression is that a nonprofit employer will view this experience as evidence of dedication and commitment. The employer won't question my commitment. Few people have the passion and dedication to do what needs to be done in the nonprofit world. For most people, the principal concern is the paycheck.

Volunteerism as a Sign of Commitment

Successful career changers reveal that nonprofit organizations do indeed view their volunteer work as a genuine sign of dedication to the sector, and that this experience does lead to employment:

> *Vera*: After being with a bank, the nonprofit sector didn't think I would
> fit in. They didn't think I was serious about it. I had to come up with a
> way to become a credible candidate. I really wanted to commit to the
> nonprofit sector. The way to show commitment is to volunteer.
>
> One reason my boss took a chance in hiring me is that she saw my
> commitment to be part of the nonprofit world. She wanted to know if I
> enjoyed it. She wanted to know how I found the people. The people
> are different. There's an intensity, but not a competitiveness that you
> find in a bank. Nonprofit people work just as hard, put in long hours,
> and are just as productive, but they focus on furthering the organiza-
> tion as opposed to squeezing out another dollar.
>
> *Nancy*: I've been volunteering for a long time. After law school, I got
> interviews with nonprofits and they wanted to hear about my volunteer
> work. Volunteering opened my eyes to what they expected from me. I
> proved, by putting in the time, that I was dedicated to the sector and
> that's what made the difference in my being hired. Four people in my
> organization were hired after volunteering for a period of 3–4 months.
>
> *Stacey*: There's a certain amount of incest in our organization. Many of us
> have been volunteers. You're comfortable with people you know. Many
> people want to hire people with international experience. Where are
> you going to get that experience? Volunteering!

In the sections above, I have described the process of peer socialization—
the process by which the corporate managers learned about and assimilated the
expectations and orientations of the nonprofit sector. And in the previous
chapter, I described certain tools such as the résumé, introduction, and mock
interview, which were intended to help the participants in the most practical
way with their job search. These tools and steps in the Program also had
another agenda of presocializing the displaced managers for their future jobs,
of remaking their occupational identities. However, selves are not resocialized
or remade without considerable emotional upheaval. No matter how well motivated, the Program participants could not go through this training and these
changes without having emotional responses. These often had little to do with
the specific skills and knowledge they were learning, and everything to do with
how they felt about themselves. In the next section, I turn the spotlight on the
responses of the dislocated corporate managers to their training experiences as
they experienced an "Odyssey of the Self."

AN ODYSSEY OF THE SELF

Mead (1934) and others maintain that individuals show different sides
of themselves based on the expectations of significant others or those most

important to the individual. Displaced managers disengage from their corporate identity—from the "significant others" who gave them their identity. As these ex-corporate managers faced various new "significant others" including the trainer, the nonprofit managers, and their peer group of dislocated managers, different selves emerged. The selves that emerged were indeed based on the expectations of others but in some different ways: ex-corporate managers often searched for comfort from the trainer, respect and empathy from their peers, and acceptance from the nonprofit employers.

It is hard to assume a new identity as evidenced by the fact that at times the selves that emerged were combative or deviant selves: ex-managers became emotional, yelling at and challenging the trainer, some spoke incessantly about nonrelated issues in front of their peers and the nonprofit guests making everyone feel uncomfortable, others refused to follow the logic and path of the class—missing homework assignments, showing up late, or avoiding class altogether. Some were unwilling to support peers through this transition, others did not come to class dressed in formal business attire. Some did not accept advice from the trainer and would not prepare for their meetings with nonprofit employers. Finally, there were some ex-managers who while having episodes of deviance, managed to continue working through their odyssey of self.

The Disengagement of Self

The dislocated corporate managers had amassed their prior workplace status and rewards by remaining good and loyal soldiers and by following the corporate "moral rules" of the game (Jackall, 1988, p. 4). Despite their loyalty and commitment, they became the casualties of a mass disengagement of the white-collar workforce. The abuse they encountered and conveyed during this period of being dislocated is extensive, as was discussed in Chapter 4 (The Nonprofit Management and Communications Program). Not only did they lose their jobs, they had essentially lost everything that gave them status: salary, job title, corporate affiliation, and co-worker friends (Newman, 1988; Trice and Beyer, 1993).

Role loss has created great psychological strain and pain among this group of workers. When the dislocated managers came for their initial intake interviews with the trainer, it was observed that while the majority came well dressed in their former corporate attire—looking like and still claiming to be businesspeople—others had already begun to disengage themselves from this identity by wearing casual clothes. A few were in total disarray and had not taken the time to comb their hair or, in a couple of cases, wash their clothes. One former manager admitted that he wore the same suit to every interview, and he had not taken his suit to the dry cleaner in weeks.

Their introductions often communicated a very bland and dispassionate chronological history of their work life. Monumental achievements including their management of people, international projects, innovative and cutting-edge ideas and their implementation were not mentioned except with the insistence and excessive "nudging" of the trainer. There was little or no attempt among the entire group of interviewees to impress the trainer with their knowledge of the nonprofit sector—the sector they wished to enter as midlevel employees earning an average salary of $50,000. Some believed that just their willingness to take a pay cut from $100,000 to $50,000 would be enough to convince the sector to hire them. They were not aware of the time and effort it would take to reinvent themselves.

Signs of "meritocratic individualism" (Newman, 1988, p. 76) or the blaming of oneself for the unfortunate demise of one's career is common among displaced managers. One thing the managers point to is age. Many managers blamed themselves as being "too old" to reenter their fields. One manager made frequent calls to the trainer distressed that his age would prevent him from employment in the nonprofit sector as well.

In essence, this is a defeated group of individuals with negative self-images and skepticism toward a new career. Many questioned whether anyone would really want to hire them if they were over age 50, viewing their age as a significant barrier to future employment. Others demanded statistical proof that the nonprofit sector is indeed a growth sector, and hires proportionally more older workers than does the corporate sector.

These are an anxious and insecure group of dislocated workers. After I spent a minimum of one hour with each dislocated worker during an intake session, many broke down, admitting both that they were hurting financially and that they had been unable to find work within the same industry or the same salary level which they had left behind. One manager in his mid-60s was bankrupt and living with his mother. Another manager over 50 had moved in with his sister. Several managers had taken jobs in the retail industry as sales clerks over the Christmas holiday "just to pay the bills." Three of these managers have their MBA degrees from Ivy League universities.

Throughout the interviews, managers shed tears because they were isolated: they had not previously encountered a support network devoted to helping them find their new sense of occupational self. Still others were petrified with the notion that they would be embarking on a new career that would require a reinvention of self. By being accepted into the Program they were hoping that the trainer and the nonprofit sector would hold the answers and give them a new and better sense of themselves.

The Reconstruction of Identity: Self-Doubt and Frustration

Throughout the Program, each member of each class was asked to shed their prior occupational assumptions of workplace rewards and values and reorient their attitudes and behaviors to a new set of values and assumptions about workplace culture. They were asked to leave their prior status behind; the status they had worked so hard to achieve; the status which gave them their identity among co-workers, family, and friends; the status which was stripped away from them. This is a difficult and arduous task for many of these liminal workers who feel lost without their prior occupational statuses and troubled by the fact that there appears to be a severe bias, on the part of non-profit employers, to their entering a world that is largely unknown to them.

In an effort to help each dislocated manager achieve a new status, the trainer worked with the class on constructing verbal definitions of self based on what the nonprofit managers were interested in hearing. In other words, the dislocated manager has to learn to become relevant to the needs of the nonprofit managers. The trainer asked each manager to construct a verbal identity that would be about 15 seconds long. After the cohort rehearsed their introductions for the first time, the trainer asked each of them to leave out negative labels like "downsized," or "unemployed," or "seizing the opportunity for early retirement." Since the majority of the managers tended to "ramble" as they introduced themselves, the trainer reminded them that they needed to make a coherent group impression as well as individual impressions. Many of the managers sought approval from their classmates and the trainer concerning the content of their introductions. One manager, in particular, called the trainer, after each class, to ask the trainer if her introduction was "OK." Not all managers sought the approval of the "significant other." Another manager challenged the trainer's 15-second time limit, requesting that a more accurate time limit be given in which to accomplish this task. The request was actually more combative in nature questioning the origin or theory behind the time limit: "Is 15 minutes an arbitrary number? Or is it really 15 minutes?" To avoid an obvious conflict between the student and the trainer, the trainer elected to assure the student that the 15-second limit was not "set in stone," but given as a guide in which to make a good impression while respecting the impressions of his fellow classmates. This seemed to reassure the student who was focusing on structure, rather than the intended content of his expression.

There were students who regardless of the sighs and nonverbal signs of disapproval from their peers would nonetheless continue to ramble pointlessly throughout their introductions. One manager would take the opportunity in his introduction to ask the nonprofit guest if he had any jobs, not realizing that the timing of his question was inappropriate and of great embarrassment to his peers. Another manager would boast her Ivy League educational credentials "à la used car salesman" again evoking great nonverbal disapproval from her peers. Despite the peer group's shunning of these individuals, both succeeded in finding jobs in the nonprofit sector.

In preparation for reconstructing one's occupational identity within the context of a résumé, the trainer also took the class through an assessment of their occupational strengths. Again, since most dislocated managers began their "biographies" with their old industrial affiliation (e.g., banker, advertiser, insurance company), the trainer helped the dislocated managers restructure their biographies stressing their functions and occupational achievements across their corporate and volunteer lives (e.g., I have raised money for both the corporate and nonprofit sectors; I have created television ads for both sectors, etc.). Since most of these managers view themselves chronologically as bankers or advertisers, often leaving their volunteer work ˄ut of their communication completely or mentioning it as something "they do in their spare time," they view this reconstruction of self based on functional achievement across two sectors as overwhelmingly difficult to accomplish.

Thus, after this class session on "assessment" concluded, the trainer learned (as this occurs for cohort after cohort) to expect that the majority of the class would line up one after another asking for a one-on-one private meeting with the trainer. Students often appeared extremely worried that they could not compete with others in the class. Typical responses to the assessment class would be: "I've listened to everybody else and I don't measure up." "I need your help." "I don't know if I can do this." Others defended their prior sense of self: "What's wrong with my corporate affiliation? I don't think we have anything to be ashamed of. If they don't want us, too bad." These are the common expressions of self-doubt, frustration, and resistance to changing workforce identities.

In the private one-on-one meetings with the trainer, students would often come to the trainer's office with blank pieces of paper, not having done any preparation or work on their new nonprofit résumé—expecting the trainer to structure their new identities on paper. While some students were paralyzed and needed reassurance and confidence from the trainer, before they attempted the first draft of their résumés, others began to show the first signs of self-confidence in changing their workforce identities. As managers changed their résumés, they were in essence changing their written portraits of self. Many remarked on how much they liked their new résumés and that these new résumés were better indicators, than their prior résumés, as to who they really were. Managers were proud to include their volunteer selves within the context of the résumé. During their final mock interviews, the verbal reaction they received from the nonprofit employers on their new résumés reinforced this pride and sense of self-worth.

During this written revision of self, there were also ex-corporate managers who began to show signs of resistance. For example, one manager refused to give the trainer a "nonprofit résumé." When the trainer urged her to try to construct this type of résumé, the manager cried, "you can't tell me what to do, you are not my mother." Eventually, she reoriented her résumé and transitioned into the nonprofit sector.

Resisting Identity Change

For some, the resistance to identity change comes at the beginning as a response to self-doubt and frustration within themselves. For others, making the commitment to changing careers becomes increasingly unbearable, creating significant barriers in their quest to change their workforce identities.

For the majority, the loss of workforce identity, an ambiguous occupational status, and fear of rejection from a new group of employers create insecurity and anxiety in the managers. Within the anticipatory socialization components of the classroom, these struggles were articulated both individually and in solidarity. Their anger and frustrations, communicated in the absence of nonprofit managers, were directed at the nonprofit employers, the trainer, and themselves.

In almost every second session of the Program, the dislocated managers became angry at the message communicated by the first nonprofit panel or nonprofit speaker featured in the first session. In order to understand the basis of the group's anger, it is important to shed light on the first (prior) session in which the cohort had been introduced for the first time to members of their new reference group—nonprofit managers. The nonprofit managers were asked by the trainer to speak about their mission (e.g., the purpose of their organization). They were also asked to talk about the need for corporate managers in their sector and the qualifications of an ideal applicant. The message in the first session was organized around new language, new values, and new goals. In order to be accepted the corporate managers were expected to understand and be familiar with this new language, values, and goals. They were also confronted with the reality of making much less money. They were faced with having to give up the rewards achieved in their prior status (Rosow, 1974).

During the second session of the Program, in the absence of the nonprofit reference group, the dislocated managers had an opportunity to grapple with these realities. In one instance, a dislocated manager began the class by confronting the trainer in a combative manner: "Was it your intention to have the nonprofit speakers talk about mission, without talking about structure, goals, and processes for achieving goals and results? Not one of the managers really talked about their missions. I was very disappointed." The trainer responded by stating that mission language is often spoken about in very general terms, stressing purpose and changing quality of life rather than highlighting the process by which to accomplish it. After the class concluded, the manager who questioned the trainer, reassured the trainer that he was not trying to give the trainer "a hard time" and was impressed with the way in which the trainer was able to respond. This deference represented the initial signs of conformity and socialization. This manager went on to become the executive director of a human services organization.

Another corporate manager was unhappy that one of the nonprofit managers present represented the organization that provided the subsidy for his nonprofit training. This corporate manager was uncomfortable with being reminded that he was out of work and really needed anyone's help. His attitude prevailed throughout the Program. Unable to find a nonprofit job, he eventually reentered the corporate sector. In another session, a former real estate manager demanded to know why nonprofit managers tended to stereotype corporate managers as authoritarian. The trainer's answer was based on the knowledge that nonprofit managers may experience authoritarian behavior from corporate managers who serve as board members or funders. If they experienced authoritarian behavior from a board member or a corporate funder, it was more likely that they would believe that the entire group of corporate managers was indeed authoritarian. Throughout the Program, this former real estate manager showed deference toward the trainer and the nonprofit managers in the class, seeking the appropriate ways to think and behave within a new organizational culture. This corporate manager eventually found work in a nonprofit housing organization.

As the class progressed, resistance to identity change was more apt to come from specific individuals who seemed to be having difficulty in internalizing new organizational values. Signs of resistance included refusal of meeting deadlines for first, second, and final drafts of résumés. One corporate manager handed in a handwritten résumé for his final résumé being submitted to an employer. When the trainer asked him why, he began screaming at the trainer—informing the trainer that he didn't have a secretary and how could the trainer expect a typed résumé from him during this very stressful time. Later he called the trainer apologizing for his outburst. He eventually found a position in his prior industry where he was obviously more comfortable. Another corporate manager had an emotional outburst telling the trainer that her nonprofit volunteer culture was drastically different from the culture in the corporate sector. "They are so slow. The money isn't good. I don't know if I can do this." The trainer reassured her that she was experiencing "culture shock" and that in time she would adjust if she truly believed the mission of the organization. Later this same nonprofit organization hired her because she had raised a significant amount of money for them.

Some corporate managers found it impossible to relinquish their prior identities. A handful of corporate managers submitted their final résumés, but did not show up for their final mock interview with a nonprofit employer. After the mock interviews occurred, some dislocated managers blamed the nonprofit employers if their interviews did not go well. One corporate manager remarked that her interviewer did not listen to her. Another who allowed her voice to drop did not understand why her interviewer kept asking her to speak up. One corporate manager told the trainer that the values of the non-profit sector continued to be so foreign to her that the class was a waste of her time. Another corporate manager told the trainer that one nonprofit manager was full of herself; another did not think the nonprofit manager was a good public speaker. Some corporate managers revealed that they had not learned to be sensitive to the values and cultures of organizational members. One corporate manager visited the interviewer's office "unannounced." Another told a fundraiser she "wasn't raising enough money." These corporate managers were unable to meet the expectations of a new reference group and consequently found jobs in the corporate sector or remained unemployed.

Cohort Solidarity

In the initial resistance to identity change, an interesting phenomenon occurs: cohort solidarity. In one case, a class who had been sitting at two different tables pushed the tables together. This was a deliberate rebellion: the organization, where the class was held, asked that the tables be left the way they were when the class arrived each day. Despite this, the class began a ritual of pushing the tables together at the beginning of each class and pulling them apart at the end of the class. The class unity was also evidenced by students leaving together after class, taking the subway together to and from class, sharing and presenting homework assignments together, and counseling each other. In one case, a manager who had decided that his stage fright would make it impossible for him to perform his mock interview was convinced by a group of his peers to do it anyway. After his performance, they applauded and cheered him. The trainer did not know until after this had happened that cohort solidarity among this class gave the student the courage to perform his mock interview and ultimately move into the nonprofit sector.

Finding Reference Group Acceptance

Ultimately, with the context of the classroom, most of the cohort members were able to regain a sense of identity within the framework of a new occupation. Meeting and networking with open-minded nonprofit managers, some of whom had been dislocated corporate managers themselves, dislocated managers began to feel a sense of achievement and acceptance by their new reference group. As the classes progressed and their introductions and questions to the nonprofit managers became more polished, they received more and more positive feedback from the nonprofit managers: "I wish I could hire all of you." "Wow, I didn't expect to hear the amount of volunteer experience each one of you has." "I have job descriptions which I will leave with the trainer." "We really do have a position and I want you to interview for it." (To the trainer) "Where did you find these people?" As each corporate manager finished his mock interview and received his "certificate of achievement," his peers, the nonprofit interviewers, and the trainer applauded him.

In reflecting on the odyssey of self, it is clear that deviance or rebellion on the part of the individual may take place during the resocialization process (Van Maanen, 1976). It appears that allowance for self-efficacy or the need to feel some control over one's actions is important to the resocialization process (Gecas, 1989). A degree of resistance encourages participation, self-evaluation, and eventual career transition.

NONPROFIT CAREER TRANSITION AND ADAPTATION IN THE WORKPLACE

Introduction

Armed with the nonprofit values and role expectations they have learned in the classroom and in their volunteer experiences, trainees are ready to assume their new occupational identities in the nonprofit sector. In terms of successful career transition and adaptation, they now encounter a new twofold challenge. First, as they encounter different attitudes toward work, are they willing to learn the requisite behaviors and attitudes of their new organizational culture? And, even if they are, will the organization provide the necessary socialization techniques that will instruct the recruit on the proper way to act and think? It is the employee's motivation to learn and the organization's ability to teach which determine if career transition will be successful.

First Encounters and Culture Shock

No matter how prepared one is for entering a new culture, one always experiences a degree of culture shock (Van Maanen, 1983). There is always a gap between anticipated expectations and what is actually demanded on the job (Hughes, 1981). Career changers talked about how their expectations differed from the realities of the job and how they began to adjust.

When recruits were asked how they were treated when they first entered their organizations, the majority discussed having a good feeling about their first encounters as employees. For example, though still wounded from their prior organizational experiences, career changers expressed a certain relief about their new surroundings. Darlene explains:

> I was treated very well. I was shocked that everyone was so nice as opposed to my last work experience. On the first day I was shown where

to put my coat. I was introduced to people and they explained the work-
ings of the organization to me.

Pat had a similar experience:

I was welcomed with open arms, respected, and given the right attention.
I benefited from this because I was coming off the hills of being fired.

Anita also noticed a different type of treatment:

People were friendly and helpful. They appreciated what I did. It was nice
to be part of a community that was concerned about the services being
provided, not just the money being taken in. It was also nice not to have
to keep time sheets.

Anne's initial treatment was radically different from the above-mentioned
experiences:

Some of the junior staff was resentful since I succeeded a woman who
was totally beloved and had worked here a long time. She didn't leave
because she wanted to, but rather because some of the top managers were
making her miserable. This happened before I was hired, and I didn't
have anything to do with it, but I was resented anyway.

I found it amusing that one woman [a subordinate] was annoyed
that she didn't get to interview me. She actually told me this and I told
her that you don't get to interview your boss. But, my predecessor had
this sort of attitude that everyone does everything together all of the time.
They resent that I don't do things the same way.

Coming from a corporate background, many career changers are surprised that nonprofits have a different approach to managing the organization. Anne, for example, didn't expect the extent to which "everyone would
have to be involved in decision-making." Mark is surprised at the "amount of
time" he has to work, "putting in many nights and working till 8 or 9 pm."
Mark is also surprised to learn that his nonprofit culture is far less "team-
oriented, friendly, and cooperative" than he had expected. Larry also feels isolated, having been placed in charge of a housing field office with little direct
contact "with people at my level that I could deal with or talk to."

Some career changers find the differences in expectations to be more
rewarding. Meredith states that as compared to her law firm, the hospital
culture is "less grueling and the goals are less strict." She finds that the hospital is more concerned with "getting the job done" than "beating the pants off
the competitor." Like Meredith, Pat finds the slower "laid-back" pace of work
refreshing. "People," she says, "walk into offices and chat more, and I'm still
not used to it. It's nice."

Kevin believes that the change actually improved his health:

I worked in the corporate sector for 20 years. While there, I had high
blood pressure. Now it's down 40 points. I have found my niche. I work
with 40 nonprofit homeless and childcare agencies. I am so satisfied.
I can't place a dollar figure on it.

Ron did not expect his healthcare organization to have such a "laid-back" culture. As a fundraiser, in this organization, he was not prepared for the "lack of a sense of urgency." In adjusting, Ron has to get used to an environment that is "not as deadline sensitive or high pressured as it was in the corporate sector." It took Cindy 2 years to adjust to a slower pace of work, as well as inferior systems, and an "unprofessional" dress code:

> Everything here goes so slowly. People here are used to saying, "if it doesn't get done today, then maybe it will get done next week. There isn't as much urgency to get things done or to do things. At the beginning I was much more involved with running around and trying to get things done quickly. I don't do that any more. I just go with the flow. I found it very annoying and most people from the corporate sector find it galling. People don't follow procedures, they just do what they do.
>
> Everything is so outdated and antiquated: things, systems, and programs. The systems aren't first class. For example, the human resource systems I have to work with still use carbon paper, if you can believe that. Maybe by the time I retire, they will have updated it.
>
> At my prior corporate job, everyone dressed so well. At first, it bothered me that people [here] dressed casually. I didn't think it looked professional. Now, I'm used to it.

Neal was "used to getting things done" when he worked in retail. He complains:

> I was used to analyzing things and setting out a one, two, three type of plan and then doing it. My ideas here don't receive a reaction or feedback. People worry about being nice so performance standards aren't set. People think that having standards and making people live up to them is not nice.

Joe is also surprised to learn the "extent to which there is a lack of expectations on the part of the nonprofit manager." He "expected more achievement from others in the organization and consequently himself."

Fred, on the other hand, expected nonprofit managers to be more laid-back and less performance oriented, but finds the opposite to be true. "Nonprofit employees are far more dedicated than I expected them to be. Many people come in on Saturdays and spend a lot of time working. I just didn't expect that." Michelle agrees:

> They are always working so hard. I never thought of them as working so hard, and they work for no money. I definitely had culture shock because I couldn't imagine people working so hard for so little money. It's unbelievable that these people are so dedicated.

Since certain nonprofit role relationships such as the volunteer–staff relationship, the board–staff relationship, and the staff–funder relationship do not exist in the corporate sector, several corporate managers experienced some culture shock with regard to these particular role relationships. Fred and Carole talk about their experiences:

> Fred: I probably underestimated the amount of personal contact that I had to keep with volunteers. I underestimated how much I had to go out and work the room, work the territory, and make contact with people. I was very used to my former corporation where I had personal contacts and most were professional contacts where we just chatted for awhile. I didn't have to constantly massage their egos. I do have to do this with volunteers. My association is volunteer driven, not staff driven. So as a staff member, you must acknowledge that the volunteers are in control and that you, as a staff person, are following their orders. I underestimated that.

> Carole: I didn't have to interact with the board in the corporate sector. I had to supply the corporate board with financial highlights, but only met with them once a year socially. In my nonprofit job, I have to attend board meetings and present a budget. At first, I found that aspect a bit intimidating. My executive director was very supportive so that helped in my getting over that.

> I am frustrated by the funding deadlines I have to meet because we are so dependent on state and federal funding. I get calls from funders asking me to make changes for minuscule amounts of dollars. For instance, "change five schedules for a discrepancy of $1."

Obstacles to Assimilation

In order for assimilation to occur, the recruit must be motivated to be socialized (Brim and Wheeler, 1966) and socialization efforts must be successful (Van Maanen, 1976). Since career changers are likely to bring bits and pieces of their corporate culture with them, they experience some frustrations in their new culture. While some repress their frustrations, others do not. Limited resources and lack of monetary incentives, for example, frustrate career changers. If their monetary goal orientation differs significantly from the nonprofit organization's goal orientation, assimilation may not occur since the majority of nonprofit organizations cannot motivate their employees by offering the monetary incentives the former corporate managers were used to receiving. Other career changers maintain that the achievement orientation they had in their instrumental organizations is not respected in the nonprofit sector. They complain that they are "used to getting things done without going through so many layers of people to make a decision." Additionally, the feedback which comes from achievement-oriented actions in the corporate sector is not forthcoming in the nonprofit sector because it is not valued. And, since the broad cultural values of capitalism (Van Maanen, 1976) and the dream of regaining their prior sense of identity are not a distant memory, some career changers are inclined to return to the corporate sector.

If organizations tend to be weak in their socialization techniques (Davis et al., 1966; Lortie, 1975; Van Maanen, 1983), in terms of guiding and training the new recruit in accepting the attitudes and behaviors of the organization, socialization is inefficacious. Frustrated career changers complain that the training they receive in "cultural orientation" is minimal or nonexistent. In the absence of this orientation, they simply do not know how to behave in their new environments. In the absence of guidance from peers or role models, career changers struggle to make their own cognitive maps (Jackall, 1988; Van Maanen, 1976) to learn the significant relationships and the expected ways to behave toward their new peer group and the managers to whom they report. Career changers describe three significant frustrations that they have to repress in their attempt to assimilate: limited resources, lack of monetary incentives, and having a different goal orientation from the nonprofit organization.

Limited Resources

Parsons (1951) argues that every social system has an ordering of rewards related to attitudes. Since profit and nonprofit organizations have different attitudes toward rewards (e.g., monetary versus nonmonetary), it can be assumed that there will a difference in the way they each order or rank their rewards. Career changers must be sensitive to this difference. In addition, according to Parsons, there is always a competition for rewards such as money, status, and facilities. Since there is less money in the nonprofit sector, it may be assumed that managers will strive to compete for scarce resources and to protect or control what they have earned. To some extent, managers who have invested their time in the accumulation of rewards may have vested interests in the maintenance of these rewards. Vested interests take the form of preventing mobility, differentiation of status (you versus us), and the devaluation of rewards (Blau, 1964). Since nonprofit organizations are more likely to have limited resources than the corporate sector, career changers find that nonprofit organizations have control and vested interest issues centered on the scarcity of resources. Some of the managers interviewed found that change within organizations is met with resistance and an attitude of "that's the way we've always done it." Organizational members have vested interests in maintaining their rewards that newcomers threaten to change. Other career changers report that this problem is rampant throughout their organizations. Here is one example:

> There are turf issues between the other departments and me. People are afraid of losing control. People are territorial about tasks and functions. They are easily threatened. They are so entrenched in their jobs they can't

change. In my corporate job, people were relieved if you were willing to do their work. Power in my nonprofit manifests itself in control rather than pay.

Eight career changers interviewed agreed that limited resources have an adverse effect on getting the job done in an effective manner:

Darlene: There are too few people to do the job right. Yes, there is too much bureaucracy. Every item purchased has got to go through a whole rigmarole. Implementation is difficult.

Fred: The only thing that frustrates me is the lack of resources. We are fairly resource poor and have to make due with what's available.

Jim: In my corporate life, I was able to delegate. Now since I'm in a smaller setting and it's more hands-on, I've had to repress not attempting to delegate. I have to roll up my sleeves and do it myself.

Jerry: On the first day, I thought that I would get an office or at least a cube. I shared a space with four other people. There is no privacy. You take for granted having privacy when you're talking on the phone. One of the shocks, for me, was the sharing of resources.

Barry: I didn't have the same support I was used to—like help in photocopying things.

Ron: The physical environment is different from the corporate sector. In my corporation, there were nice plush offices. My office now is not as nice. In the corporate sector, I just took supplies when I needed them. But in the nonprofit sector, it's different since there is less money. I needed to learn to become more sensitive to spending money on basic things.

Walt: You bring in certain expertise, but you have to alternate your time between doing the budget and making sure the toilet gets fixed. In the last year, I spent a lot of time shoveling snow.

Paul: There are no layers and layers of resources to be mined to get things done. The scale is dramatically different in the sense that if you have to send out letters, you buy and lick the stamps yourself.

Reward System

While career changers know there is a difference in reward systems, some have a difficult time adjusting to this significant reality as Jerry and Cindy report[1]:

Jerry: I always used to bring this expensive briefcase to work, but I realized that in the nonprofit sector, this might be perceived as flashy. I realized I needed to downplay the finer things in life.

Cindy: The lack of pay frustrates me. Not necessarily for me, but for attracting the best candidates. We can't compete in the marketplace. People are leaving all of the time and that is frustrating.

Different Goal Orientation

A significant obstacle to assimilation is the ability to manage their frustrations concerning goal orientations between the profit and nonprofit sectors. Since there is minimal training and weak socialization efforts in many nonprofit organizations, corporate managers are more likely to utilize "corporate techniques" in achieving nonprofit goals within their new organizational cultures. Of course, this is often met with great resistance. While frustrated by consensual decision-making and the length of time it takes to make decisions, many career changers are motivated to "fit in" and weather the differences in management styles. Here are seven examples:

> *Pat*: Sometimes it takes a long time to get things done and for decisions to be made. Things that should take a day or a week take a month or weeks. Results in lost productivity mean less money coming in. People are not aware of the degree of urgency that should be attached to things [which will] ultimately raise more money. I think that my frustration comes from working in my prior environment. People that come from a social work background think we work too quickly and that we are always in a rush to raise more money. They think that we should step back and plan more, think more. I think it depends on what your perspective is.
>
> *Ron*: I needed to repress the sense of urgency in myself. I am high strung and driven, and I've had to repress that. My co-workers have given me a hard time for the way I dress [suit and tie], but I haven't really changed that.
>
> I'm used to working long hours, but people tell me to go home and quit working. So, I've repressed the urge to work late. I was conditioned to work this way.
>
> I'm frustrated with the amount of time it takes to get things done. Simple requests like getting people paid. I have to go through all these different steps that I didn't have to go through in the corporate sector.
>
> *Cindy*: I had to learn to slow it down and lose my edge. I learned to go with the system. You get used to it. You learn to deal with people without being offensive. Sometimes, coming from the corporate world, you have to be very aggressive if you want to get things done. You can't do that here.
>
> *Larry*: I saw that there was a lack of motivation among employees. I expected everyone to do it the way I wanted him to do it. I became frustrated and tried to micromanage people. They resented me. It didn't work.
>
> *Neal*: I'm frustrated with the slow decision-making and the lack of performance standards. I've had to repress initiative, imagination, and drive.
>
> *Kevin*: I've had to repress my desire to take charge; to grasp the vice president by the throat and yell "decide!"
>
> *Paul*: I had to repress the sense to insist that business logic carried the day. If there is an argument for doing something a certain way and it

> could be made clear that there was an economically rational way to do it, I had to adjust to the idea that this organization wouldn't necessarily do it. There was a realization that people valued the way in which they worked together, rather than the amount that could be saved by working a different way. I had to learn to share their values.

In the most severe cases when the career changer is not able to repress his frustrations, the career changer is asked to leave the organization because he will not adopt the values of the organization. In some cases, it is believed that career changers are dismissed because they are not motivated to internalize the values of their new nonprofit cultures. In other cases, it is believed that since most nonprofit organizations conduct minimal training, their socialization techniques are weak and ineffective in properly helping the recruit learn the requisite behaviors and attitudes.

Minimal Training: Weak Socialization

How did these career changers learn to meet the expectations of a new organizational culture? Though the majority of career changers are expected to learn the appropriate attitudes and behaviors on their own, a small proportion of the newcomers are formally trained by the nonprofit organization. Formal socialization implies that recruits are formally oriented and trained around specific organizational rules and guidelines. Formal socialization takes the form of educational training outside the organization or on-the-job training (apprenticeship) by a designated individual(s) within the organization. One career changer believes that his human services nonprofit organization has "the most extensive training program of any I've been involved in. My organization trains everybody. We learn about the clientele we serve and the whole reason for the organization."

Another career changer maintains that each department, within her human services organization, has a formal orientation of employees. Every newcomer is paired off with a veteran employee and shown everything she has to do in her job. Two other career changers were given a formal on-the-job 2-week training course in presentation and solicitation skills before they were each placed as volunteer fundraisers within the same human services organization. As volunteers, they learned the expectations of the job through working with experienced peers in their groups. When these career changers made the transition from volunteer to employee within the same human services organization, they knew what to expect.

It is more common to find career changers who are expected to come in with a certain set of skills and learn the details on their own or through trial and error. One career changer mentions that when he entered the association, there "was no one who I could have as my mentor; no good role models. You had to just jump in and start swimming."

Another career changer was also expected to learn his role on his own through trial and error: "I was thrown into the situation and I learned as I went along. There wasn't a formal orientation, but I learned on my own by going through the manuals and interfacing with the system. There was a fairly steep learning curve." This career changer also asserts that he was "expected to come in with a certain amount of skills and that he had responsibility for learning computer skills on his own."

While most of the career changers interviewed are expected to bring the skills of their prior culture with them, the following career changer experienced an attempt to strip away her entering characteristics such as having the independence and authority to get the job done without the constant approval of her boss:

> Since there was no training process, I did what I would normally do in a new situation. I just came in and tried to do what I do best. My boss was quick to tell me that this was not the way it was done in the past. After running with the ball several times, I realized through trial and error that I needed to get my boss to sign on.

Some career changers report learning by both formal and informal means. When Pat first entered her human services organization, she received three to four days of formal orientation by the organization itself (e.g., writing and presentation skills). However, it is through the informal mentoring of peers and observation that Pat learned "the unspoken language of the organization" (e.g., who the powerbrokers are, when to press for something, and when to take a break for lunch) (Van Maanen, 1977). Schein (1990) calls this unspoken language the "basic assumptions" of the organization (p. 111).

In learning the unspoken language of the organization, Neal relied exclusively on learning by trial and error. It is through this method that he learned that his department has no clout within his organization. It was also through trial and error that he learned the mechanics and the relationships important to doing his job:

> I had no job training. Maybe a half an hour of orientation with my manager, but nothing substantial. Learning the mechanics of the job wasn't hard, but I had no help with the direction of the job, and the relationships within the organization.
>
> My boss, who hired me, was very bright and businesslike and she gave me encouragement and feedback. However, since she was atypical of the culture, she didn't help me in adjusting.

Since Cindy was hired to create a new role in her department, she tried to both create and learn her role by talking to other human resource people in other departments within the university. She learned the basic assumptions of the university by informally speaking to a veteran 25-year employee and through trial and error. She maintains:

> At first, I was much more aggressive in trying to get things done, and it just didn't happen, and it antagonized people. I also learned that if I used certain people's names [a higher power] things could get done.
>
> In terms of learning the work hours, I watched people. People have flexible hours here. I'm an early person and come in around 7:30 a.m., but others come in at 10 a.m. This is not the kind of place where if you come in at 9:05, you will get fired.

Career changers believe that there needs to be greater emphasis on formal training within the nonprofit sector and that this lack of formal training has an adverse effect on retaining people:

> *Mark*: I wasn't taught how to operate and what the rules of the game were. Everything that is learned is still learned through trial and error. I have redefined myself, in the course of the first year about ten different times.
>
> *Myron*: I know that money is hard to come by in the nonprofit sector, but in order for people to do their jobs, there needs to be a commitment from management or by the board to train staff. I think the turnover in the nonprofit sector wouldn't be as great if there were the potential for people to come in and get an objective sense of where they are, what they are part of, and what is expected of them.

Weak Socialization

In the absence of clear direction or formal training, corporate managers are unable to decipher, practice, and meet the expectations of their bosses and peers. One nonprofit "career manager" observed this to be true with a corporate manager who transitioned to his organization:

> *Career Manager*: Corporate culture is a mind-set. This individual was hired from the beauty industry to market [nonprofit] arts events. This person could not react to the day-to-day selling of the "product." This person had no sensitivity to the live performance as opposed to the product she had been selling. She couldn't make the transition. Mentally, she and the culture were not in synch. The support she needed to make the transition was not there. She had to do the brochure herself. She wasn't used to this.

Since they do not know how to behave, corporate managers, like this one, use their prior experience in making decisions resulting in culture clash. In the following excerpts, both Myron and John used their prior experiences in making decisions. This did not serve them well. They were both asked to leave their organizations.

> *Myron:* In the corporate sector, I was used to handling myself in a certain way. I was surrounded by a structure that I could lean on. In my non-profit organization, since decision-making was centralized, I had to go to the top to get answers. I had been used to picking up a phone or walking over and asking someone. In the nonprofit organization, I had to go to my boss all of the time, and he was busy all of the time. It meant delays on everything that I did and it left me with a sense of being left out. I didn't feel I was contributing. I didn't feel important. I decided to just keep busy, rather than doing something to feel productive.
>
> My boss called me in and chewed me out for writing a letter and sending it out without being reviewed. I set up an appointment, with the expectation that my boss was going to meet with me and go through some things. My boss sat right there, in front of me, and said that she had better things to do than sit in a room with me. After a few of those things occurred, I had to take a wait-and-see attitude.
>
> *John:* I had a conflict with the senior manager and she decided to let me go. I was asked to write a letter introducing my organization to a corporate funder. I had a good idea about how to do this and who the audience would be. Three versions of the letter were sent back to me for more revisions. I suggested that my manager write the letter and that generated a rebellion. The organization didn't respect my knowing the audience that I was writing to better than they did. It came to a dead end.
>
> I realize now that things are different in the nonprofit sector. You have to go through a chain of command, and people don't make instantaneous decisions and execute them like they do in the corporate sector. I didn't realize that when I was going through it.

Lack of Motivation

Some career changers appear to have a lack of motivation in learning the new values of their employer. Walt talked about one career changer who continued to resist his new cultural expectations:

> One of the new people seems to have expectations of being taken care of like he was taken care of in the corporate sector. I run the business office and most people have learned to get by with less, but this person still is resisting that. For example, here, I don't charge things to the institution that I would have charged in business. None of us ever do, and this person does.

Lack of motivation on the part of the career changer may cause culture clash within the organization. Susan, a career changer who moved from banking to a trade organization, reveals how one particular career changer clashed with his culture:

> *Susan:* A business-oriented financial guy, who was all about numbers and the bottom line, came in to the nonprofit and pissed everybody off—to the point where negative stories were being told about him. He was a good business leader and he wanted to run it like a business. The non-profit people, on the other hand, were devoted to their mission. You have to keep the mission in mind. You want to carry a big stick, but speak softly.

Jerry's and Anne's lack of motivation caused them to clash within their cultures: This is what they have to say about their experiences:

> *Jerry:* No one at the lower levels can make a decision. It always has to go through a consensus team. There are a lot of forms to fill out and a lot of people that you have to get to concur. This was one of the frustrating aspects of the nonprofit sector. I had to get acceptance from outside constituencies and the organizations with which I was working.
>
> I left my position because it didn't allow me to accomplish anything. It was more like babysitting and making sure people's feelings weren't hurt.
>
> *Anne:* Everyone in my institution considers himself to be an expert on creating special events. Give me a break. Everyone has to have input on the food [for a special event]. I believe that you choose the food and decor based on who it is that you are entertaining. Here, everyone always likes to get involved in those decisions. You get so frustrated and angry. This was one part of the corporate world where no one got involved. I did it, and it was done, and it didn't take all the time it takes here.
>
> Also, I find that there is a lot of nickel and diming that goes on here. I know we have to save money, but it is absolutely outrageous that people will spend time bickering with the vendor over $10. It's a waste of time. There are other things that need to get done.

The lack of training or formal socialization techniques in the nonprofit sector creates an environment where the career changer is expected to learn by trial and error. While many career changers are successful (30 of the 35 interviewed remain in the nonprofit sector), others are unable to adapt (5 returned to the corporate sector). In addition, if nonprofit organizations are organized around a "nonprofit" model of management where consensual decision-making is considered the norm, corporate managers like Anne and Jerry who find this style frustrating and are not motivated to conform will tend to look for other opportunities more in line with their previous management style, e.g., the corporate model of management. If indeed, more nonprofit organizations are seeking to hire managers from different occupational backgrounds, they must be willing to reveal their expectations regarding the appropriate management style within a formal training process. If the appropriate style is "nonprofit," the career changer must be aware of this expectation from the beginning. If the prior skills of the manager are needed in order to affect culture change within a nonprofit organization, this must be communicated as well. Without knowing the perspective of the nonprofit employer, it is difficult to adapt and to become a member of the new reference group.

Note

1. Please refer to pages 47–51 for a more detailed explanation of rewards.

Chapter 7

Conclusion—Implications for Management Approaches

Nonprofit and corporate employee attitudes and behaviors are shaped by their organizational cultures. It is the culture that determines value orientations of managers (Deal and Kennedy, 1982; Ott, 1989; Trice and Beyer, 1993). It is the culture that creates the profile of the employee within each sector of the economy: his gender, race, age, and compensation. It is the difference in cultures that produces the difference in value orientations among employees. Differing value orientations distinguish the identities of employees within sectors of the economy. Occupational identities are laden with the values of the occupation (e.g., reward system, personal, and professional networks). Since employees are rewarded for investing time in their occupational identities and the core values that support them, they may not find it necessary to build alternative occupational networks (Blau, 1964; Trice and Beyer, 1993).

When limited opportunities within one's chosen industry caused by culture changes within the industry threaten the employee's survival, he may be motivated to seek alternative careers within other industries. Without having the necessary occupational networks, this may be a difficult task. Those who do not have links to an industry through occupational networks are often viewed as outsiders (Epstein, 1970, 1981, 1988, 1995; Lorber, 1984). Outsiders who are perceived as not having a similar occupational identity or value orientation may pose a threat to those insiders who guard the rewards and statuses achieved within their occupations. In order to guard these rewards, insiders categorize or stereotype these differences, regarding them as dirty and dangerous (Douglas, 1966; Schur, 1984). Branded as a manager with differing value orientations, the corporate manager is believed by nonprofit managers to be unable or unwilling to adapt within a new occupational culture. Insiders guard their precious rewards through established hiring practices which screen out and negatively stereotype those without

165

a shared occupational background (Abbott, 1988; Epstein, 1970, 1981, 1988, 1995; Lorber, 1984; Milkman, 1987; Trice and Beyer, 1993; Walsh, 1977).

Breaking these occupational hiring barriers, while not easy, may take the form of building a new occupational network through joining voluntary or nonprofit organizations (Granovetter, 1995). Through association with voluntary organizations one can meet individuals with differing occupational backgrounds.

Outsiders may also break hiring barriers through learning the expectations of their reference group (Merton, 1968; Rosow, 1974). Internships, volunteering, and classroom training which emphasize anticipatory socialization expose the outsider to behaviors and attitudes of the new peer group (Becker et al., 1961; Brim and Wheeler, 1966, Clary et al., 1996; Elkin and Handel, 1984; Rosow, 1974; Van Maanen, 1976, 1977, 1983). Interaction with the new peer group is a necessary component to effective socialization and adaptation within the new reference group. Peer socialization minimizes culture shock and maximizes assimilation of the newcomer (Brim and Wheeler, 1966; Rosow, 1974). Without informal mentoring by peers, recruits may not successfully adapt (Van Maanen, 1976, 1977, 1983). Of course, the recruit must also view the new values of the reference group as relevant and be motivated to conform to these new values (Merton, 1968). Finally, peer socialization enables the new reference group to get beyond negative stereotypes and to accept differing management styles as necessary means of growth and survival.

IMPLICATIONS

This study found that while profit and nonprofit managers view their cultures to be different, they recognize the need for strong management in the nonprofit sector. The greatest single fear that nonprofit managers have, which may lead to the maintenance of distinctions through negative stereotypes, is that the sacred values of the nonprofit culture will be altered through the management practices of corporate managers. At the same time, nonprofit managers believe that good management practices are important to the survival of their organizations. This type of rational thinking is being fostered by funding organizations seeking accountability for the funds allocated, by the public wanting greater scrutiny of nonprofit organizations, and by the organizations themselves who want to survive in this new century (Smith and Lipsky, 1993). Thus, nonprofit organizations may be more likely to consider hiring individuals with corporate backgrounds because funding sources and the opinion of the broader society maintain that interdependence between the profit and nonprofit sectors will influence the survival of many nonprofit organizations in this new century.

In addition to these external forces, one additional factor is driving the need for interdependence between the two sectors: a competition for qualified managers. While interdependence and competition seem to be at odds with one another, they are not. Due to a shrinking labor pool of qualified managers, the nonprofit sector, now more than ever, must think about changing the way it recruits, trains, and retains its workforce.

This new type of interdependence between the corporate and nonprofit sectors is the creation of an organization development[1] model which utilizes a combination of corporate and nonprofit reward systems to recruit, train, and retain a new breed of nonprofit manager. A comprehensive organization development strategy should be aimed at recruiting and retaining a nonprofit manager who understands the mission of the nonprofit organization, is loyal to that mission, and is rewarded for his loyalty. A nonprofit peer group should train this breed of nonprofit manager in a formal or informal setting. This breed of nonprofit manager could be a career changer, or a career manager, and/or an older manager.

An increasing demand for nonprofit services and a competition with the other sectors for qualified managerial talent are driving the need for a nonprofit culture that utilizes the assets of the corporate culture—its recruitment and retention systems as well as its employees.

A War for Talent

According to one nonprofit manager, there "is a war for talent" (Billitteri, 2000, p. 4). This war in recruiting talented nonprofit managers is being waged with all sectors of the economy. By 2015, it is estimated that the number of workers aged 25 to 54 will grow by less than 1 percent; the number of workers aged 35 to 44 will decline by 16 percent (DeSantis, 1999, p. 3). At the same time that workforce numbers are declining, human services and healthcare services jobs are expected to account for one out of two nonfarm wage jobs and managerial and executive jobs are expected to grow faster than average (Bureau of Labor Statistics, 1999, p. 1). The need for technology managers is apparent in all sectors of the economy. The growth in technology jobs and the shortage of technology managers are forcing nonprofit organizations to compete for talent at salaries that just a few years ago would have been unthinkable in the nonprofit sector:

> With the demand for skilled technology workers outstripping the supply—
> 1 out of 10 technology jobs is currently unfilled, according to experts—
> for-profit companies are offering salaries that charities can't afford ... .
>   A survey by *Computerworld* magazine found that the average salary employers paid to a director of information technology was $83,000 last year; among the nonprofit groups in the survey, the average was $56,000 (Sommerfeld, 2000, p. 1).

Executive recruiter James Abruzzo maintains that nonprofit organizations are finding their "salary offers outpriced by as much as $50,000 to $100,000 by businesses competing for the same pool of labor" (Sommerfeld, 2000, p. 2).

Not only are nonprofit organizations losing potential applicants to the corporate sector, but they are losing members of their own sector as well. Nonprofit managers with expertise in planned giving are being "plucked" by banks, brokerage houses, and mutual fund companies to create services and products for financial services companies (Blum and Marchetti, 2000, p. 25). Nonprofit managers are leaving the nonprofit sector because as one former nonprofit manager states, "there's a lot more opportunity for additional benefits than the nonprofit arena just doesn't have to offer (Blum and Marchetti, 2000, p. 25). Pedro Martinez, controller of the Catholic Charities of the Archdiocese of Chicago, believes that "in today's economy, people are realizing how much they can make" (Billitteri, 2000, p. 2).

In a tight labor market, it is the employee who has numerous opportunities. It would appear from the paragraphs above that compensation alone is driving this new breed of employee. While compensation may be driving job or career choice, it is important to take a closer look at the values of the worker aged 25 to 54. This group, having been exposed to corporate downsizing for the past 15 years, understands that "the potential for layoffs has become a fixture of corporate life, and job security is increasingly a component of middle-class culture" (Davis, 2000, p. 15). The lack of job security has perhaps created a more cynical and less loyal worker:

> Today many bright workers are getting their revenge by fleeing their
> fickle employers for better-paying rivals—or dot-com startups. Indeed,
> quitting has become so fashionable in Silicon Valley that the turnover rate
> for companies there has reached an estimated 25 percent a year. The aver-
> age American 32-year-old has already worked for nine different compa-
> nies (Wooldridge, 2000, p. 82).

RECOMMENDATIONS

Given the fact that this shrinking pool of talent has an ever-increasing number of opportunities, it is critical for nonprofit organizations to rethink how it recruits, trains, and retains its employees. The nonprofit sector must create an organization development model that reinforces its traditional culture of commitment to its employees with an improved monetary reward system. It must view graduate educational programs as recruitment vehicles and work closely with them in recruiting a pool of talent. It should widen its applicant pool to include members from the corporate sector and offer anticipatory socialization to help them assimilate. Finally the nonprofit sector should consider widening their applicant pool to include a growing segment of the population, workers aged 55 to 64.

Developing an Organization Development Strategy

As has been discussed throughout this book, nonprofit organizations, for the most part, do very little in the way of organization development. Corporations have long used organization development strategies to recruit, develop, and retain their employees. In order to compete for qualified managers, nonprofit organizations must develop a strategy that capitalizes on the strengths of its culture, while finding ways to incorporate an improved monetary reward system.

Reinforcing a Culture of Commitment

Rosabeth Moss Kanter of Harvard Business School maintains that "companies must earn loyalty...you can't buy loyalty with just a paycheck" (Wooldridge, 2000, p. 82). Since most nonprofit organizations find it difficult to match corporate salaries, they are creating organization development strategies that reinforce their culture of commitment. For example, nonprofit organizations are creating strategic print, radio, and Web page advertising campaigns that fortify the traditional values that come from working for a mission-oriented organization. Campaign slogans with mission-oriented themes such as "where your heart and mind go to work" (American Red Cross) and "pour your heart and soul into our land and waters" (Nature Conservancy) are being used to attract employees.

Once employees are recruited, how can nonprofit organizations retain them, given the tight labor market? Nonprofit organizations are creating organization development departments just to tackle this issue. In an effort to nurture staff, nonprofit organizations are promoting from within, hiring volunteers as employees, orienting new employees, creating training programs, flexible work schedules, and encouraging a life after work. Jumpstart for Young Children, a national organization that supports preschool children, has an organization development staff of three to recruit, retain, and develop staff. They promote people from within and also hire people who have served as Americorp volunteers. Since the Americorp volunteers have been oriented and socialized by Jumpstart, they make committed and loyal employees. The Nature Conservancy created a three-person recruiting department that revamped their pay system and began a three-day orientation for every new worker.

Rethinking the Role of Compensation

In addition to creating recruiting and retention strategies that reinforce traditional values, nonprofit organizations are rethinking their reward system. While you may not be able to buy loyalty with a paycheck, nonprofit organizations are losing qualified managers to corporations who can pay more. One career changer who moved from a corporate technology company to a nonprofit job in the low 30s says that she can "barely afford to live in the Bay Area" on her salary (Sommerfeld, 2000, p. 2). Eric Dawson, national executive director of the Peace Games, said that he spent a year searching for a director of finance who had an MBA and "didn't want to make $120,000 a year and who was committed to social justice" (Billitteri, 2000, p. 3). Pedro Martinez is trying to do more to increase salaries at Catholic Charities:

> Our employees come to work for us because of our mission to help the poor. But when they see that we also are trying to come close to matching what they could get in the for-profit world, that helps to retain them because they see the appreciation of their work (Billitteri, 2000, p. 3).

Goodwill Industries International raised its salary range to attract high-level technology managers, offering between $50,000 and $70,000 (Sommerfeld, 2000, p. 1). In a survey conducted by the National Society of Fund Raising Executives, "one in five fundraisers reported that their annual pay had increased by at least 10 percent" (Hall, 2000, p. 1). In 1998 "compensation for top executives of major nonprofit institutions grew at nearly double the rate in 1997, and slightly outpaced business executives." The median increase in executive compensation for nonprofit managers was 5.7 percent, 4.6 percent for corporate managers (Labaton, 1999, p. 2). In addition to salary increases, nonprofit organizations are paying finders fees and cash bonuses to nonprofit employees who refer other employees.

Thus, nonprofit organizations are utilizing corporate reward systems to attract and retain both career managers and career changers. As the war for talent continues, what more can nonprofit organizations do to increase the pool of talent? One answer may lie in working more closely with graduate education programs in nonprofit management to recruit and presocialize career changers. Since nonprofit organizations, for the most part, have limited resources for orienting and presocializing career changers, graduate nonprofit education programs may be able to fill this need.

Graduate Programs in Nonprofit Management: Recruiting and Presocializing the Career Changer

The resocialization of white-collar corporate managers for careers in the nonprofit sector is possible, but not easy. It was found that dislocated white-collar managers were often so invested in their prior corporate roles that they were not able to present themselves as relevant members of another occupational group. It was found that when these managers were given a structure in which to start, an anticipatory socialization structure where they were able to try on new roles, develop new competencies, and make mistakes, they were likely to be successful in transforming their occupational identities.

Since there is unlikely to be formal training in the attitudes, behaviors, and values within nonprofit organizations, this type of anticipatory socialization process becomes critical if corporate managers are to become relevant members of a sector that is in great need of their skills and expertise. Alan J. Abramson, director of the Nonprofit Sector Research Fund of the Aspen Institute in Washington, D.C., states that "people who move to nonprofit work from business or government jobs may have leadership experience, but they want more training in nonprofit issues" (Cohen, 1999, p. 11).

Graduate programs in nonprofit management can develop curricula that help corporate managers understand the everyday challenges of nonprofit organizations and how to manage those challenges within the confines of the culture. These same curricula could be used to help nonprofit practitioners (earning their graduate degree) better understand the prior cultures of their corporate classmates, helping to eliminate bias in hiring practices. As nonprofit management programs within higher education continue to develop their curricula, and they look at the interdependent relationships between the profit and the nonprofit sectors, it is important that the curricula include a cross-sector management perspective. A cross-sector management perspective would be organized around the expectations of the career changer and the nonprofit employer. It would provide classes on human resource management and the creation of nontraditional applicant pools. Such a class would, for example, teach students how to prepare job descriptions that use inclusionary language to attract a wider pool of nontraditional candidates. It would draw attention to the ways in which incumbent networks restrict opportunities to bringing in managers with different perspectives and new resources. These new curricula might focus on the peer training of nontraditional candidates as well as students coming right out of college. Internships, community service, and volunteer experiences could become a structured part of the peer socialization process. The nonprofit employer and the student could present case studies, based on the volunteer experience or internship, in the classroom. Such case studies would highlight the way in which leadership roles are negotiated within the organization between experienced members and the newcomer. These internships would also help the nontraditional students and students right out of college build the necessary occupational networks for employment opportunities in the nonprofit sector.

Volunteerism: A Necessary Part of Anticipatory Socialization

In working together, nonprofit organizations and graduate programs in nonprofit management must view volunteerism as a necessary part of anticipatory socialization for the career changer.

Members of an organization determine the acceptance of a newcomer into the group (Merton, 1968). It is their approval that governs a newcomer's membership. In order to earn the respect of the group, the newcomer must be able to demonstrate an understanding of the group's core values (Wax, 1983).

For the career changer, anticipatory socialization learned within a class-room may be coupled with on-the-job learning through volunteerism. These techniques enable the corporate manager to practice the requisite behaviors and attitudes before being hired as a nonprofit employee. Within the anticipatory socialization process, the corporate and nonprofit managers can create an informal interactive relationship where both the peer and the newcomer can learn to accept and appreciate each other. It is in the mutual acceptance of each other that they can begin to negotiate the extent to which the newcomer must adapt and the degree to which his prior skills, attitudes, and behaviors will be accepted by his new peer group (Van Maanen, 1976, 1977, 1983). Anticipatory socialization of corporate career changers is critical because it not only earns them respect by their new nonprofit peer group, but also helps the career changers distinguish the important nonprofit significant others within the nonprofit organization culture before they arrive as employees.

A Growing Segment of the Labor Force: The Older Worker

As the nonprofit organizations continue to experience a critical shortage of workers between the ages of 25 and 54, one segment of the workforce is expected to increase its numbers by 10 million by 2008—the older worker. By the year 2020, 18.4 percent of the population or 59.4 million people will be 55 to 69 years of age (Goldberg, 2000, p. 21). Burbridge (1994) found that older workers were more likely to transition into the nonprofit sector from the corporate sector. This being the case, how might nonprofit organizations utilize this trend to attract an older worker with business skills? Nonprofit organizations are already thinking about how to retain the older worker utilizing corporate reward systems such as deferred-compensation packages to supplement pension plans. It is estimated as many as "40 percent of all tax-exempt organizations are offering such plans to newly hired officials" (Lipman, 2000, p. 1). Under this type of plan, the employee only receives the cash if he stays with the organization until retirement. Since the older worker is viewed as the institutional memory of an organization, there is an incentive for the nonprofit organization to keep them by using corporate reward systems.

There is also an incentive for the older worker to stay employed. According to the Administration on Aging (1999), two-thirds of the men and one-half of the women now work at ages 55 to 64 (p. 11). One reason for this, according to the Employee Benefit Research Institute, may be that "36 percent [of retirees] are not confident that they will have enough money to remain comfortable through retirement" (Goldberg, 2000, p. 94). If this is the case, nonprofit organizations must take advantage of this trend and create an organization development strategy designed to entice the older worker. This organization development system is an integration of mission-oriented values, training and orientation, and increased monetary rewards. It is a system open to recruiting nontraditional candidates as well as career managers. It is interdependent with the corporate sector in that it uses its business and management models as a means of survival and growth in this new century.

Note

1. Organization development is the development of managerial talent through methods which "improve levels of performance, sharpen conceptual skills ... and increase job satisfaction by facilitating self-development and career interests" (McFarland, 1974, p. 466).

References

Abbott, A. D. (1988). *The system of professions.* Chicago: University of Chicago Press.

Administration on Aging. (1999). Aging into the 21st century. http://www.aoa.dhhs.gov/aoa/stats/aging21/program.html, pp. 1–17.

Attewell, P. (1995). *Dislocated worker interview questionnaire.* Graduate School and University Center, City University of New York.

Attewell, P. and Stein, T. S. (1996). *Career transition follow-up questionnaire.* Graduate School and University Center, City University of New York.

Becker, H. S., Geer, B., Hughes, E. C., and Strauss, A. L. (1961). *Boys in white.* Chicago: University of Chicago Press.

Billitteri, T. J. (2000, September 21). Keeping the best on board. *The Chronicle of Philanthropy.* http://philanthropy.com/cgi–bin/printable.cgi, pp. 1–5.

Blalock, H. M., Jr. (1982). *Race and ethnic relations.* Englewood Cliffs, NJ: Prentice–Hall.

Blau, P. M. (1964). *Exchange and power in social life.* New York: John Wiley and Sons.

Blum, D. E. and Marchetti, D. (2000, November 16). Fundraisers find for-profit jobs give them best of both worlds. *The Chronicle of Philanthropy,* p. 25.

Bodenhausen, G. V. and Wyer, R. S., Jr. (1985). Effects of stereotypes on decision making and information-processing strategies. *Journal of Personality and Social Psychology, 48,* 267–282.

Brim, O. G., Jr. (1968). Adult socialization. In J. A. Clausen (Ed.), *Socialization and society* (pp. 182–205). Boston: Little, Brown, and Company.

Brim, O. G., Jr. and Wheeler, S. (1966). *Socialization after childhood.* New York: John Wiley and Sons.

Burbridge, L. C. (1994). *Government, for-profit, and third sector employment. Differences by race and sex, 1950–1990.* Washington, DC: The Aspen Institute.

Bureau of Labor Statistics. (1999, November 30). BLS releases new 1998–2008 employment projections. http://stats.bls.gov/emphome.htm, pp. 1–6.

Bureau of Labor Statistics. (2000a, August 9). Displaced worker summary. http://stats/bls.gov/newsrels.htm, pp. 1–5.

Bureau of Labor Statistics. (2000b, February 9). Table 3a. The 10 industries with the fastest wage and salary employment growth, 1998–2008. http://www.bls.gov/news.release/ecopro.t03.htm, p. 1.

Bureau of Labor Statistics. (2000c, February 9). Table 3c. The 10 occupations with largest job growth, 1998–2008. http://www.bls.gov/news.release/ ecopro.t07.htm, p. 1.

Bush, R. (1992). Survival of the nonprofit spirit in the for-profit world. *Nonprofit and Voluntary Sector Quarterly, 21,* 391–410.

The career network. (2001, March 22). *The Chronicle of Philanthropy,* pp. 51–63.

The Chronicle of Philanthropy. (2000). Tax–exempt organizations registered with the IRS. http://philanthropy.com/premium/articles/v12/114/ 14003801.htm, pp. 1–3.

Clary, E. G., Synder, M., and Stukas, A. A. (1996). Volunteers' motivations: Findings from a national survey. *Nonprofit and Voluntary Sector Quarterly, 25*, 485–505.

Cohen, T. (1999, April 18). Managing when profit isn't the goal. *The New York Times*, pp. 3, 11.

Collins, N. W. (1983). *Professional women and their mentors*. Englewood Cliffs, NJ: Prentice–Hall.

Cunningham, K. (1995). [Cohorts one and two: Interviews, taped recordings] Unpublished raw data.

Davis, C. (2000, July 16). Orange County voices; Layoffs show the once-sacred employer–worker pact is gone. *Los Angeles Times*, p. 15B.

Davis, F., Olesen, V. L., and Whittaker, E. W. (1966). Problems and issues in collegiate nursing education. In F. Davis (Ed.), *The nursing profession* (pp. 138–175). New York: John Wiley and Sons.

Deal, T. E. and Kennedy, A. A. (1982). *Corporate cultures*. Boston: Addison–Wesley.

Deaux, K. and Lewis, L. L. (1984). Structure of gender stereotypes: Interrelationships among components and gender label. *Journal of Personality and Social Psychology, 46*, 991–1004.

Deaux, K. and Ullman, J. C. (1983). *Woman of steel*. New York: Praeger.

DeSantis, V. (1999, June). Composition of working age population to change. *Employment in New York State, 1*, p. 3.

DiMaggio, P. J. (1988). Nonprofit managers in different fields of service: Managerial tasks and management training. In M. O'Neill and D. R. Young (Eds.), *Educating managers of nonprofit organizations* (pp. 51–69). New York: Praeger.

Douglas, M. (1966). *Purity and danger*. London: Routledge and Kegan Paul.

Drucker, P. F. (1990). *Managing the nonprofit organization*. New York: Harper Collins.

Eisenberg, P. (1997). A crisis in the nonprofit sector. *National Civic Review, 86*, 331–341.

Elkin, F. and Handel, G. (1984). *The child and society: The process of socialization*. New York: Random House.

Emanuele, R. (1997). Total cost differentials in the nonprofit sector. *Nonprofit and Voluntary Sector Quarterly, 26*, 56–64.

Epstein, C. F. (1970). *Woman's place*. Berkeley: University of California Press.

Epstein, C. F. (1981). *Women in law*. New York: Basic Books.

Epstein, C. F. (1988). *Deceptive distinctions: Sex, gender, and the social order*. New York: The Russell Sage Foundation.

Epstein, C. F. (1992). Tinkerbells and pinups: The construction and reconstruction of gender boundaries at work. In M. Lamont and M. Fournier (Eds.), *Cultivating differences* (pp. 232–256). Chicago: University of Chicago Press.

Epstein, C. F., Saute, R., Oglensky, B., and Gever, M. (1995). Glass ceilings and open doors: Women's advancement in the legal profession. *Fordham Law Review, 64*, 295–448.

Etzioni, A. (1975). *A comparative analysis of complex organizations*. New York: Free Press.

Farber, H. S. (1998). *Working paper #400: The dynamics of job change in labor markets*. Princeton, NJ: Princeton University.

Gardner, J. (1995). *Displaced workers 1991–92*. Washington, DC: U.S. Department of Labor.

Gecas, V. (1989). The social psychology of self-efficacy. *Annual Review of Sociology, 15*, 291–316.

George, L. K. (1993). Sociological perspectives on life transitions. *Annual Review of Sociology, 19*, 353–373.

Goffman, E. (1959). *Presentation of self in everyday life*. Garden City, NY: Doubleday.

Goffman, E. (1961). *Asylums*. Garden City, NY: Anchor.

Goffman, E. (1963). *Stigma*. Englewood Cliffs, NJ: Prentice–Hall.

Goldberg, B. (2000). *Age works*. New York: Free Press.

Golden-Biddle, K. and Linduff, H. A. (1994). Culture and human resources management: Selecting leadership in a nonprofit organization. *Nonprofit Management and Leadership, 4*, 301–315.

Goode, W. J. (1957). Community within a community. *American Sociological Review, 22,* 194–200.

Granovetter, M. S. (1995). *Getting a job.* Chicago: University of Chicago Press.

Greene, S. G. (1994, June 28). Non-profit groups' expanding world. *The Chronicle of Philanthropy,* pp. 1, 28–29.

Gudykunst, W. B. and Kim, Y. Y. (1984). *Communicating with strangers.* Reading, MA: Addison–Wesley.

Hall, H. (2000). Fundraisers: In demand, in the money. http://www.philanthropy.com/premium/articles/v12/io8/08002301.htm, pp. 1–2.

Hipple, S. (1999, July). Worker displacement in the mid-1990s. *Monthly Labor Review, 122,* 15–32.

Hochschild, A. R. (1973). *The unexpected community.* Englewood Cliffs, NJ: Prentice–Hall.

Hodgkin, C. (1993). Policy and paper clips: Rejecting the lure of the corporate model. *Nonprofit Management and Leadership, 3,* 415–428.

Hodgkinson, V. A., Weitzman, M. S., Abrahams, J. A., Crutchfield, E. A., and Stevenson, D. R. (1996). *Nonprofit almanac 1996–1997.* San Francisco: Jossey–Bass.

Hodgkinson, V. A., Weitzman, M. S., Noga, S. M., and Gorski, H. A. (1993). *National summary: Not-for-profit employment from the 1990 census of population and housing.* Washington, DC: Independent Sector.

Horner, S. (1996–1997). [Career transition follow-up interviews, tape recordings]. Unpublished raw data.

Hughes, E. C. (1945). Dilemmas and contradictions of status. *American Journal of Sociology, 50,* 353–359.

Hughes, E. C. (1981). *Men and their work.* Westport, CT: Greenwood Press.

Hutchens, R. M. (1988). Do job opportunities decline with age? *Industrial and Labor Relations Review, 42,* 89–99.

Jackall, R. (1988). *Moral mazes: The world of corporate managers.* New York: Oxford University Press.

Joyner, T. (2000, May 28). Left behind: Despite record employment, millions aren't participating in prosperity. *The Atlanta Journal and Constitution,* p. 1R.

Kanter, R. M. (1977). *Men and women of the corporation.* New York: Basic Books.

Labaton, S. (1999, November 17). New rules lift the lid on nonprofit pay. *The New York Times,* p. 2H.

Levy, R. (1985, May). *Talent matters: Attracting and retaining gifted managers in the third sector.* Paper presented at the Independent Sector Professional Forum, Washington, DC.

Levy, R. (1988). Curing benign neglect: Alternative approaches to nonprofit management education. In M. O'Neill and D. R. Young (Eds.), *Educating managers of nonprofit organizations* (pp. 22–31). New York: Praeger.

Liedtka, J. M. (1991). Organizational value contention and managerial mindsets. *Journal of Business Ethics, 10,* 543–557.

Lipman, H. (2000). Retirement perks help keep workers. http://philanthropy.com/premium/articles/v12/i23/23004801.htm, pp. 1–2.

Lipton, J. P., O'Connor, M., and Terry, C. (1991). Neutral job titles and occupational stereotypes: When legal and psychological realities conflict. *Journal of Psychology, 125,* 129–151.

Lorber, J. (1984). *Women physicians, careers, status, and power.* New York: Travistock Publications.

Lortie, D. C. (1975). *Schoolteacher.* Chicago: University of Chicago Press.

Mason, D. (1992, November/December). Invasion of the soul snatchers: Aliens in our midst. *Nonprofit World,* pp. 27–30.

McFarland, D. (1974). *Management principles and practices.* New York: Macmillan.

McMahon, M. B. (1996, January 25). Business ventures are not the only gospel for charities. *The Chronicle of Philanthropy,* p. 38.

Mead, G. H. (1934). *Mind, self, and society.* Chicago: University of Chicago Press.

Merchant, K. E. (1991, March/April). Guilty of nonprofit bashing? *Nonprofit World*, p. 3.

Merton, R. K. (1968). *Social theory and social structure.* New York: Free Press.

Merton, R. K. (1972). Insiders and outsiders. *American Journal of Sociology, 78*, 9–47.

Milkman, R. (1987). *Gender at Work.* Urbana: University of Illinois.

Miller, J. (1997, April 12). Harvard to establish center to study nonprofit sector. *The New York Times*, p. A7.

Mirvis, P. H. and Hackett, E. J. (1983). Work and workforce characteristics in the nonprofit sector. *Monthly Labor Review, 106*, 3–12.

Moen, P., Dempster-McClain, D., and Williams, R. M., Jr. (1992). Successful aging: A life-course perspective on women's multiple roles and health. *American Journal of Sociology, 97*, 1612–1638.

Montagna, P. D. (1974). *Certified public accounting.* Houston: Scholars Book Company.

Moore, J. (1992, April 21). Charity workers' job market jitters. *The Chronicle of Philanthropy*, pp. 1, 28–31.

Moore, M. H. (Draft, 1996, October). Notes toward a curriculum in nonprofit policy and management. Cambridge, MA: Harvard University, Hauser Center on Nonprofit Organizations, John F. Kennedy School of Government.

Moore, M. H. (2000). Managing for value: Organizational strategy in for-profit, nonprofit, and governmental organizations. *Nonprofit and Voluntary Sector Quarterly, 29*, 183–204.

Moore, W. (1969). Occupational socialization. In D. A. Goslin (Ed.), *Handbook of socialization theory and research* (pp. 861–883). Chicago: Rand McNally.

More than 43 million jobs lost reaching every walk of life. (1996, March 3). *The New York Times*, p. 27.

Moses, N. (1997, April). The nonprofit motive. *Arts and Business Council's Partners*, p. 5.

Neugarten, B. L. and Datan, N. (1973). Sociological perspectives on the life cycle. In P. B. Baltes and K. W. Schaie (Eds.), *Life-span developmental psychology* (pp. 53–69). New York: Academic Press.

Newman, K. S. (1988). *Falling from grace.* New York: Vintage Books.

Occupational Outlook Handbook. (2001). http://stats.bls.gov/oco/ocoitz.htm#T.

O'Neill, M. (1989). *The third sector.* San Francisco: Jossey–Bass.

O'Neill, M. (1998). Nonprofit management education: History, current issues, and the future. In M. O'Neill and K. Fletcher (Eds.), *Nonprofit management education: U.S. and world perspectives* (pp. 1–12). Westport, CT: Praeger.

O'Neill, M. and Young, D. R. (1988). Educating managers of nonprofit organizations. In M. O'Neill and D. R. Young (Eds.), *Educating managers of nonprofit organizations* (pp. 1–21). New York: Praeger.

Ott, J. S. (1989). *The organizational culture perspective.* Chicago: Dorsey Press.

Parsons, T. (1951). *The social system.* Glencoe, IL: Free Press.

Philanthropy and volunteerism in higher education initiative: Building bridges between practice and knowledge in nonprofit management education. (1997). *W. K. Kellogg Foundation Program Initiative Overview* [Brochure]. Battle Creek, Michigan: W. K. Kellogg Foundation.

Professional Opportunities. (2000, October 5). *The Chronicle of Philanthropy*, pp. 63–79.

Reskin, B. F. (2000, Spring). The proximate causes of employment discrimination. *Organizations, Occupations, and Work Newsletter*, pp. 3–8.

Reskin, B. F. and Hartmann, H. I. (1986). Explaining sex segregation in the workplace. In B. F. Reskin and H. I. Hartmann (Eds.), *Women's work, men's work: Sex segregation on the job* (pp. 37–82). Washington, DC: National Academy Press.

Rosemarin, J. (1995, November 13). Building bridges from profit to nonprofit. *The New York Post*, p. 28.

Rosow, I. (1965). Forms and functions of adult socialization. *Social Forces, 44*, 35–45.

Rosow, I. (1974). *Socialization to old age*. Los Angeles: University of California Press.

Ruhm, C. and Borkoski, C. (2000). *NBER working paper no. W7562: Compensation in the nonprofit sector*. Cambridge, MA: National Bureau of Economic Research.

Salamon, L. M. (1997). The United States. In L. M. Salamon and H. K. Anheier (Eds.), *Defining the nonprofit sector: A cross-national analysis* (p. 296). New York: St. Martin's Press.

Salamon, L. M. and Anheier, H. K. (1996). *The emerging nonprofit sector: An overview*. New York: St. Martin's Press.

Schein, E. H. (1990). Organizational culture. *American Psychologist, 45*, 109–119.

Schur, E. M. (1984). *Labeling women deviant*. New York: Random House.

Smith, L. (1996, June). Moving to the nonprofit sector. *Right Associates New York News*, pp. 1, 4.

Smith, S. R. and Lipsky, M. (1993). *Nonprofits for hire*. Cambridge, MA: Harvard University Press.

Sommerfeld, M. (2000). A good techie is hard to find. *The Chronicle of Philanthropy*. http://philanthropy.com/premium/articles/v12/i13/13002901.htm, pp. 1–5.

Souccar, M. K. (2000, December 18). At nonprofits, execs make big personal profits. *Crain's New York Business*, pp. 23, 28.

Stein, T. S. (1991–1996). [Tape recordings of nonprofit management and communications program class sessions]. Unpublished raw data.

Stone, G. P. (1962). Appearance and the self. In A. M. Rose (Ed.), *Human behavior and social processes* (pp. 86–118). Boston: Houghton Mifflin.

Trice, H. M. and Beyer, J. M. (1993). *The cultures of work organizations*. Englewood Cliffs, NJ: Prentice–Hall.

Tschirhart, M. (1998). Nonprofit management education: Recommendations drawn from three stakeholder groups. In M. O'Neill and K. Fletcher (Eds.), *Nonprofit management education: U.S. and world perspectives* (pp. 61–80). Westport, CT: Praeger.

U.S. Census Bureau. (2000). 1997 economic census: Comparative statistics for United States. http://www.census.gov/eped/ec97sic/E97SUS.HTM, pp. 1–4.

Van Maanen, J. (1976). Breaking in: Socialization to work. In R. Dubin (Ed.), *Handbook of work, organization, and society* (pp. 67–130). Chicago: Rand McNally.

Van Maanen, J. (1977). Experiencing organization: Notes on the meaning of careers and socialization. In J. Van Maanen (Ed.), *Organizational careers: Some new perspectives* (pp. 15–45). New York: John Wiley and Sons.

Van Maanen, J. (1983). People processing: Strategies of organizational socialization. In R. W. Allen and L. W. Porter (Eds.), *Organizational influence processes* (pp. 240–259). Glenview, IL: Scott, Foresman, and Company.

Waldinger, R. (1992). *The ethnic politics of municipal jobs*. Unpublished manuscript, University of California, Los Angeles.

Walsh, M. R. (1977). *Doctors wanted, no women need apply*. New Haven, CT: Yale University Press.

Walshok, M. L. (1981). *Blue collar women*. Garden City, NY: Anchor Books.

Wax, R. H. (1983). The ambiguities of fieldwork. In R. M. Emerson (Ed.), *Contemporary field research* (pp. 191–202). Prospect Heights, IL: Waveland Press.

Wethington, E. and Kessler, R. C. (1986). Perceived support, received support, and adjustment to stressful life events. *Journal of Health and Social Behavior, 27*, 78–89.

Wilder, D. A. (1984). Intergroup contact: The typical member and the exception to the rule. *Journal of Experimental Social Psychology, 20*, 177–194.

Wolpert, J. (1993). *The patterns of generosity in America*. New York: Twentieth Century Fund Press.

Wooldridge, A. (2000, March 5). Come back, company man! *The New York Times*, p. 82.

Zey, M. G. (1991). *The mentor connection*. New Brunswick, NJ: Transaction Publishers.

Zuckerman, H. (1977). *Scientific elite*. New York: Free Press.

Appendix A

Dislocated Worker Interview Questionnaire

© 1995 PAUL ATTEWELL

code: date of interview:

gender:

Thank you for agreeing to participate in our research.

This interview is part of a study of careers and workplace culture in the private sector, and about peoples' ideas about moving from the corporate to the nonprofit sector.

All the information we are collecting is strictly confidential.

No names will be mentioned in any publications, or even stored with the data.

The data will be used to look for general trends and patterns, to understand what professional and managerial life in the corporate and nonprofit sectors is like.

I would like to use a tape recorder, because that enables my notes to be more complete. But if you don't want me to use the tape recorder, or if you want me to stop it at any point, please let me know.

Could you please sign this consent to be interviewed form?

I would like to begin by talking first about your experiences with, and perceptions about, the nonprofit sector. A bit later on I will want to ask you a series of questions about your work experience in the corporate sector.

1. Perceptions of the Nonprofit Sector

I know you have been attending workshops about jobs in the nonprofit sector.

a. Before you attended Tobie's class, what were your links to the nonprofit sector, i.e. Were you a volunteer, a board member, a manager, a consultant? What roles have you had in the nonprofit sector? Did your friendship networks include friends who are managers in the nonprofit sector?

b. What reservations, negative beliefs or stereotypes do/did you have about the nonprofit sector as a place to work?

(Probes: slower pace of work; nonprofits as less goal and bottom-line driven; less hierarchical, more consensus; more people oriented, less numbers-oriented; more tolerant of diversity; requiring more commitment to ideals; nonprofits as less demanding of quality performance).

c. What things appeal(ed) to you about the nonprofit sector as a work place? Why do you want to work there?

(Prompts: more sense of community; can't find anything in the profit sector; economics; more tolerance of age, gender, etc; slower pace; more time with family; better sense of self).

d. What perceptions do/did you have of the nonprofit culture and management style?

2. Experiences in Interviewing with Nonprofits

a. Did you apply for any jobs in nonprofit organizations prior to starting Tobie Stein's course? What types of nonprofit positions are you inquiring about?

b. How did you find out about those nonprofit job openings?

c. Did you get interviews? And if you did, what were your experiences in those interviews? If not, why do you think you didn't?

d. Did you feel recruiters in nonprofits had a particular view of you, as someone coming from the corporate world?

e. What barriers were/are in your way of getting a job in the nonprofit sector? (prompts: anger; loss of confidence; loss of identity; no networks; poor communication).

3. Corporate Job History

Okay, I'd like to shift to your experience in the corporate or private sector. Could you please walk me briefly through your private sector job history, from the time you left college until the present?

I'm interested in the two or three main jobs you held, roughly for how long, and why you left.

4. Job culture in last, longest, or most important corporate job

I would like to focus on your job at _____. I am interested in getting a sense of the corporate culture and the atmosphere of the place when you worked there.

a. Could you describe what you like most about working there?

b. Could you describe what aspects you liked least about working there?

Now I would like to go through several individual features of corporate culture, and ask you about where your company fit in relation to them:

c. The pace of work

Some companies seem to really pile on the pressure. The pace of work is very intense, people have to take lots of work home. There is a lot of stress. Other firms are more relaxed. People work hard but there isn't the same feeling of time or workload pressure.

What was the pace of work like at your firm? Did it change while you were there?

d. Work measurement

Some people I have interviewed say that their firms use a lot of performance targets and quotas or work measurement. They measure every aspect of performance and are constantly scrutinizing numbers. Managers have to spend a lot of time looking over these statistics and explaining to higher management why the numbers look like they do.

What was your firm like? (Could you describe what it felt like?)

How were you evaluated in your work?

e. Politeness at work

Some people I have interviewed describe their corporation as having a very cordial and polite culture. Bosses are polite and friendly to their subordinates and try to be supportive or understanding when people make mistakes. They use praise rather than criticism.

Others describe their firms as having a more rough and tough style: Managers are hard–driving and often sarcastic to their subordinates. They may criticize people quite publicly. Lower level employees may be fearful of their bosses.

Could you describe what your corporation was like on these issues?

(Possible follow-up: Did this change during the time you were there?)

f. Identification with the firm (loyalty)

Some firms manage to make employees feel like they are a member of a family or a team. People become very loyal to the company itself. They identify with the company, and feel the firm cares about them.

Other firms have a much cooler relationship towards their employees, and employees have less loyalty. How was this in your firm? Did it change over time?

g. Competition among professionals

In some firms, managers or professionals are very competitive among themselves, even to the point of deliberately making one another look bad. They seem to enjoy conflict and intrigue as a way of seeing who is top dog. Other firms seem to build a feeling of mutual support among employees. Decisions are less ego-driven. In fact there is an effort to build consensus, and not to offend anyone.

Could you describe your company in this regard? (How did you feel in that kind of an environment?)

h. Connections, networks, and alliances

Some people say that in their firm, connections, who you know, are very important. If you aren't allied or connected in certain ways, or don't have friends looking out for you, you won't get promoted, or you won't get information that is critical for doing your job well.

Other people describe their firms very differently: networks and alliances don't seem to be important. Could you tell me how it was in your firm?

i. Hierarchy and centralization (authority, discretion)

Some people I have interviewed describe their firms as being very hierarchical or centralized. All important decisions (and sometimes even unimportant decisions) need someone's approval high up in the firm.

Other firms seem to delegate a lot of authority and give a lot of discretion to lower managers. Decision-making is not so centralized.

Could you describe your firm's pattern of authority and responsibility?

(Follow-up: Are people in your firm often held responsible for things they can't really control?)

j. Jargon, slogans, belief systems (new thinking)

Some firms seem to use a lot of slogans and jargon, or they have an official value or belief system. There is a certain language one has to talk if one is to be a successful manager. Sometimes this is Total Quality Management talk, sometimes it's "empowerment," or some other managerial theory.

Did your firm have this quality of language, slogans, or an official belief system?

(Follow-up: Was this official belief system sincere? What was it like working in that environment?)

k. Honesty and speaking one's mind (politics)

Some of the people I've interviewed describe their workplaces as very honest up-front places. People speak their minds. They aren't worried about being outspoken, so long as they do their job well. They feel they can argue against a policy if they believe it is mistaken.

Other people describe their workplaces as very political. They say you have to be very careful what you say in public. People censor themselves, and don't feel they can be honest to their bosses or others. If they oppose or are even lukewarm about a proposed policy or initiative, they feel they will be viewed with suspicion, as disloyal or something. Could you describe how things like this were in your company?

l. Top-down communication

Some firms seem to be relatively open in terms of top-down communication: employees are told what is going on. Communication up and down the company works well.

Others are more secretive at the top. People speculate and gossip a lot about what is really going on. And there may be collusion in the middle ranks not to let those at the top know when things are going wrong, or what one is up to.

Could you describe how it was in terms of communications and secrecy in your company?

m. Restructuring and innovation

Some people I have interviewed say their firms are constantly undergoing restructuring: who reports to whom, how many layers of management, new programs, or procedures. Sometimes the pace of change is quite frantic.

Others say their companies change very slowly, and may even be resistant to change.

Could you describe how your company was in terms of change?

(Probe if they say it was frantic. How did people cope? Did change create disorganization?)

n. Social conformity

Some corporations seem to stress conformity for their employees. They tend to select people of a certain background, or require a certain style of dress and behavior. Others encourage more individuality. What was your firm like?

o. Diversity

Some companies seem to deal with diversity very well. Women, minorities, older workers all blend in. Other companies seem to be less open. They may make older workers, for example, feel like they are viewed as deadwood. What was the situation in your company?

p. Opinion of management

Did you feel your company was well managed? Was top management in touch with the realities of the rest of the company? What is your assessment of that company's direction and management?

(Follow-up: Were there occasions when you felt that a bad decision was made, either by top management or by your immediate superiors? Could you give an example of such a decision, and what resulted from it?)

Appendix B

Career Transition Follow-up Questionnaire

© 1996 PAUL ATTEWELL AND TOBIE S. STEIN

code: date of interview:

gender:

1. *What do you think are the major differences between the nonprofit and for-profit sectors?* (Probe: decision-making processes; language; professional development; support of outside interests and commitments e.g. family, volunteer activities; governance (board of directors role); rewards; workforce characteristics; tolerance of diversity e.g. women, older workers, people of color; goals and methods of achieving goals; the way results are measured; leadership styles; types of entrepreneurs who are attracted; feedback on performance; structural differences e.g. chain of command; dress codes.) Anything else?
2. *When you decided to make a transition to the nonprofit sector, how did the people closest to you react?* (Probe: spouse, children, family, colleagues, friends, members of your community.)
3. *What influenced your decision to transition into the nonprofit sector?* (Probe: lost your job, your values conflict with corporate values, no jobs left in the industry, job security.)
4. *What were the major obstacles that stood in your way?* (Probe: did not have a nonprofit network, did not have an understanding of nonprofit culture, not able to get interviews, was not able to convince perspective nonprofit employer that I would "fit in," did not have the proper résumé, did not fit the nonprofit employer's image of the nonprofit ideal type, lack of money to "fund your search," lack of family support, unemployed status, age discrimination.)
5. *What are the ideal qualifications for a nonprofit job in terms of work experience, skills, educational credentials, values of nonprofit manager?*
6. *How do these qualifications and values differ from your last for-profit job?*
7. *During your corporate career, what was your involvement with nonprofit organizations?* (Probe: volunteerism, philanthropy, served on board, serviced by nonprofits, had nonprofit clients, funded nonprofits, responsible to building nonprofit business.)
8. *If you volunteered, what did you learn about the nonprofit culture? How did you learn? Did it prepare you for the transition, how?*
9. *Did your volunteer experience lead directly/indirectly to your present job? Explain.*

10. *If you had a mentor during your volunteer experience, what role did he play in helping you make the transition?*

11. *How did you find the nonprofit job you finally took?* (Probe: How did they become aware of you, how were you contacted, who interviewed you, how many interviews occurred?)

12. *How did this process differ from the hiring process of your last for-profit job?*

13. *In addition to your skills, why do you think you were hired?* (Probe: volunteer experience, types of resources (examples), interpersonal connection.)

14. *Who was most helpful in helping you get your nonprofit job?* (Probe: direct relationship with employer; knew someone who knew employer.)

15. *What adjustments did you make when you were transitioning from volunteer to employee within the same organization or between one organization to another?*

16. *When you first entered the nonprofit organization as an employee, how did your expectations differ from the actual demands of the job and culture?* (Probe: extent to which there is culture shock; in what way did employee attitudes/behaviors differ from your expectations?)

17. *How would you characterize the way you were treated when you first entered the organization?*

18. *What obstacles did you face in assimilating?*

19. *What types of attitudes/behaviors have you had to repress for this job?* (Probe: What frustrates you?)

20. *What situations have led you to repress these behaviors/attitudes?* (Probe: How does the organization let you know that a certain behavior is not acceptable?)

21. *What types of training processes did you experience?* (Probe: trial/error; on-the-job training through seminars, mentoring; formal orientation.)

22. *How did you learn the "unspoken language" of the organization?* (Probe: who the powerbrokers are and their significance to you; when to press for something/or not e.g. promotion, new programs, strategy implementation; when to share an idea/or not; when to take a break e.g. go to lunch.)

23. *What kinds of situations generate conflict in your present job? Did this differ from conflicting situations in your last for-profit job?*

24. *Are there other people working in your organization who have made the transition from the profit to the nonprofit sector?*
If so, who?

25. *Do you know anyone in your current nonprofit organization who was forced to leave? Why?*

26. *Are there official rules and unofficial rules in your organization which conflict with your values? Explain.*

27. *Did this ever happen in the corporate sector? Explain.*

28. *What types of nonprofit practices make it difficult to carry out the mission?* (Probe: bureaucracy, conflicting values of staff, board, constituencies, goals not clearly defined, two equally valued goals compete for primacy; competition between staff members.)

29. *What types of business practices has your nonprofit organization adopted?* (Probe: strategic/financial planning, restructuring, language, computers, furniture, dress code, decision-making, rewards e.g. monetary incentives.) Describe these in detail.

30. *What types of for-profit practices have worked/not worked in your nonprofit organization and why?*

31. *How did Tobie Stein's Program prepare you for making the transition?* (Probe: job search skills résumé, interviewing, presentation, networking, formal strategies e.g. ads, Internet, recruiters; build confidence; learned to anticipate employer's expectations during interview; learned to anticipate employer's expectations on the job; learned to anticipate behaviors/attitudes of significant others e.g. peers, boss; learned role expectations of other managers in the organization.)

Appendix C

Recruitment of Applicants

During 1991 and 1992, I contacted the corporate and nonprofit press about the Nonprofit Management and Communications Program (also called the Career Transition Program) with the expectation that press would help me recruit students for the early phases of the Program. The press along with word of mouth attracted students between 1991–1993. From 1994 on, the Consortium for Worker Education provided me with the majority of applicants. Here is a listing of the 21 articles that were written about the Program as well as four articles that I published for purposes of recruiting students:

Academics. (1991, August 20). *The Village Voice*, p. 14.

Alumni news. (1991, Fall). *Emerson College Beacon*, p. 29.

Bernstein, A. (1995, September 24). Author envisions a world without work. *New York Newsday*, p. 6.

Breznick, A., Moss, L., and Parker, M. (1991, October 7). Switching direction. *Crain's New York Business*, p. 6.

Bulletin board. (1991, Fall). *The Professional Communicator*, p. 44.

Course set on shift from profit to nonprofits. (1991, October 10). *Gannett Suburban Newspapers*, p. 1.

Gatewood, D. (1991, October 27). Profit from nonprofits. *New York Newsday*, p. 62.

Gatewood, D. (1992, April 19). Trading corporate paychecks for some nonprofit satisfaction: People are finding out there's more to work than just money. *New York Newsday*, p. 62.

Jackson, T. (1992, March 9). Calendar listing. *New York Newsday*, p. 34.

Making the switch to not-for-profit. (1993, January). *FWA New York News*, p. 2.

Managing your portfolio of careers: Five career-changers tell their stories. (1991, November). *FWA New York News*, p. 6.

Mangan, D. (1991, November 7). Profit from nonprofit boom. *New York Daily News*, p. 43.

Mason, M. E. (1992, June). Education in nonprofit field a growth industry. *Nonprofit Times*, pp. 8, 20.

Moss, L. (1991, October 14). For publishing refugees, new horizons. *Crain's New York Business*, pp. 3, 43.

Nonprofit training program at Baruch. (1991, September). *The Graduate School and University Center Newsreport*, p. 2.

NYRAG members' memorandum. (1995, October 16). *NYRAG Newsletter*, p. 7.

Olcott, W. (1992, December). Crossing over to new careers. *Fundraising Management*, pp. 23–24.

Pool of high-level executives looking for work with nonprofits. (1992, February). *Nonprofit Marketing Report*, p. 7.

Roscetti, M. (1994, May). Going back to school. *Community Jobs*, pp. 1, 4–5.

Save these dates. (1991, Fall). *New York Women in Communications: Connection*, p. 1.

188 TOBIE S. STEIN

Stein, T. S. (1992, February 7–13). Transfer your skills to the nonprofit sector. *The Wall Street Journal: National Business Employment Weekly,* pp. 29, 33.

Stein, T. S. (1992, March/April). Letters to the editor. *Nonprofit World,* p. 3.

Stein, T. S. (1992, May). Career crossover: From profit to nonprofit. *Community Jobs,* pp. 1, 4–5.

Stein, T. S. (1993, Spring). Making a successful career transition. *Interface,* pp. 5–6.

Stern, G. (1991, October 29). Nonprofit-group jobs take getting used to. *The Wall Street Journal,* p. B1.

Index

Volunteer (*cont.*)
   159, 166, 169, 171; *see also*
   Anticipatory socialization;
   Nonprofit Management and
   Communications Program; Role
   expectations; Roles (work);
   Volunteerism
Volunteerism, 6, 38, 57, 82–83, 89,
   127, 131, 140, 143, 172; *see also*

Volunteerism (*cont.*)
   Anticipatory socialization;
   Nonprofit Management and
   Communications Program; Peer
   socialization; Volunteer

Workforce transition, 3, 19; *see also*
   Career transition